Legally Kidnapped

Legally Kidnapped

Oliver Kaye

authorHOUSE®

AuthorHouse™
1663 Liberty Drive
Bloomington, IN 47403
www.authorhouse.com
Phone: 1-800-839-8640

First published by AuthorHouse   09/23/2011

ISBN: 978-1-4567-9816-1 (sc)
ISBN: 978-1-4567-9824-6 (ebk)

Printed in the United States of America

Table of Contents

Chapter 1

Early Days

Mark sat staring at the dusty garage wall. He wondered why he had kept the old rusty watering can with the hole in it that stood on the shelf he had been meaning to fix. He smiled to himself. What did it matter? What did any of it matter? He looked at the unopened pack of cigarettes on the dashboard. He had given up many years ago but had thought that just once more he would like to savour that 'just opened pack smell', light one of the fragrant cigarettes and inhale the acrid fumes. But he knew that after so long the first drag would make him cough, and would probably taste rank. He hesitated, his hand half way towards the pack before he dropped it back into his lap again. Tears were coming now, streaming down his face and making his nose run. His brain was working overtime. Almost as though it knew what was coming. He thought about his childhood, happy innocent days. He thought of the photo he still had of his 5 year old self, standing with bruised knees in short trousers, his hand being held by someone out of the picture. His face was unlined, his gap toothed smile wide. The tears were coming faster now as he thought about another little boy whose hand he should have been holding, on his first day at school. The pain of his loss was like a heavy weight on his chest and he wondered if he was having a heart attack. He smiled through his tears. What did it matter? He got out of the car and checked the hosepipes he had connected to the exhaust. They were in place. He looked at the pack of cigarettes again and opened them, breathing the fresh smell of tobacco in. But he did not light up. Instead he held a small tee shirt with Thomas the Tank Engine on the front to his face smelling the familiar child smell and as he did so, he turned the key in the ignition. As he closed his eyes he was immediately transported back as his mind took inventory of his journey to this point.

1980

It had been another hot and dusty day in a rare spell of soaring summer temperatures in the Berkshire countryside. Everywhere grass was parched and with hosepipe bans in full force, flowers drooped and died in gardens and on the dusty banks of the country roads. The ground that Mark was trying to dig was rock hard and his fork made little impression on the baked earth even when he stood on it.

"Bit of a job that!" his employer came up behind him with a glass of water.

"I should leave it for today Mark, you've done pretty well, here's your money, have a good weekend. Mark took the glass of cold water, draining it in one gulp and thanking old Mr. Williams. The heat of the day had accumulated to make the pavements and road shimmer. As he walked through the village he wiped sweat off his face with the rolled up sleeve of his shirt and banged the dusty earth off his trousers. Approaching the Hare and Hounds Pub he saw two of his former student friends going in through the little side door that led to the snug. Jogging the rest of the way Mark burst through the door. "Mine's a cider!" he said.

"Typical, I swear you can bloody smell the drink!" Jim grumbled pulling another note from his wallet, giving the order for the cider to the barmaid. Mark looked at the young woman pulling the cider from the draught tap. This was the second time he had seen her and he gave her a smile. She looked down and plonked the glass in front of Jim a tendril of her dark hair that had come free from her ponytail falling over her heart shaped face. She brushed it away and shot a wary glance at Mark before turning her back on them as she put up another pork scratchings card.

"Here you are you sponging bastard, some of us are surviving on student grants you know!" Jim said and Mark smiled.

"Perpetual student syndrome, that's your problem, the rest of us are out at work and you two are hiding behind your PhD's, anyway you miserable bugger, next round's on me, I got paid today!"

"Paid for standing round in a garden like a tit, nice work if you can get it!" Tony said as Mark lowered himself onto the long bench seat at the table in front of the bar. The barmaid now on the other side of the bar, Mark said

"Do you know what her name is?"

"Who?"

"The new barmaid."

"Miss frosty knickers you mean, no, that one ain't giving *nothing* away!" Tony drawled in a mock American twang.

"You mean you've tried?"

"Asked her to the gig next weekend, she knocked me back good and proper!" Tony said.

Tony was the good looking one of the group, a rugby player with broad shoulders and a shock of dark hair above a handsome face; he was certainly not used to girls refusing his advances. If she wasn't interested in Tony, Mark thought doubtfully, still, there was something about her . . . .

It was a full week later before Mark got more than a few words out of Emma. He was doing a shift behind the bar and she was on duty with him. He had tried to get her into conversation from the other side of the bar but she resolutely stuck to her one word answers, not exactly rude, but certainly not encouraging. It was tennis that finally broke the ice. Mark had brought his racket with him to work after playing a match for his club that afternoon. When she saw it propped up against the crisp boxes in the hall she said.

"Where do you play?"

"At the Whitfield Tennis Club, do you play?" Mark felt his heart begin to beat a little faster.

"Yes, I do, but I haven't for a while." She looked up at him a tiny smile playing around her lips and Mark noticed the hazel flecks in her dark eyes.

"Maybe you'd like a game sometime?" he said holding his breath for her reply. She was lovely, dark naturally curling hair that fell down her back, a long graceful neck and a truly exciting figure. She had an athletic build but still had curves that made his pulse race.

She seemed to study him in return for a moment and then with a smile that lit up her lovely eyes she said. "Maybe." In the years to come Mark was to think back on that day, on the elation he had felt on that hot summer afternoon and more than once he had wondered if that had been the highlight of their relationship, the antithesis of the hell he was to live through.

Over the next few weeks he had to endure a lot of teasing from his friends. Emma was a very private person, almost paranoid in insisting that he tell no one anything about his or her relationship. In public she barely acknowledged him and he knew that his friends were half convinced that his relationship with Emma was all in his mind. In private it was a different matter altogether and the fact that she was so reserved in public made her warmth towards him, when they were alone, all the more exciting. They played tennis and took long walks together in the cool of the summer evenings, and one weekend drove down to the coast in Mark's beat up old mini. Emma laughed as he folded himself into it, his head brushing the roof as he sat behind the steering wheel.

Oliver Kaye

As they parked the car in the Hengetsbury Head car park they could see the sea reflecting blue under a cloudless sky. As they left the car Emma pointed to a group of starlings sitting in the sand, their legs tucked underneath them, Emma was taken aback, she had never seen birds sitting like this before.

"Are they OK?" She asked worriedly shielding her eyes from the sun as she looked up into Mark's face. He smiled at her and caught her nose between his thumb and finger, in the way he often did, giving it a little wiggle.

"Yes. They're fine, just waiting for the next picnic to be laid out!"

"I've never seen anything like that before" Emma said. They had got quite close to the birds now, and although they pulled their feathers in exposing their feet, they did not fly off.

"They're here all through the summer, making the most of the picnickers on the dunes and the crumbs shaken off picnic rugs by the cars. In fact this beach is called Starling Beach, so they must have been at it for some time!"

As they walked over the dunes to the beach, Emma followed Mark, his strong brown hand holding their cold box, a tartan rug under his arm.

They found a quiet spot in the dunes and stripped down to their swim things, racing each other to the water. Emma's laughter warmed Mark's heart and he pulled her to him as the waves swelled around them, putting his salty lips to hers.

Her mouth was warm and inviting and they kissed until she wound her leg around his, toppling him over in the water. Chasing back up the beach they threw themselves down on the blanket and as she lay on her back Mark noticed her nipples, tight underneath the top of her bikini. Lying beside her he kissed her again stroking the side of her breast with his thumb. He could feel the sun on his back and moved his hand slightly, brushing his thumb over the tender point of her breast. For a moment she allowed him to caress her then she sat up and looked at him, her eyes wide.

"Mark look, I've got to tell you, I'm not going to sleep with anyone 'till I'm married." She looked down, taking in the obvious sign of his excitement, then looked away.

Mark was speechless. He was hardly a playboy but he had not met anyone at his age who was still a virgin.

"You mean you've never . . . ?"

Emma shook her head. "No" she said quietly. Mark rolled over onto his stomach. "Right well, that's OK, of course it's OK!" Emma smiled at him shyly from under her long lashes, in the way that she knew he could not resist.

"You're sure?"

"Of course I'm sure!"

On the way back from the beach Emma hummed softly to a song on the radio. Mark glanced at her, there was still sand dusting her face, and her soft skin was glowing from the sun. He felt a tenderness that he had never felt before when he looked at her. He knew he was falling in love. She glanced up at him and her dark eyes smiled as she put her small hand on his brown leg. The no sex business was going to be tough, but she was worth it Mark thought, covering her hand with his.

"I was wondering Mark, would you like to meet my mother?"

It was the first time that Emma had mentioned her mother, or any of her family and Mark knew he was being considered as someone special.

"Yes, I'd love to, if you think she would approve of me?"

"Why wouldn't she?" and all of a sudden a dark cloud blotted out the warmth of the day as she shot him a glance, the eyes that moments before had been warm and gentle now dark and cold as she snatched her hand off his knee.

"No reason, sorry I didn't mean to suggest that I had any skeletons in my cupboard" Mark looked at her. Her head was down now but when she looked up again her smile had returned.

"Of course, sorry, I didn't mean to over-react." They held hands again and when he dropped her off at home that evening she kissed him warmly pressing her body to his.

He groaned with pent up desire and made his way home, the scent of the sea and her perfume seeming to linger around him.

As he let himself into his rented farm worker cottage Mark picked up the post from the mat. He leafed through them and then stopped and putting the rest of the post unopened on the hall table he carried the letter he had been waiting for into the small lounge. For a moment he sat, the evening sun shining in on him through the latticed windows looking at the outside of the envelope. Mark knew what it was. He shook his head and smiled ruefully to himself. Just a week ago he would have had his heart in his mouth hoping against hope that the envelope contained the offer of work that meant so much to him. But that was before Emma had got under his skin. That was before he had fallen in love.

Now Saudi Arabia seemed a very poor alternative to the lovely woman that he had just spent a magical day with. His agricultural background was, it seemed, in demand as the Saudi Government set up a huge desert reclamation project outside the capital city Riyadh, with crop and livestock farming. When Mark had applied for the job he had been captivated by the thought of carving out green and fertile pastures in the middle of one of the most inhospitable places on earth, coaxing life out of dry unyielding soil.

The advert had tempted him as soon as he had read it.

On behalf of a leading dairy farm in the Middle East we are urgently seeking Dairy Farm Project Managers to be based outside the capital city of Riyadh in Saudi Arabia. Responsible for the overall management of up to 1000 milking cows, developing and maintaining Pastures. Knowledge of milking procedures and use of Dairy Herd Improvement Records. Ability to motivate employees. A hardworking, dedicated professional who gets the job done. Computer literate. Proven knowledge of managing stocks for herd management raw materials and goods, stock rotation and control are essential. Personal drive and initiative, and the ability to communicate effectively with a wide range of people. The Project Manager will implement project strategy, supervise the local project team, and manage expenditure and project reporting. Supervising employees in all phases of the dairy

Skills

Suitable applicants must have a University degree in agriculture or dairy production with experience handling cow dairy projects of not less than 1000 milking cows. Gulf experience will be given priority with the ability to lead a team and achieve successful outcomes

And now here was the reply to his application. It was, of course, a yes. Mark smiled to himself again. He would take it, he knew he would, but the shine was definitely off the thrill of the acceptance. He would tell Emma when they met the next day. Now he called Tony.

"Hi Tony mate!"

"Hello you old bastard, where you been? I swung past your way early today and no sign of you or the Mark-mobile. Not out on another phantom date were you?"

"I was actually and you're getting boring Tony, listen, I got the Saudi job."

Tony let out a low whistle. "Well done mate, how much is it again?"

"Two thousand a month."

"Tax free"

"Yep, tax free"

"God, it's alright for some!"

"Well I've told you Tone, if you ever get the balls to leave school, you too could have a job like that! You're going to have to take the plunge one day."

"Yeah ha ha very funny, listen what about miss frosty . . . I mean Emma?"

"What about her?"

"How are you going to tear yourself away, or can her apparition appear anywhere in the world to you?"

"Shut up Tony, just because you can't get a woman."

"Hold on there loser. What or rather who do you think I was doing last night?"

"I dread to think."

"Well it doesn't matter, she is merely one of many, as you well know. Anyway back to Arabland. Drink tomorrow to celebrate?"

"OK, H and H tomorrow, sixish?"

"See ya!"

Emma was working the next day and Mark got to the pub early to speak to her before joining Tony for a drink. Tony was already there. She leaned on the bar smiling at him and he caressed the soft skin of her arms as he told her about the job offer. And there it was, once again he witnessed the shutters come down, her warmth instantly replaced by a hostile wariness.

"You didn't say anything about going to work overseas?"

"To be honest I applied so long ago I had almost forgotten it."

"So why bother to start, well, you know, us?" she spat at him Mark was taken aback. He felt genuine dismay.

"I applied before we started going out, how did I know that I was going to meet the girl of my dreams? If I had known, obviously there is no way I would have applied, but Emma, surely you didn't think the height of my ambition was to potter around Mr. Williams' garden?" Despite herself Emma smiled briefly.

"I applied for the Saudi job because it is an exciting project, one to really get my teeth into."

"I assumed you were looking for something around here."

"That's the ultimate aim yes, but I need to get some money behind me, the job out there pays more in a year than I could earn in five here. But if it is going to come between us, then I won't go"

Emma looked up at him from under her eyelashes again; she looked mollified, for the moment.

"We'll talk after my shift." She said and Mark made his way to where Tony was sitting at the back of the pub. When he got there his friend's usually playful jollity was nowhere in evidence.

"Seriously Mark mate you need to be bloody careful!"

"What?"

"Emma, I've seen her type before. Sex kitten one minute and iron maiden the next."

Mark was about to say that Emma and he were saving themselves but thought better of it, Tony would not understand. Instead he said

"Don't know what you're talking about."

Tony leaned forward. "All lovey-dovey, kissey-kissey one minute then bam, frozen out the next! Ring any bells?"

"For fucks sake Tony, I've just told her about Saudi, what do you expect her to do? Dance for joy?" Mark was irritated now.

Tony put his hands up "Ok mate, okay, but just think on!"

"You don't know what you are talking about!" Mark said taking a swig of his pint. The celebration had fallen flat, and after half an hour the two men went their separate ways.

As the summer heat continued unabated, Emma took him to meet her mother. The thatched cottage on the outskirts of the village was surprisingly cool inside and smelled of freshly cut flowers. Emma's mother was a gentle, sweet, lady. She welcomed Mark warmly although he noticed that Emma seemed on edge glancing continuously at her mother as if looking for a sign of approval.

"Now then Mark, you take a seat on the patio and I'll bring you some cold beer, would that suit?"

"Yes, thank you very much Mrs. Channing" As Emma and her mother went to the kitchen Mark looked around the little cottage sitting room on his way to the patio. Surprisingly there were very few photos, and certainly none that could be Emma's father.

He had asked Emma about her father as they had lain together on the sand dunes at the coast. He had felt her slender body tense in his arms and immediately regretted asking the question. After a moment she shrugged.

"I don't know anything about him really. He had a shop selling rare books and was a book restorer."

"Oh that's interesting." Mark said. She had wriggled out of his embrace, "He died when I was about 6 months old. Mother doesn't ever talk about him, so when you meet her don't bring it up. It's private." She shot him a warning glance.

He had not pushed any further.

Now standing in her mother's cottage he could find no trace that there ever had been a man in her life. For a moment the image of a preying mantis eating its mate flashed into his mind and ducking to avoid the low lintel he chuckled to himself and went out onto the little patio. Everything about the cottage and indeed Emma and her mother was as neat as a new pin. Even the old flagstones of the patio had not the slightest hint of a weed growing in the cracks.

As they sat shielded from the heat of the afternoon sun by an oversized patio umbrella Mark complimented Mrs. Channing on her garden.

"Please call me Mary" she said smiling warmly at Mark patting his sun-browned hand with hers. Mark noticed that Emma watched every move her mother made, almost, it seemed to Mark, in the way the owner of a dog of uncertain temperament would watch for any sign of aggression, which surprised Mark as Mary Channing seemed the epitome of a little England gentile lady of leisure.

"Tell me Mark, do you have any brothers and sisters?"

Mark laughed. "Oh yes, I call them 'the clan' there are dozens of us; brothers, sisters, cousins, aunts and uncles."

Mary Channing's smile faltered slightly.

"Really, how nice for you." But the friendly manner had been replaced by a slightly clipped tone. The difference was almost imperceptible and if it had not been for Emma's' tense watchfulness Mark probably would not have noticed. Now though, Emma leaned forward a little in her chair, her cup of tea half way to her lips as if waiting for her mother's reaction.

Reaction to what? Mark asked himself bemused. It might be a little out of the experience of this single mother and her daughter to imagine a huge extended family but it was not as though he had said he was a descendent of a Moors murderer. People did have big families.

By the time that Mark left the little cottage the conversation had been steered into safer waters and Mary Channing waved them off insisting that he visit again soon.

Mark put any misgivings he had had to the back of his mind as Emma, her dark hair tumbling over her brown shoulders skipped like a child beside him, obviously delighted that the visit had gone so well. As he looked down at her he felt an overwhelming love for her. Picking her up and kissing her deeply he whispered in her ear.

"Emma, I love you so much." She kissed him back and when he set her down again he saw tears in her eyes. He held her to him, her head on his chest, stroking her sun-warmed hair.

"I love you too Mark" she murmured into his tee shirt. Holding hands they walked through the village to his cottage.

Inside the cottage evidence that he was packing up was everywhere. The cottage had come furnished so he did not have that to worry about, but it was surprising how much stuff he had accumulated.

In the tiny bedroom upstairs his suitcase lay open on the floor and they had to step over it to get to the bed. As they lay next to each other, as they had often done, the desire to make love to Emma was almost overwhelming. As their kisses became more passionate and his need more urgent he wondered if she would be overcome by desire and maybe this time they would . . . . He could feel her breasts swelling under his caressing hands the hard nipples pressing into his palms. He stroked the contour of her waist and her hip to where her short skirt ended and the smooth skin of her tanned legs began. He groaned as he stroked her warm flesh and began to stroke her soft thighs under her skirt. Instinctively she rolled over slightly onto her back and Mark let his hand rest on the slight swell of her belly above her panties. He looked down at her face. Her eyes were half closed her lips apart and a flush of desire suffused her face. His hand inched lower and under the elastic of her panties until he could feel a line of gently curling hair under his fingertips, his breathing was coming hard now and he was almost in physical pain. Emma's breathing had quickened too, and she was making no move to stop his probing fingers. Holding his breath Mark pushed his hand down his fingers exploring her warmth.

With almost an agonised groan Emma suddenly sat up.

"Stop Mark! You know what I said, why do you *always* push it too far?" Her tone was irritated and acted like a bucket of cold water. Mark could scarcely believe this was the same woman he had been caressing moments before. For a moment he remembered what Tony had said in the pub. But he dismissed it. He loved Emma and she loved him. He would just have to be patient.

Chapter 2

Emma

Emma woke up with a headache the next day. She felt irritated, out of sorts. She frowned at her reflection in the mirror. Her dark eyes looked darker in the way they always did when she was annoyed. And she was annoyed. Mark always took things too far. She was only human and he knew that she wanted to save having sex until she was married, yet he always tried to trick her into letting go. Did he really love her? She was beginning to doubt it. Why would he get them into such situations where she always had to be the one to put the brakes on? She tugged at her sleep tangled hair and winced as another wave of annoyance swept over her, the pain of her hair pulling viciously away from her scalp making her grit her teeth.

At breakfast she studied a copy of the parish news intently hoping her mother would leave her be. She didn't

"So Emma, it was late when you came in last night."

"Yes."

"Were you with Mark *all* that time?"

"No, for part of the time I was dancing naked in the village square." Emma said caustically.

"No need for sarcasm young lady." Her mother said.

"Well, for God's sake mother, I'm 24, I shouldn't have to answer to you for everything I do."

Mary Channing pursed her lips.

"While you live under my roof, you are my concern."

"Concern, yes, prisoner, no!" Emma said through clenched teeth, the day was going from bad to worse.

"Well I know I've said it before but I am going to say it again Emma."

Emma clamped her hands over her ears but her mothers piercing voice and her familiar mantra still filtered through.

"Make him value you for more than what is between your legs. The fastest way to lose a man is to sleep with him."

Emma wanted to scream. She pushed away from the table so violently that her chair fell back clattering onto the flagstones of the kitchen floor. As she passed her mother she saw that far from concern or alarm her mother was smiling, a quiet triumphant smile.

In the back garden Emma paced up and down. She had dug her nails into the palms of her hands and now as she fished a packet of chewing gum out of her shorts pocket, she noticed flecks of blood on her palms. She made for her favourite spot under the willow by the pond, between carefully tended flowerbeds. She threw herself down, wiping away the blood on the dewy blades of grass.

This was all Mark's fault. Rage rose in her again and she saw white spots in front of her eyes. She felt her breakfast in the back of her throat and all of a sudden she had thrown up, the half digested remains of her toast an incongruous heap amongst the summer flowers in their beds. Holding her hand under the pond's waterfall feeder pipe she wiped her mouth. She closed her eyes and leaned back against the tree, breathing deeply.

When she returned to the house her mother was nowhere to be seen. Emma took the stairs two at a time and brushed her teeth, tying her hair back in a ponytail with a white tie. She changed her shorts for a tennis dress and grabbed her racket. She was running late. She had stayed in the garden longer than she should have but she felt calmer now, more in control.

Mark looks nervous, she thought to herself as she arrived at the club. The sight of his face anxiously trying to read her expression pleased her. She did not smile, instead she handed him the tube of balls she had brought and walked past him towards the court they had booked. She could hear him behind her and the feeling of power made her feel good for the first time that day. She would let him suffer a little longer, he deserved it!

They played the first game in silence. Mark was a good player, but he was off his game today. Emma beat him easily.

"Game to me!" Emma said cheerily.

"Yes, well done!" Mark said

"You don't seem to be on form today?" She said smiling at him

"No I'm fine!" the relief on his face was obvious.

"Well come on then, make a fight of it!" she teased, flicking her ponytail over her shoulder.

The next game was a close call, and Emma had a feeling that in the end Mark let her win. Good, she thought. Very good.

After the game as they sat on the benches watching the other games he put his hand tentatively on hers. She left her hand where it was for a moment and then curled her fingers around his. He smiled at her lovingly and she rested her head on his shoulder for a moment. She let him smooth the damp tendrils of hair away from her flushed cheeks and felt his lips graze the top of her head.

As the hot days of August dragged on they took trips out, sometimes to the beach but on one bright day to Oxford. As they walked hand in hand along the streets amongst the ancient colleges of Oxford University Mark brought them to the Botanical gardens. Occupying 4 ½ acres in the centre of Oxford, this unexpected oasis was a vibrant splash of green in the middle of the city. As she wandered through the gardens with Mark he asked her if this the first time she had been to the gardens

"Yes, they're lovely."

"Especially at this time when the University is on holiday. Otherwise it's usually full of students. I haven't explored it all yet, I did come here when I was a student to look at some of the rarer species.

"Wasn't one of the Alumni JRR Tolkien? I read that he liked to relax in the gardens, under a certain tree." Emma said.

"Ah ha, that I can help you with!" Mark took her hand and led her through the gardens pointing out the walled garden. "If you look you'll see it is surrounded by the original seventeenth century stonework. The garden's oldest tree is in there.

"Its' a Spruce, isn't it ?" Emma asked

"No, it's actually an English Yew". Mark said " but close! For someone whose mother is so passionate about the garden, you don't know a lot do you?"

"It's not my area of interest" Emma said shortly.

"Hey I wasn't criticising!" Mark put his arm around her shoulders.

"Over that way are the glasshouses for the plants that can't stand the British Weather "Maybe we can look around them later?"

"I'd like that" Emma said.

They stopped under an enormous Austrian Pine.

"Pinus nigra" Mark announced "People think that it might have been the inspiration for the Ents of the Lord of the Rings, the walking talking tree people of Middle-earth."

Emma stood under the tree looking up. "Of course! I can see that!" she said excitedly.

"You know Lord of the Rings?" Mark asked

"Almost by heart, I've read it so many times" Emma said

Mark threw back his head and laughed. "Me too." They sat down together on the bench Mark staying silent to give Emma a few moments to imagine the great Tolkien looking out over the same view that they now enjoyed, from this very spot. While she did he watched her beautiful face, her eyes bright and alive with her thoughts. He loved her so much and when she turned her animated face to him, he could see the love shining in her eyes. They kissed deeply, the warm sun shining down on them as they sat, only the gentle rustling of the trees and distant traffic noise reminding them they were not in their own private garden of Eden.

"Oh Mark, I love you so much, I'm going to miss you so badly!" Emma said looking deep into his eyes. The hazel flecks in her eyes seemed on fire as her emotion shone through her tears.

"God Emma," he crushed her to him. "I'm going to miss you as well, but this will be such a step up for ou . . . the future. If it wasn't for that I couldn't drag myself away, you know that."

Emma buried her face in his broad shoulder loving the feeling of his strong arms around her. She had noticed the slip he nearly made, mentioning 'our' future. He obviously thought it a bit presumptuous to use that word at the moment, but it was a very good sign! Emma often fantasised about living her life with Mark. He was kind and soft hearted, and he loved her, as far as she could see they were made for each other. She had had boyfriends before him but they had never lasted long. They either wanted to get her into bed, and ran for the hills when she told them she was waiting for marriage or they got tired of her moods. She knew she had moods, but she couldn't help herself. Mark seemed to understand that.

There were many other idyllic days in the run up to Mark's departure and Emma felt more relaxed in his company as each day went by. Emma felt herself falling more and more in love with this quiet, gentle man. She felt safe with him, she could see how much he cared about her and she wanted so badly to trust him completely. She wanted to but something was stopping her.

The night before he was leaving for Saudi Mark told her that he planned to have a get together with his friends in the pub. Sitting in his cottage Emma felt irritation sweep over her.

"You mean you prefer to spend the night with the lads rather than me? Oh well that's a clear enough message I suppose." She stood up

"Hey hey, not only with them, with you too, all of us!"

"No." Emma said flatly, she felt anger bubbling inside her and felt her fists clenching.

"No?"

"No! Tony doesn't like me, don't think I don't know that, I'm not spending the last evening you are here, with him!" she spat

"He does like you." Mark said although his eyes told her that he was not being entirely honest.

"Very convincing Mark! No you go and enjoy yourself and forget about me, in fact you might as well forget about me full stop, you're going to Saudi, I'm staying here, not much point is there?"

Despite herself Emma felt slightly mollified by the stricken look on Marks' face.

"Emma, darling, no, I never want it to be over, I want us always to be together, when I come back I was hoping . . . ."

"Hoping what?"

"Hoping you would marry me" he said miserably.

Silence hung between them for a good minute. This was hardly the romantic proposal Emma had imagined, but it was a proposal. She ran across the room and flung her arms around Mark's neck.

"Of course I'll marry you!" she said into his neck.

Mark looked stunned, he could not keep up with her fluctuating moods, she knew that, but she felt his comforting arms around her, holding her tight as he smiled down at her, his eyes full of love for her and said.

"I'll buy the biggest diamond I can find for you!"

They spent his last evening together curled up on his bed talking and planning for their future. Emma loved the way Mark's face became animated when he told her of his plans for them. He wanted to have a farm, and to raise rare breeds. His experience on the farm in Saudi was going to be a great grounding for him and the money he would earn would ensure they got off to a great start.

Just before 10.30 pm as Emma lay sleepily, her head on his shoulder, he said.

"Emma, let's go down to the pub, just for last orders, I can't wait to tell everyone our news. I'm so happy. I want the world to know!"

For a moment Emma hesitated. But then the thought of Tony's face when they told him made her jump up from the bed.

"Come on then!" she laughed and jumped into his arms making him carry her down the stairs laughing as he nearly dropped her as his head hit the low ceiling. As they arrived on the bottom step he pretended to stumble and they collapsed together on the couch laughing and kissing each other. It would be so easy to let go, to sleep with him, it would mean so much to Mark, on his last night . . . .

"Come on then lover boy, lets go!"

Reluctantly Mark disentangled himself from her arms and they ran together down the road to the Hare and Hounds.

Inside the pub Tony and Geoff and a few other friends from the tennis club were about to call it a night. Tony felt hurt that Mark had stood them up, hurt and unutterably sad for his friend.

As they burst through the door laughing Emma looked intently at Tony. He had another one of his bimbo's in tow. He changed women as often as he changed his socks, and his bimbos were all no better than they should be, 'girls of easy virtue' her mother would call them. This particular peroxide blonde was sitting beside Tony, her erect nipples visible through her tie dyed tee shirt under which she obviously was not wearing a bra. Tony had his arm around her shoulders, and his fingers occasionally brushing over the hard nipples under the thin cloth.

Normally Emma thought the sight of such a common slut would kill her enjoyment of the evening, but this evening she had something special to tell them all.

Then as she watched the girl stood up and hugged Mark kissing him on the lips. Aware that her eyes were on him Mark quickly held her away from him and said

"Tilly, long time no see! What are you doing here?"

"Oops I forgot you two had been an item once!" Tony said with fake sincerity looking at Emma mockingly waiting for her reaction.

Emma felt bile rise in her throat and a vice tighten around her chest but she kept the smile on her face, taking Mark by the arm brushing roughly past Tilly

"Tony, I'm so glad you're here" she said, "We wanted you to be the first to know! We're engaged! I'm *so* sorry, we're late too—private celebration" She stood on tiptoes to kiss Mark on the lips, " I'm sure you understand?"

Tony was looking at Mark. He seemed about to speak and then with an almost imperceptible shrug he got up and shook his friend by the hand.

"Well done, Emma" he said flatly. The fact that he had said well done, rather than congratulations was not lost on Emma. Still, she thought with delicious satisfaction, Mark's mine now.

As some of their friends from the tennis club crowded around to congratulate them, out of the corner of her eye Emma could see Tilly congratulating Mark, her unfettered breasts squashed against his chest as she planted another kiss on his lips.

Mark glanced at Emma aware that she was watching him and once again pushed Tilly away from him, winking at Emma.

As they walked away from the pub that evening Emma said casually

"Who *was* that utter tart with Tony?"

"She's not really a tart, Em, more of a free spirit, if you like. She comes from a very good family, she's just, well, unconventional."

Emma felt irritation and a cold loathing well up in her.

"Well I bet they're *delighted* with her peroxide hair and awful dress sense!"

"Her hair's not dyed, that's its natural colour." Mark said.

"You seem to know a lot about her?" Emma fought to control her voice.

"Yes, we used to go out, a long time ago."

"Oh really? And now she's got her claws into Tony? Not fussy then?"

"That's a bit unfair Em, she's a lovely girl, and if you got to know her I know you would like her."

"I doubt that, but you obviously still care a lot about her!" Emma said through gritted teeth.

"Anyway, why are we talking about ancient history when I've got the most beautiful exciting girl in the world, the future Mrs. Richards, right by my side?" Mark picked her up and swung her around, and despite herself Emma felt the tension go out of her.

Mark kissed her deeply and with the warm night scented air around them she surrendered to the urgency, the promise and the reassurance of his embrace.

And then he was gone. Emma was surprised at how bereft she felt without him. At the pub whenever the door opened she still looked up expecting to see him coming in, dusty from working in Mr. Williams' garden, his face lighting up as he saw her. She hardly spoke to anyone and stopped playing tennis. Nothing was the same without Mark, her big handsome protector.

Tony and Tilly came in almost every day although Emma tried to ignore them. They seemed to be getting very close and rarely spoke to her except to ask how Mark was doing when they ordered at the bar. That suited her just fine, Emma thought.

Mark wrote to her every day and she replied immediately. As the heat of summer was fading into cooler autumn days in England, he reported that it was hotter than hell in Riyadh.

The farm that he was working at was about 40 miles from the capital city so he and his colleagues only went there at weekends, which in the Moslem world was Thursday and Friday, Emma learned.

Her mother was not pleased with the daily deliveries from the postman, sometimes, two or three letters at once.

"For goodness sake, I thought he had gone there to work. He can't be doing much of that if he has time to write so much?"

Emma said nothing but she felt the hackles on the back of her neck rise as she eagerly ripped the latest envelope open.

"And not just one sheet, either, how many is that?"

"Three" Emma said through clenched teeth, making for the stairs.

"Lucky for you that he's not in a normal country or he'd be tomcatting around by now, I'm sure!"

Emma stopped on the middle of the staircase.

"I'll have you know, *mother*, that Mark has asked me to marry him."

There was silence for a moment and Emma took in her mother's startled expression with triumph.

"When? When did he ask you?"

"On his last night here!" Emma said

"Oh I see. Would that also be the night you lost your virginity by any chance?" Mary Channing's voice dripped sarcasm

"No!" Emma shouted. She was shaking now, she felt more vulnerable without Mark close.

Mary Channing shrugged seemingly oblivious to her daughter's distress

"Well it's your look out. I've tried to warn you, but that's really all I can do."

"I HAVEN'T SLEPT WITH MARK! Emma shouted and then collapsed in tears on the stairs. In an instant Mary was by her side, stroking her hair and pulling her up so that her face was buried in her shoulder. Sitting together on the stairs, Mary rocked Emma as though she was a child.

"There there, little Emma, mummy knows you're a good girl, mummy only wants to keep you safe from the nasty man.

"He's not a nasty man!" Emma sobbed

"No, no, but no one can love you and look after you like mummy does, can they?"

Emma shook her head miserably.

In Riyadh Mark had spent a hot evening in the gold souk looking at the jewellery. He had already bought a few gold chains for his sister and a couple of his cousins but now he was looking for the ring that he would present to Emma when he got back. It had to be something special. There was no shortage of choice and with prices much lower than in the UK, he was going to be able to get her something really stunning. The sights and sounds of the souk fascinated him. The gold souk was as far removed from his idea of a traditional Arab market place as it was possible to be, all white brick built air-conditioned shops with grills over the windows, extending left and right along numerous corridors, as far as his eye could see.

The other souks were far more atmospheric, the smells of the schwarmas, a kind of sandwich made with meat sliced off a big rotating spit and wrapped in warm pitta bread always led him to one of the little stalls to buy a couple. He bought lovely bright material for his mother and Arab hunting daggers for his brothers. Unlike the gold souk the other souks were outside and not air-conditioned and Mark felt sweat trickling down his back. Still it killed time and one of these nights he knew he was going to find the perfect ring.

As he walked through the streets of the old city where some of the original ancient buildings still remained, he watched the Arab women covered from head to toe in black moving around the souks behind men dressed in brilliant white thobes with red check head-dresses, most dangling worry beads from their hands. Brightly dressed children ran in and out of the thronging crowds. As he watched a little girl of about 10 playing an energetic game of tag with her younger brother, he wondered how long it would be before she was hidden away behind the mysterious veils of adult womanhood.

Returning with a couple of the other farm workers to the compound Mark checked the post. There was a letter from Emma. He ripped it open and scanned it avidly. He frowned slightly. This was the fourth letter since he had asked about how her mother had taken the news of their engagement and still no answer to his question. Did that mean that Emma hadn't told her, or that she did not approve? Still, he reassured himself Emma seemed full of excitement about their future together, full of plans about where they would live and what they would do. She would be starting back at College soon. And by the time he finished his year in Saudi she would have finished her dog-grooming course, and they would be able to be together. At this distance his frustration at not being able to sleep with Emma had become a kind of awe at her self-control and conviction. She was truly unusual. He felt privileged that she had chosen him. He had worried at first that she might not want to sleep with him because she did not like sex, or the thought of it. But there had been plenty of evidence that she got as aroused as he did, he knew how hard for her to pull away from him while her body was responding to his caresses. Their wedding night was going to be something special. Lying on his bed underneath the droning air conditioning unit reading her letter he felt the familiar urgency that his body always exhibited at the thought of her, and groaned. It was going to seem years instead of months before he saw her again.

Back in Berkshire Mary Channing had walked Emma up to her room and despite the fact that it was nearly midday, helped her back into her nightie and tucked her back into bed sitting beside her smoothing Emma's hair away from her flushed tear stained face, humming to her until her furrowed brow smoothed in sleep. Then taking the letter from her sleeping daughters hands, she took it downstairs to read.

Emma's dreams were vivid. In them she was running towards Mark, who was standing at the foot of his cottage stairs. As she ran to him he reached out to pull her to him and she realised she was naked. He stood just out of her reach as an invisible force held her back. The anticipation of his hands on her put her every nerve on fire, her breasts ached for his tough, her nipples were distended and painful and the heat between her legs almost unbearable. Her sensitive flesh felt swollen and ripe, ready to burst and then suddenly she was awake, her hand between her legs and stars bursting in her brain. She gasped for air as spasm after spasm wracked her body. For a moment she thought she was having some kind of seizure but the rhythmic throbbing of her most sensitive part and the intense pleasure unlike anything she had ever felt before, drowned her fear in an achingly delicious ecstasy. She slept again, this time quietly, a small smile playing around her lips.

Downstairs Mary Channing sat in her favourite chair, Mark's letter open on her knee, her lips pursed. She obviously had a lot of work to do with her daughter. She sighed and began to fold the letter carefully back into its envelope. She was ready for the fight.

Chapter 3

Planning

As the weeks turned into months Mark's letters kept coming. Emma loved receiving them and enjoyed being in her private little world with his words cocooning her. She felt loved and protected and as she continued her dog-grooming course she looked forward to the day that she and Mark would be able to start their life together.

She kept herself to herself at the college and refused all invitations to 'girls nights out'. She did make friends with a quiet girl called Linda that most of the other girls ignored and the two of them occasionally met for a drink or a game of tennis. Linda was Emma's only opportunity to talk about Mark and she took every chance to do that.

"Wow it must be great to have someone who loves you that much!" Linda said pushing her glasses up her nose.
"It is." Emma said quietly.

At home she kept herself to herself as much as she could as well. She was aware that her mother thought it was a bad idea that she marry Mark but that was not going to stop her. But her mother had said nothing for a while so Emma was daring to hope that she was coming around to the idea. They never spoke of Mark and the only time that he was acknowledged was when her mother would hand over his latest letter with her trademark pursed lips.

As the heat of the desert Kingdom increased through the summer months Mark threw himself into his work. The milking parlour for the herd of cows that he was working with was state of the art and although he could never hope to be able to afford the same for any farm he bought, he tried to study methods that he might be able to adapt to his own operation when he got it. Although he desperately wanted to go home and had the leave to do so, Mark chose to work on. He reasoned that if he went home it would be even harder to leave and come back again, and as he only intended to do a year, he would crack on with it and then come home to Emma. He asked her frequently how the plans for the wedding were coming along but she never answered him except in the vaguest terms. In his last letter he had asked if she was having second thoughts, but her passionate reply had reassured him. He was aware she had never answered his question about how her mother had taken the news and he had a sneaking suspicion that she might be the problem. He hadn't really spent enough time with Mary Channing to form an opinion about her but he had not got the impression that she didn't like him, but he still had the feeling that this was where the problem lay.

Mark decided that he would write to Mary Channing. Sitting under the air conditioner in his room Mark started and discarded one letter after another before he finally arrived at a version he was happy with.

Dear Mrs. Channing

I wanted to write to tell you how proud and happy I am that Emma has agreed to marry me. I realise that I should probably have come and spoken to you first, and I apologise for not doing that. As you know I proposed the night before I left for Saudi Arabia I want you to know that I will do my best to look after Emma.

The only reason I am now so far away from her is so that I can earn enough money to secure our future together.

I am looking forward more than you can ever know to returning to you both at the end of this year in Saudi. As Christmas has now past I am at least in the year of my return!

I am sorry that I did not speak to you about my intentions before I left and that I have left it this long to write to you. I know that Emma will appreciate your help and guidance as she prepares for our wedding.

Yours truly,
Mark Richards

When Mary Channing got the letter from her future son in law she read it once and then threw it on the fire.

As winter turned to spring and then summer, Emma did begin to make some plans for the wedding and tentatively showed her mother the list of people she wanted to attend. The list included all her aunts and uncles and cousins.

"What do you think?" Emma held her breath.

"No." Mary threw the list aside.

"Mother, what do you mean 'no'? This is the list of my wedding guests, I *am* getting married, and these *are* the people I want to invite."

"Then I won't be there." Mary said shortly turning her back on her daughter.

Emma fought back tears of rage.

"Mother why are you doing this?"

"Doing what?"

"Trying to ruin everything for me!"

"You're doing a good enough job yourself Emma as far as I can see!"

"What do you mean?"

"Look Emma, Mark is not to be trusted, you found that out yourself on the last night, the way that woman in the pub threw herself at him."

Emma went cold.

"How did you know about that, I didn't tell you?"

"You left one of your letters from *him* lying about and I read it." Mary said flatly.

"You did what?"

"I read it, and good job I did, it showed me what he was like, apologising for his tomcatting behaviour, pathetic, if he's like this before you're married what is he going to be like after?"

"It wasn't like that, she was an ex girlfriend, and she was the one who approached him!"

"Oh and I suppose he immediately pushed her away did he?"

Emma hesitated.

"No? I thought not, look Emma if you go ahead with this wedding you'll be sorry!"

"Well then sorry is what I'll have to be mother, because I am going to marry Mark!"

Eventually Mary agreed not to object if Emma's cousins came to the wedding In her letters sent in the weeks before Mark came back to the UK, Emma seemed to think that the fact that her mother had even acknowledged that there was going to be a wedding was a triumph. Mark felt angry and hurt. He had no idea why Mary Channing was so against their marriage. Emma said that it was because she did not want to lose her daughter, that she was frightened of being alone. Mark immediately softened. It must be tough to consider being alone when she had had Emma with her all these years. He resolved that he would make sure that they included Mary in a lot that they did, that they invited her often to stay with them, made sure she was involved with the grandchildren when they came. In the week before he was leaving Saudi that Emma dropped the bomb-shell. Her mother had said that as so few of Emma's family were going to the wedding, Mark would have to cut down the invites to 'the clan' to match the numbers. As he sat on his bed reading the letter Mark felt a cold chill go up his spine. This was supposed to be the happiest day of his life and it was turning into something torturous and painful. He was so full of excitement and pride about the wedding that he had written to everyone he could think of telling them that they would be invited. The reception, Emma told him was to be at the cottage, which presented an obvious limitation to the number of guests that could be invited and despite the numerous options of wedding reception venues nearby, Mary would consider none of them.

Mark poured his heart out to his father on one of their rare phone calls.

"It's bloody disappointing dad, I wanted everyone to be there!"

"Look son, maybe it's a financial thing, weddings and wedding catering can be very expensive you know. Look, give me her number. Let me ring her. There's no reason why she should bear the financial burden on her own. I would be delighted to chip in!"

"I've already offered that dad, but she turned the offer down."

"Well maybe it was because it was from you, it's the parents of wedding couples who have to dig deep, not the couple themselves!"

"Maybe years ago, but it's not uncommon these days."

"Well she's probably a proud lady. I'll give her a ring anyway, it can't do any harm."

"Thanks dad!" Mark hung up relieved

His father's words, saying that it could do no harm to ring Mary were to haunt Mark as the last letter that Emma would send him in Saudi arrived. Mary, it seemed had been appalled and taken a serious dislike to his father when he asked if he could help with any of the costs of the celebrations. Mark felt his heart sink. In the same post he got a letter from his father.

Dear Mark

Well, what can I say? I phoned Mary Channing and asked her if we could share the expense of the wedding, maybe move the reception to a larger venue so that everyone we wanted to invite could be accommodated. To say that she reacted badly to that suggestion is an understatement! She was extremely annoyed that I would even suggest it, accused me of insinuating that she could not 'do right' by her own daughter! You must believe that I was as tactful as I could be and I really did try to make it clear that I was not trying to offer charity, rather chip in so that you and Emma could have the wedding you wanted. She really was very aggressive with me Mark, the bloody woman virtually said that she did not want you marrying Emma, I got the impression that she is very protective of Emma, and that you would do well not to cross her.

It probably won't do any good to say this Mark and I don't want to throw a dampener on things, but think carefully son. I know how these over protective mother/daughter things can be and Mary Channing seems about as difficult as anyone could be. All I'm saying son, is to think about it carefully, to really know what you are getting into.

By the way, it doesn't look like I'll be able to make it to the wedding. I really am sorry but you know the trip that I had been planning to the states, well I will be away for the whole month. I don't suppose you could re-arrange? Or maybe it's a good thing I won't be there given the impression I have made on old Ma Channing!

See you soon

Dad

Mark felt a guilty sense of relief, if his father could not attend that should calm Mary down, but why was she being so difficult? His father's warning played on his mind as he made the rounds of the friends he had made in Saudi and visited the herd for the last time. As the sound of the imam calling the faithful to prayer hung on the evening air, Mark left the compound for the last time. In his pocket he had the ring he had chosen, a brilliant cut solitaire diamond. He was ready to start his life with Emma.

Emma had managed to get the farm worker's cottage back for Mark to rent. She and Linda had been looking through the local paper trying to find a premises to rent for dog grooming. The course was finished now and both girls had qualified with distinction. They had been to see many places but most were on industrial estates and not really likely to attract people looking to have their dogs groomed.

"Here, how about this one?" Linda had said pushing her glasses up her nose.

"Hicks farm. It is a converted stable block for rent. Looks like it would be perfect for us!"

"Hicks farm? Mark used to rent a cottage from them just outside the village." Emma took the paper from Linda.

"Look at that! The cottage is up for rent again too. Let's get over there and see what we can do. I've been looking for something for Mark to rent when he gets back, that would be perfect, especially if he have our business in the stable block. It's literally just down the track!"

The farmer remembered Emma and eyed her tan legs in her short skirt appreciatively.

"Well now, I remember young Mark, nice chap. You say he wants to rent the cottage again?"

"Well, yes, we both do, we're getting married!"

"Getting married you say?" the farmer licked his lips in a way that made Emma's flesh crawl. She was beginning to think renting from him might not be a good idea.

"Well as far as the stable block is concerned, you two young ladies can have it for the dog groomin' and there's a little fenced in pen outside so those waiting from their shampoo and set can 'ave a bit of a run around" the farmer laughed and Emma relaxed slightly. The rent was more than reasonable both on the cottage and the stable.

She and Linda asked for a few moments to talk it over and Emma could feel the farmers eyes mentally undressing her as she and Linda looked around the stable block again. It had electricity and plumbing and a stone floor that would be easy to keep clean.

"What d'you think?" Emma asked Linda

"Well that farmer's got the hots for you, that's for sure."

"Yes well never mind that, what about the stable?"

"I think we should go for it." Linda pushed her glasses up her nose again and smiled.

"Well then, it's yes to both!" Emma said holding her hand out to the farmer.

He shook it holding on to it for a bit too long.

"Righto, I'll get the leases over to you to sign. You're Mary Channing's girl aren't you?"

"How did you know that?" Emma was genuinely surprised

"Ah well there's not much I don't know around these parts!" Tom Hicks tapped the side of his nose,. "I knew her when she was a girl, your age, you're just like her too!" his eyes roamed freely up and down her body again. Emma felt an unease, something that felt like an itch, which if she scratched it could turn into something really nasty. She nodded curtly and said she would wait for the paperwork.

"Boy he's a bit creepy!" Linda said when they were back in the car. "You sure you're going to be alright with him perving around?"

"Don't worry about me Lind, I can look after myself."

"Well if you're sure." Linda pushed her glasses up her nose and fastened her seat belt.

On the way back to Emma's cottage they talked about the grooming parlour they were going to set up. " We'll have to get a bank loan for the equipment and work out what we are going to charge." Linda said excitedly.

"Yes, but I think we're in a pretty good position there, as long as we advertise well, there's loads of parking and the little pen to the back of the stables so that the dogs can wait there or go out there after their clips."

"I think it's going to be great!" Linda said, as they walked into the Channing's cottage.

"What's going to be great?" Mary Channing smiled charmingly at Linda, she approved of Emmas' friend, a real plain Jane of a girl. No-one who was likely to turn Emma's head any more than that wretched Mark had done.

"We've been to look at the stable block that is for rent at Hick's farm" Emma said. "We met the farmer and he said he knew you when you were young."

For a moment Mary Channing's smile faltered, but only for a moment.

"He must be mistaken, dear, I've never met him."

As he sat in the 747 that would take him back to Heathrow, Mark thought about the future. He was looking forward to being back in the little cottage but as Mary and Emma's cottage had four bedrooms, he had hoped they would offer him a room there. After all, the wedding was just one month a way now. Still at least he and Emma could be alone in the cottage and it could be a stop-gap until they could find their own place. He had made contact with various farming agents giving his requirements. Prices were higher than he had remembered and he might have to scale his operation back a bit but the thought of having his own place, albeit a rented farm, with his own stock filled him with a thrill of anticipation. As he watched the cabin crew answering the little insistent pings and small flashing lights above passengers' seats in the darkened cabin that broke into his thoughts, Mark wondered how Tony was doing. He had lost touch with him when he was in Saudi, he had written to him once but had had no reply. Hardly surprising he thought, regretfully, his last evening had hardly been his finest hour as far as Tony was concerned.

As Emma prepared to leave for the airport in the little car that Mark had sent her the money to buy for them, Mary came into her bedroom pulling the cord of her velour dressing gown tight around her. Her hair looked as it did during the day, set in corrugated grey waves, but without make up Emma noticed, her mother looked older, sterner, and deeply disapproving.

"It's very early isn't it?"

"Yes, mother, it is, but the flight gets in at 7 in the morning and I have an hour to drive to get there and then I have to park!"

"Well surely he could wait for a more reasonable hour to be picked up, it's hardly very considerate to drag you out in the middle of the night!"

"Mother it's 5.30 hardly the middle of the night, and I don't mind, I'm marrying Mark in a few weeks and as surprising as you may find it, I am actually looking forward to seeing him again."

"Sarcasm doesn't suit you my dear." Mary said sitting down on Emma's bed.

"Well I had a good teacher, didn't I mother, now I'm off" Holding her hair back she leaned over to kiss her mother on the cheek. "Go back to bed, I'll see you later."

At Heathrow, in terminal three arrivals, Emma stood at the barrier eagerly craning her neck to catch the first glimpse of Mark through the straggling line of disembarking passengers. Most were businessmen. There were a few families and Emma stared fascinated at the women head to toe in black, just their eyes visible, following behind their husbands. And then there he was, eagerly looking for her. As their eyes met he left his trolley and ran to the barrier, lifting her off her feet and kissing her hard on the mouth. The crowd clapped and laughed at the young couple in love.

"Oh my God Emma, it is so good to see you, I love you so much!" Mark held her face in his hands and showered it with kisses.

"I love you too!" Emma sobbed into his shoulder, he was back, her strong protector was back and everything was going to be wonderful.

One of the other passengers, a man that had been sitting next to Mark brought his luggage trolley around to the other side of the barrier and clapped him on the back.

"You're a lucky bloke!"

"I know that!" Mark beamed, and right there in the arrivals hall of Heathrow airport he got down on one knee, taking out the ring he had chosen for Emma. The crowd closed in around them, some people took photos and everyone clapped and cheered when Emma, through her tears took the ring and nodded her consent to Mark.

On the drive back to Berkshire they held hands; Mark keeping her hand under his even when he changed gears. They talked about their plans about how they had missed each other and then they sat quietly content to be in each other's company again. Mark looked at Emma, she was so beautiful, her profile delicate and totally enchanting. The thought that their wedding night was not far away now had had an immediate physical effect on him. He saw Emma glance over at his lap and look away. The fact that he would be her first and her only lover thrilled him and despite his desperate longing to be with her, he valued her all the more for it.

They reached the cottage and Emma handed the key to Mark to open the door. She had filled the little house with flowers and their scent hit them as they came in. A trail of rose petals led up the stairs and taking his hand Emma led Mark up, unbuttoning her blouse as she did so. Without saying anything more she led him into the bedroom where she had made up the bed with crisp white sheets. She had left one side of the bed covers folded down in an invitation to get into the exquisitely made bed. As Mark looked from Emma to the bed and back to her again, she stepped out of her jeans, and took off first her bra and then her panties, standing naked in front of him. The morning sun streaming through the window highlighted the curves of her perfect body, the swell of her full breasts, their dark nipples erect, her flat stomach and downy mons. Looking from her body to her face Mark saw there were tears in her eyes.

"Are you sure?" he croaked.

Emma nodded and he picked her up carrying her tenderly to the bed. Then keeping his eyes on her he stripped off his clothes, his erection so engorged that he was in physical pain. As he stepped out of his boxers Emma's eyes flickered to his manhood briefly and then back to his face and he saw fear in her eyes. His heart felt as though it would burst with love for her. Getting into bed beside her he held her to him and slowly and gently began to explore her body. As she relaxed he felt her breathing quicken and her hands begin a tentative exploration of their own. Finally when he thought he could stand it no longer he moved above her watching her eyes widen with his first gentle thrust. Gritting his teeth to try and prevent the inevitable Mark watched as her face softened, the fear replaced by building desire. And then it was over and as white hot lightening bolts wracked his body Mark knew that Emma was his, at last.

Around lunch time, after they had made love three more times, Mark asked Emma if she would like to go to the pub for lunch. She smiled at him. I'll have to shower first, we both will! They tried to shower together but the rickety shower over the bath had a mind of it's own and ran first cold then boiling hot before jumping off its catch and writhing like a snake spraying the whole bathroom with water.

As they laughed and Mark kissed Emma's flushed face he thought that he was the luckiest man on earth. He had hoped that he would give Emma her first orgasm but that had not happened, despite his gentle coaxing. Still there was time, he had to remember it was her first time. He could barely believe that they had made love at last.

In the pub at lunch time Mark and Emma ordered a ploughmans and sat together talking about their plans. To Mark, Emma looked more radiant since their love making, her lips slightly puffy, bruised form the intensity of his kisses, her face slightly red from the bristles on his unshaven face. He should be exhausted. He had not slept on the flight, but he was so happy to be home and now that he had made love to Emma, the tension that had been building in him since he met her had finally been released. His muscles felt almost fluid and his groin ached, but he was content.

Emma felt different as well, she was disappointed that she had not waited until their wedding night but at the same time she was relieved that she had got her first time out of the way. She knew that Mark had wanted her to have an orgasm but although she had been incredibly aroused there was something, some small part of her brain that would not switch off. She hoped that it would come in time.

The bar staff had all changed since they had worked there, and they knew no-one. Emma breathed a sigh of relief, she really did not want to share Mark with anyone at the moment. She thought about asking him if he had heard from Tony but she didn't want to spoil the magic of their first day together.

Now that she had slept with him she knew she had him. And this close to the wedding her mother's warnings about saving herself meant nothing. Mark was hers now.

Chapter 4

Marriage

As the last two weeks before the wedding sped past Mark split his time between helping Linda and Emma set up the dog grooming parlour and visiting his bank and various farms for rent in the area. The money he had earned in Saudi was tax-free and had impressed the bank manager enough to get him a very generous mortgage offer.

As he sat in the hot office of the old bank building Mark showed the manager the detailed business plan he had drawn up for his venture.

John Abbot was about the same age as Mark, with an open friendly face. Mark had imagined some kind of monocled old fossil of a bank manager and was pleasantly surprised. The two men sat on either side of ancient desk that had probably been in the bank since it was built and Mark took his papers out of his file.

"This is what I estimate the equipment will cost for the milking parlour and this is the amount I will need to pay for the rare breed cows.

John Abbott studied the papers.

"So what's the difference between common or garden cows and these rare breeds, where milk is concerned?"

"Well, rare breeds or at least the Shorthorn which I am interested in, are primarily a dual purpose breed. Beef Shorthorns have been developed as a separate breed and dairy breeders have also worked to improve the dairyness of the animals. Also, a blending scheme to introduce outside blood from other breeds has been introduced to maximise advantage"

"I see, so the whole of this rare breed has been bred to these standards?" John asked and Mark smiled.

"Actually some breeders did not participate in this scheme, and so there is now quite a diversity of type within the Shorthorn breed. This diversity of type means that the Shorthorn can be used in a variety of different systems. In Ireland, for instance the majority of Shorthorns are used for their suckler/beef capabilities, whereas in the UK the milking qualities of the breed have been developed. That's what I am interested in."

"So why the Shorthorn in particular?" John asked and Mark leaned forward, warming to his subject.

"The importance of the Shorthorn breed in the development of other cattle breeds is enormous, and Shorthorn genetics have been used worldwide in the development of over 40 different breeds. The breed has a very long and distinguished history, and developments on both the beef and dairy sides have ensured that the breed also has a very bright future."

"So are you planning to breed these cattle for beef as well?"

"Yes, there is a big demand for organic and rare breed beef and I am also keen to breed bulls for semen donation." John raised his eyebrows.

"Sounds like a nice life to me!" The two men laughed. John got up from his desk, running his finger inside his collar.

"God it's hot isn't it? We can't have air conditioning in the building, grade two listed and all that, and it's like an oven in here, I'm sorry about that!"

Mark got up, putting his papers away.

"No problem, it's like a cool spring morning compared to where I've been!" Mark said and John held out his hand.

"Leave this with me, I'll look through your plans and get back to you as soon as I can, but I don't think there'll be a problem." Mark shook his hand, the meeting had gone well.

When he got back to the cottage he found a note from Emma.

AT THE STABLE BLOCK X

As Mark walked down the track to where he could see Emma's partner Linda's battered Mini parked he thought how lucky he was. He had been back a week and although Emma had not stayed at the cottage with him and had repelled any amorous advance he made, he did not have long to wait now until they were man and wife. He replayed their first lovemaking time and time again in his head, it had been magical and it could only mean that they had the greatest time ahead of them when they were free to enjoy each other whenever they liked. He had worried that Emma might have become pregnant, he had not used anything, he asked her if she had started taking the pill. Her reaction surprised him.

"Why the hell would I do that? I'm not like a man, sleeping around everywhere whenever the opportunity presents itself. " Mark had physically reeled from the unexpected attack.

"God Em, I didn't mean . . . of course I didn't I just thought that you might have started on it in preparation for our marriage, don't doctors advise you to take it for a while before it's effective?" As soon as the words were out of his mouth Mark regretted them as Emma flashed her dark eyes at him, her face contorted.

"Well you obviously know all about it, more than I do in fact! Oh yes I had forgotten the lovely Tilly and however many others there were!" she spat at him.

"I do have a sister you know!" he countered weakly.

"Who discusses her sex life with you? Well *that's* healthy!" her voice dripped sarcasm.

Mark tried to take her in his arms, to hold her but she was rigid and unyielding and flashing him a hateful look, she had stalked out of the cottage and gone home.

He had sat stunned for a while in the little lounge of the cottage. He had forgotten about this side of Emma while he had been away. He knew he should feel angry with her, but he couldn't. He did not know where her insecurity came from but he was quite sure he was going to dispel any doubts she had about him. He was going to make her the happiest woman in the world.

She had arrived back at the cottage the next morning, her hair tied back in a ponytail, wearing shorts and a tee shirt that accentuated her exciting body. She had pressed herself to him and he could smell her shampoo and the fresh perfume she wore.

"Sorry Mark!" she whispered and he had kissed her deeply. He was due at the bank in an hour and he had felt that he could conquer anything with her by his side.

Now with the successful meeting under his belt Mark dispelled his thoughts of Emma's outburst of the day before. He found her with Linda, scrubbing the floor of the old stable that they were going to use as a parlour. Along one side of the stable was an old stone manger that Linda was washing out. It was cool in the stable and it smelt a bit musty, but not unpleasantly so.

"Hi girls!" Mark said coming in to the stable, from the bright sun, his eyes struggling to adapt to the gloom

"How'd it go?" Emma looked up at him from the floor, blowing at a tendril of hair that had escaped her ponytail and was hanging over her eyes. Her face was flushed.

Mark reached down and tucked the lock of hair behind her ear.

"Pretty well, I think!" he said dropping to his haunches in the cool of the stable.

"So will he give us the loan?" Emma leaned back on her heels looking at him hopefully.

"Well I don't want to jinx it, but he seemed pretty happy with the work I had done putting the business plan together!"

"Well done you two" Linda said, pushing her glasses up her nose. They kept steaming up as she bent over the bucket of hot water but she couldn't see a thing without them!

"Thanks Linda!" Mark said. "How's the fitting of the bridesmaid dress going?"

Linda blushed.

"Fine thanks, it's a lovely dress. He looked back at Emma. She was looking at him questioningly.

"What are you asking her that for Mark? Can't you see you're embarrassing her?"

Something in Emma's voice told Mark there was no right answer to her question and he jumped to his feet.

"Right, well I better get on, how about I buy you two ladies a pub lunch to celebrate?"

"We haven't got the loan yet!" Emma snapped

"No but we will have, my darling!" Mark said flashing her his most winning smile. It seemed to do the trick, she gave him a half smile back and they arranged to meet at one.

In her cottage Mary Channing was looking at the guest list for the wedding. She tutted. Despite her stipulation that the guest list should be even, there were still four more guests on Mark's side. The last four he had added were relatives visiting from South Africa; he said especially for the wedding, but Mary did not believe him. So that made twenty-four guests in total, not including the top table, which would be herself, Emma and Mark and Mark's brother, Tim or Tom or something. She knew that both Mark and Emma had wanted more guests but small and intimate was definitely better than big and showy, she had told them firmly. She sighed deeply, she supposed it was too late to do anything about it now but the whole thing seemed to be getting out of her control. That she did not like at all. She had always taught Emma that to be in control meant having power, and she was not ready to have her power challenged. She smiled to herself. The caterer would be coming round in the afternoon, she would have the last word. Not only was she not ready to have her authority challenged, she would make sure it wasn't!

Driving into town Mark was going to pick up the tickets for their honeymoon. He had kept it a secret from Emma, he wanted to surprise her. She had guessed at all sorts but so far not at the safari and beach holiday that he had booked for them in Kenya. He was glad about that as he did not think he would have been able to keep a straight face if she did guess at what he had planned. He hoped that she would love it. He had been to Kenya many times, several times in recent years with Tony, who had family there. Relics from the country's colonial farming past. Mark loved the Norfolk Hotel in Nairobi: its old world elegance and huge peaceful veranda at the front from where you could sip tea and watch the life of Nairobi go by. The hotel was wrapped around an inner courtyard where brightly coloured captive parrots squawked and all manner of fragrant and exotic plants flourished under the practiced eye of the hotel's gardeners. In the rooms, enormous ceiling fans moved lazily above large beds with crisp Egyptian cotton sheets. He imagined himself and Emma making love for hours cooled by the fan and the solid walls of the old colonial building. He couldn't wait!

Mark thought about Tony. He wondered where he was. He knew that he would have finished his PhD by now and probably gone back to London where his parents lived. He felt a twinge of regret that he had lost touch with his friend. They had had some good times together. He wondered if Tony and Tilly were still together, they were a good match, Mark thought. Tilly had been too much for him to handle. He had loved their wild abandoned lovemaking and her 'Zen' outlook on life but Tilly was a restless soul and a risk taker, and Mark knew that he would never be comfortable or relaxed with her. He thought of his Emma, feeling slightly guilty about his reminiscence of the wild times he had spent with Tilly. No, Emma was more his style, innocent and private and even more conservative than he was. They, too, were a good match.

Later that afternoon Mary Channing opened the door to the caterers.

"So where is the blushing bride?" the camp young man said clasping his hands together.

"Oh she apologised for not being able to be here, but don't worry I've been fully briefed!" Mary said brightly leading the young man and his harassed assistant out to the garden where the marquee was to be erected.

"Excellent, excellent," the camp young man clapped his hands enthusiastically, "such a *beautiful* garden."

"Thank you" Mary said demurely

"So then we will bring the tables and set them up in the marquee just here!" the young man spread his arms to encompass the area, then half squatted and simulated eating.

"How many guests will we be laying places for?" he said

Mary hesitated.

"Twenty" she said firmly.

The day of Mark and Emma's wedding dawned bright and clear. The humidity that had dogged the Berkshire village lifting slightly, as though in honour of the occasion.

As Emma woke up for the last time in her single bed she blinked in the morning light. She had not thought she would sleep but she had and she felt fresh and alive and ready to face her big day. Her dress was laid out in the spare room; the headdress resting on top of a vase on the wide windowsill. On her way to the bathroom Emma looked in on it. The virginal white of the dress seemed to reproach her and for a moment she felt a twinge of guilt. She should have waited for the wedding. But on the other hand her mother's dire warnings had been unfounded. Mark had not run for the hills as soon as he had made love to her; if anything he seemed keener than ever, and obviously very eager to repeat the experience. She was less so. It had hurt a bit but she thought she would get to like it. And Mark was very gentle and tender. She smiled to herself as she thought of him, his open honest face and his obvious love for her. She was a lucky girl.

Her mother had kept up her campaign to the end, telling Emma it was not too late to change her mind. Her parting shot, when all else failed was to say.

"Your wedding night will be an ordeal but always remember that sex can be your friend. Men are animals, it's really all that motivates them and it is in your power to take control by managing that side of things. Use it as a reward, withhold it as a punishment!"

Emma clapped her hands over her ears. "Mother, I can't believe you would say anything so.. so.. evil!" She said. She had been determined not to let her mother get to her, but this was so horrible that she ran upstairs to her room, slamming the door behind her.

Emma shuddered as she remembered what her mother had said. She looked outside, trying to distract herself. From the window of the spare bedroom she could see the marquee that had been erected the day before.

Late the night before, long after Mary Channing had gone to bed, Emma had let herself out of the cottage and walked barefoot around the inside of the marquee. The tables were dressed beautifully with white ruffled table cloths, the chairs covered in the same material. Elegant flower stands with white organza ribbons tied in huge bows stood ready for the flowers that would be delivered the next day. The top table where she would sit as Mrs. Richards stood at the head of the two tables at which their guests would sit. The caterers would lay the tables up while they were at the church but already the tablecloths had been strewn with a glittering confetti of tiny hearts in different colours. Under the bright moon that seemed to Emma almost as bright as sunlight in the clear summer night sky, the scene looked almost ghostly. A lovely ghostly tableau waiting for her and Mark to animate it.

Emma returned to the house, running her hands over all the familiar things that she had lived with from childhood. The old bookends above the mantelpiece, the grandfather clock that had marked the minutes of her life as a single woman. Back in her bedroom, she looked at the old battered teddy bear, missing an ear and threadbare in places, that she had slept with every night since she was born. Most of her clothes and possessions had been moved to Mark's cottage now, but teddy had to be here for her last night in the cottage. And he would be waiting for her when they got back from honeymoon. She sighed as the first butterflies began to flex their wings in her stomach, and made her way to the bathroom to shower.

And then before she knew it, she was at the alter. Mark looked down at her lovingly, his nervousness eclipsed by the almost ethereal beauty of her lovely face, her long dark hair curling softly on her bare shoulders. The summer warmth of her skin made the white of her dress all the more striking in its stark simplicity, a floor length sheath with a short train and an understated headdress fastened to her glossy dark hair with a simple tiara. She looked serene and beautiful and he felt a lump come to his throat.

The ceremony passed in a haze for both of them and as they stood on the steps of the church, Emma looked up at Mark as confetti rained down on them. As he leant over to kiss her he whispered.

"I am going to make you the happiest woman in the world, I can't wait for tonight!" Emma stiffened. "Was that all he could think about?" Seeing her eyes darken Mark said.

" . . . so that we can be alone and plan our future together." Emma softened and smiled back at him.

As the wedding party arrived back at the cottage, Mark and Emma took their places at the top table, Emma's mother to her right and Mark's brother Tom who had been his best man to his left. The guests had been told that there was no seating plan and they should seat themselves. As people took their seats Emma noticed four of the guests standing at the back of the tent. She looked up and down the tables. There weren't enough seats. The wedding coordinator was flapping around them looking at his notes and at the table and then back at the guests. Mark had noticed the commotion.

"Aren't there enough seats?" he asked Emma getting up from his chair.

"I thought your mother had briefed them about the numbers?" he strode to the back of the marquee. Emma looked across at her mother. Mary Channing was sitting staring at her hands a small smile playing around her lips.

"Mother! How many did you tell the caterers to lay up for?" Emma asked angrily

"Twenty, that was right wasn't it dear?" Mary looked at her daughter, all wide-eyed innocence.

"Mother you knew *very well* it was 24, Marks' family from South Africa?"

Mary put her hands to her face.

"Oh no, how awful, I am a silly old woman, I'm so sorry my darling, I must have got confused, I've had so much to do to prepare for this wedding" She sniffed loudly a convincing quaver in her voice. Emma glanced at the guests within earshot. All of them were looking at Mary sympathetically. Emma bit her tongue.

"It's OK mother, Mark is sorting it out. Luckily it looks like the caterers had extra cutlery and he's brought some chairs out from the dining room, so no harm done!" Emma said cheerily.

Mary glanced at the waiters scurrying around laying up the extra places. Only Emma recognised the annoyance in her mother's eyes.

And then at last the newly married Mr. and Mrs. Richards were heading for the airport, the obligatory cans and balloons tied to the back of their battered old car.

"Well this will be the first thing to go when we come back!" Mark said. As they stopped in a lay by to remove the clattering tins.

"Oh I see, I'm sorry I thought you were pleased with the choice of car I made, it wasn't easy with you away and everything!" Emma said petulantly. Mark glanced at his bride, was she joking? It didn't look like it!

"Hey hey! Of course I was pleased with it, it's done the trick, all I meant was that we will need to be thinking about four wheel drives, tractors and the like for our new life as farmers, Mark squeezed Emma's hand. Mollified she squeezed back.

When they arrived in Heathrow Mark would still not tell her where they were going. And it was only as they approached the check-in desk that she read the sign—BA 126 Nairobi

"Oh Mark, Nairobi? We're going on Safari?"

Mark nodded happily, he knew it was something she had always wanted to do and he was delighted to have been able to make sure that they did it in style.

The flight was a night flight although Mark didn't sleep much. He looked down tenderly at Emma's sleeping face on his shoulder, her long lashes sweeping her cheeks and her lips slightly parted. He supposed that he should have booked them a night in the UK before they set off and there was no doubt that he could not wait to make love to her as his wife, but they were on their way now. Soon they would be in the Norfolk Hotel and they would be able to consummate their marriage.

The African morning greeted them with a deep humidity and leaden skies. It was the coolest season in Kenya but the humid atmosphere still hit them like a wet slap in the face. The airport felt stuffy and smelt musty. Emma looked around her with wide eyes. The noise and the colour, the smells and the sights, all new to her. Their drive to the Norfolk was hair-raising and had her laughing and gasping with horror in equal measure. Being used to the enthusiastic driving of Saudi Arabia, Mark held her hand delighting in her obvious excitement.

They arrived at the hotel in the midst of the disgorging of a tour coach full of Americans. As they elbowed their way in, Charlie the concierge recognised Mark.

"Mr. Richards! I heard you were coming and this must be your lovely new wife?"

"Yes, this is my wife, Emma Richards." Mark felt a thrill of excitement and Emma blushed.

"Well now, I think that this is your first time to Kenya, Mrs. Richards?" Emma nodded and smiled at the man, his gentle lilting voice enchanted her.

"Well, we welcome you to the Norfolk Hotel!" he said as they followed him to their room.

"The Norfolk Hotel has played a leading role in Kenya's colourful history, and continues to be Nairobi's finest and best-known luxury hotel. The town and later the modern city of Nairobi grew up around The Norfolk Hotel, which still has its own private tropical gardens." He led them into the inner courtyard and Emma caught her breath

"It's beautiful!" she said.

"Thank you," Charlie beamed "Our hotel is still the traditional starting point for safaris and the Lord Delamere Terrace that you entered through, is modern Nairobi's most famous meeting place, where drinks and light meals are served continuously from morning until midnight. Well here is your room," he said throwing open the door to a large cool room, the bed sheets invitingly turned down. "Everyone at the Norfolk would like to offer their congratulations and we hope you have a wonderful stay with us."

Emma thanked Charlie and at last they were alone.

"Shower?" Mark said

"You go first!" Emma said opening her suitcase.

"I was kind of thinking we could shower together" Mark came up behind her putting his arms around her. She wriggled out of his grasp.

"No, you go ahead, I've got a bit of headache, I just want some sleep."

Mark stepped back as though he had been slapped. He got into the shower feeling numb. He had thought she would be as keen as he was to consummate their marriage and somewhere in his brain warning bells were sounding. He shook his head. He was being unreasonable. Emma must be exhausted after yesterday and the long flight. By the time he came out of the bathroom Emma was asleep curled up in the foetal position on the edge of her side of the bed. Mark got into his side of the bed and closed his eyes.

The ringing of the bedside phone woke them a few hours later. Mark answered it groggily.

"Hey Mark how's it hanging?" Mark sat up in bed.

"Tony?"

"Got it in one, I heard you were here, you old bastard, and I thought I would see if you were up for a wedding?"

"What are you on about?" Mark croaked.

"Tilly and me, we're in Nairobi to get married, then heading out to Naivasha to the old family homestead. Just a little civil thing but we wouldn't be too put out if you and Mrs. Richards, congrats by the way, came to the reception at the Carnivore."

Mark knew the Carnivore; it was a meat eaters paradise on the outskirts of the city.

"Yes, We'd love it Tone, when is it?"

"Tomorrow, about 2 ish."

"Great see you and Tilly then."

"Hey imagine that Em, Tony and Tilly are here tying the knot, they've invited us to their reception tomorrow . . ."

"I heard!" Emma said shortly, getting out of bed. "And we're not going."

Chapter 5

Honeymoon

In the malignant silence that hung between them after Emma's blunt dismissal of the idea of going to Tony and Tilly's wedding; Mark felt a cold knot in his stomach. There was no sign of the wonderful dewy-eyed girl that he had married not even 48 hours ago. Instead a hard faced and uncompromising woman with a set to her shoulders that was like a repellent force field had materialised in her place.

"Emma darling" Mark said, although he was aware that his voice sounded strangled and forced.

"I want to show you off to everyone, please say you'll go, after all I'm the proudest man in the world!" he tailed off, hell he wasn't even convincing himself.

"Hah!" Emma snorted. "More likely you want one more chance to drool over that tart Tilly before she marries your loser friend Tony. "

Mark flinched. It hurt him to hear Emma speak of his friend and ex lover like that. He knew they weren't bad people, just normal fun loving young adults, like he was. But, he thought, obviously a million miles away from what Emma was. Light years away from what he had thought she was. He sat miserably, his hands in his lap. He had no idea what to do now. A deep gloom started to take hold of him. He had no idea that depression could come on with such tangible and instant effect. Emma was fussing around putting her clothes into drawers. If it was not for the rigidity of her back and jerky movement, the scene would have looked entirely normal. But it was as far from normal as Mark could imagine.

"So shall we go out and about then?" Emma said brightly looking at him with raised eyebrows.

Mark got up wearily, he did not know what to say. They walked outside, he felt as though he was on automatic pilot. Emma tucked her arm through his and chatted about the sights and sounds that they passed.

"You're very quiet Mark, well, I suppose you've seen it all before, but you've got to remember that it's all new to me! Oh look at that woman carrying those bananas on her head. How on earth can she carry such a heavy load like that?"

They were opposite the old market in Nairobi now with all its noise and bustle. Normally Mark would have delighted in it but he felt numb, as though he had had a terrible shock. He stood on the pavement, unhappiness washing over him like a tidal wave. Emma was bending over a collection of carved wooden animals spread out on an old newspaper at the side of the road. Suddenly from out of the crowd a young man appeared snatching her bag from her shoulder and made off like a gazelle through the crowd. Instinctively Mark chased after him. He could hear Emma screaming his name and as he half turned his head he stumbled and fell into a big storm drain. As he pulled himself out of the drain Mark winced in pain. It felt as though he had twisted his ankle. God he was lucky he hadn't broken it. He limped back to where Emma was standing, sobbing at the spot at which he had left her; a curious crowd around her, jostling to see what was going on. Men, women and children with big bellies and snotty noses all stared at her.

"Mark what the hell do you think you're doing?" She flew at him hitting his shoulder.

"How could you just leave me here like that?"

"I was going after the thief!" Mark said, blood was oozing from a cut on his leg now dripping down onto the pavement. The crowd of onlookers chuckled as Emma continued to rant at Mark. He started to limp back in the direction of the hotel.

"WHERE ARE YOU GOING?" Emma shrieked running after him.

"I have to get this leg seen to!" he said.

"What about my bag?" she sobbed

"Well I tried to get that back and that didn't suit you, so you tell me Emma what the hell do you want from me?"

he shouted. Emma recoiled from him as though he had hit her. The crowd that were keeping pace with them stopped as they stood face to face, Emma with her fists held in front of her, Mark with blood trickling down his leg. Then as if seeing the crowd for the first time Emma said

"Mark, you're making a scene! Lets go back to the hotel." Dumbstruck Mark limped behind her back to the hotel.

When they got into their room Mark went and sat on the edge of the bath stripping his trousers off to reveal a large gash on the side of his leg.

"I think this might need stitches" he said

"Rubbish!" Emma said "We haven't got time for that now, we need to get down to the police station and report my cards missing."

Charlie who had seen them come in was tapping on the door.

"Mrs. Richards is everything all right?" Emma let him in, explaining tearfully about the fact that she had had her bag snatched.

"Oh no this is terrible, I will call one of the officers from the station to come here and see you."

"Oh thanks so much, I'm really too frightened to go out again, especially as Mark left me in the middle of the market on my own!" she said.

"But he's here now? I thought you both came in?"

"Yes, he's in the bathroom. He's cut his leg." Emma said dismissively.

"In here Charlie" Mark called and Charlie appeared at the bathroom door.

"That looks like a bad cut, I think I better call a doctor for you. It may need some stitches!" Charlie said his friendly face the picture of concern.

"This is a terrible thing to happen on your honeymoon, I'm so sorry! Both of you just wait here and I will let you know when the police and the doctor get here. I will send some tea for you."

The policeman that arrived in a smart uniform took the details of the crime but did not hold out much hope that any of Emma's possessions would be recovered.

"Unfortunately there are a lot of thieves in the market, we always advise our lady visitors to wear their bags on a long strap across their body to make it harder for the thieves to strike."

The police officer wanted to know what had happened to Mark's leg and when Mark told him about how he chased the thief he shook his head."

"That is not a good idea Mr. Richards, some of these miscreants carry knives and it could have been a lot worse for you!"

"Yes, imagine that, running off and leaving me alone like that!" Emma said viciously.

Mark felt his depression deepen. This was turning into a nightmare, very far from the idyllic honeymoon he had imagined. He glanced at his watch. It was approaching noon. He knew without even broaching the subject with Emma again that going to the Carnivore to meet Tony and Tilly was out of the question. The doctor arrived soon afterwards and stitched his leg, dressing it and announcing his attention to come back the day after to change the bandage. His bill took a big chunk out of the money Mark had brought with them to spend but he would be able to get it back from the insurance armed with the police report and the doctor's bill.

That evening they sat out on the veranda sipping cocktails and watching the hotel guests getting ready to go out for the evening. Emma had calmed down a bit now that she realised that there was no danger of them having to go to Tony and Tilly's reception. As Mark looked out into the Nairobi night Emma said.

"I'm sorry we couldn't go to Tilly and Tony's do." Mark looked at her sharply. He knew she wasn't.

"I know I didn't want to go but it was only because I wanted to be alone with you, after all it is our honeymoon. I was just about to say that we *should* pop out and see them, when my bag was snatched. After that I didn't feel like it, and with your leg, it wouldn't have been a good idea would it?" she looked at him pleadingly and Mark softened. It was true the bag snatching and his fall had been a huge shock, and he had to remember this is the first time Emma had been out of the country. It must have been terrifying for her.

He reached over and squeezed her hand. "Well I'm glad you want to be alone with me and I want to be alone with you too. It occurs to me that we haven't consummated our marriage yet, and that's a situation I don't want to continue!"

"Me neither" she said brightly although he felt her hand tense slightly in his. "But what about your leg isn't it too painful?"

"No, I'll be fine!" he said watching for her reaction. But she smiled warmly at him and even leaned over to give him a kiss.

They were about to go back to their room when he heard someone calling his name.

"Mark, you miserable no-show! Don't think you get away that easily, I thought if the mountain wouldn't come to Mohammed, then, well you know the rest!" It was Tony, obviously slightly drunk and hand in hand with a tanned and radiant looking Tilly. Mark experienced a mixture of emotions, he was delighted to see his old friend but at the same time he realised that this was very likely to put pay to any chance he had of making love to Emma tonight. He glanced at her. She was sitting stony faced her back up handbag on her knees like a middle aged matron. Mark could not help contrast his frosty faced bride with the carefree and lovely Tilly who had thrown her arms around his neck and was giving him a kiss. She smelt of flowers and sex. He extricated himself and shook Tony by the hand. When he looked around again Emma was kissing Tilly on the cheek offering congratulations. As the two couples sat down, Emma began to tell them of their ordeal. She pointed at Marks bandaged leg visible below the hem of his shorts..

"It was a *very* bad gash, the doctor had to put, how many stitches was it darling?" she looked up at him.

"Six." He answered stunned. Emma had shown no interest in his injury at the time, in fact she hadn't even wanted him to see a doctor.

"Oh you poor things" Tilly said hugging Emma. "We are so sorry, no wonder you couldn't make it!"

"Yes what with the doctor and the police, we were tied up for ages! When we were finished it was too late and to be honest we weren't in the mood, but I'm *so* glad you both came here!" Emma said

Mark was speechless. Both Tilly and Tony seemed to have been taken in by Emma. He supposed at least that was better than the actual version of Emma's reaction to their invitation. Mark scrutinised his friend's face for any hint that he had seen through Emma's earnest protestations. He saw none. Although he was pleased that Emma had not made a scene the cold knot in his stomach tightened as he felt a deep disquiet at how easily his wife could lie. It was to be something she used against him in years to come, to massively detrimental effect.

Tony and Tilly left an hour later and the two newly married couples waved goodbye like long lost friends.

"Listen you two when you're out on Safari, if you get close to Naivasha make sure you pop in and see the family. We're going down the coast now then up to the parks afterwards."

"We will, and thank you!" Emma said waving them off and as she said it Mark knew without the smallest doubt that there was absolutely no chance, even if theirs was the only home left in the country, that Emma would be visiting Tony's relatives.

Back in their room they undressed for bed. Emma had not spoken since Tony and Tilly left and Mark was bracing himself for her attack. But it didn't come. Instead as they lay together under the huge fan in the restless African night, her hand found his and when he turned on his side to kiss her she did not resist. Despite himself Mark felt the beginning of his physical response to her closeness and although they still had not said a word to each other, she did not stop him making love to her. Looking down at her impassive face Mark felt almost guilty for taking her body when she was so obviously not interested. But he needed to claim her as his bride and as her beautiful eyes opened to watch him in the final throes of his passion she smiled and kissed his lips and he collapsed on top of her, tears pricking the back of his eyelids , For a moment the tight cold fist in his stomach slackened.

As he lay with her curled up in the crook of his arm he said.

"Emma, why did you let me . . . you know, when you really weren't in the mood?"

"Because I love you." She said quietly.

The next morning they set off on Safari. They were heading for Mount Kenya and the Mount Kenya Safari Club via lakes Naivasha and Nakuru. Emma was her brightest most excited adorable self during the day as they drove through wildlife parks and marvelled at the sights and sounds of the country. At night they stayed in hunting lodges and park hotels where Emma showed sometimes more but mostly less interest in sex. Mark was desperate to give her her first orgasm but that, it seemed, was a long way off. In fact the abandon she had shown the first night they had made love before they were married had never been repeated. But left to themselves with minimum contact with other holidaymakers Emma was the lovely warm girl he had fallen in love with.

As their dusty jeep approached the Mount Kneya Safari Club Emma clapped her hands to her face at the impressive view. The majestic Mount Kenya rose behind the hotel and as they drove through some of the 100 acres of landscaped gardens, Emma pointed out the peacocks, their haunting cries hanging on the air as they passed.

"They do riding, golf, croquet, they've got a bowling green, table tennis, swimming, and they've got a beauty salon, not that you need it!" Mark said.

"I don't know about that?" Emma laughed, "10 days on Safari have taken their toll!"

Emma could hardly comprehend the beauty of the place.

"Look Mark," Emma said," there's a sign for an animal orphanage. Can we visit it?"

Mark laughed, "Of course we can!"

The concierge met them at the door snapping his fingers for the porters who whisked their luggage away to their room.

"Mr and Mrs. Richards, Welcome, we want our guests to be able to relax and appreciate the superb setting, the personal attention lavished on all our visitors, the numerous activities and superb cuisine. One night is just not enough. Fairmont Mount Kenya Safari Club! I am sure we will be able to persuade you to stay with us for another night or two?"

"Well we do have a schedule" Mark said doubtfully.

Emma was looking at the heads of hunted beasts mounted on the walls of the old hunting lodge, relics of a bygone era. Huge skins lay on the floor and despite the fact that she loved animals she was surprised to find she was not upset. These magnificent creatures had lived and died in a very different age to the one they were living in now.

"Oh please Mark, can we stay another night? I just love this place!"

Mark smiled. It was the most animated Emma had been since they had been on honeymoon.

Their room, when they reached it, was even more breathtaking. A huge bed with thick blanket draped over it stood in the centre of the high ceilinged room and a fire blazed in an enormous fireplace in front of which a sheepskin rug practically begged to be made love on.

"At this time the weather can be cooler and we like to make our guests comfortable at night." The porter said with a wide smile.

Emma clapped her hands and danced around the room. "I love it, look at the view Mark!" Outside the large window the slopes of Mont Kenya rose gently; the lush green giving way to imposing rock as the mountain disappeared into the low cloud.

That night they made love in front of the fire and for the first time since they had been married Mark felt that they had got close to the passion and closeness that had been a feature of the only time they had made love before they were married. The cold knot in his stomach had almost dissipated now as he and Emma lay entwined in each others arms naked on the sheepskin rug, the dark mountain looking down on them under a star strewn sky.

The next morning they made for the animal orphanage. The sanctuary had been set up for animals that had been orphaned or were vulnerable in other ways. The animals of all shapes and sizes were housed in pens or left to roam freely. As they arrived one of the keepers brought out a baby chimpanzee who made straight for Emma and hugged her legs. Emma dropped to her knees and the young animal climbed onto her lap and put his arms around her neck.

Looking into his eyes, eyes, they had been told, that had seen his mother butchered in front of him. Emma burst into tears. The young animal looked at her curiously, gently touching her face and putting her salty tears to his lips. Mark felt close to tears himself. It was not the story of this young animal's ordeal that touched him as much as seeing this genuine and heartfelt reaction from his wife. He knew now that Emma was a self contained individual with a capacity for inflicting emotional pain that often left him breathless, maybe this was the beginning of her thaw? He hoped so.

As the young animal clung to Emma Mark looked at his wife lovingly. He knew she loved animals and something in the way that she was holding the chimpanzee, the tenderness that she showed and the sadness she felt for its predicament, stirred him. All of a sudden and for the first time he thought about their future together and the children they would have. Emma would obviously be a great mother.

As they left the Safari Club each of them deep in their own thoughts Mark put out his hand to rest it on her brown leg. She put her own small hand over his and they sat for a long time without speaking. The cold fist that he had had in his stomach had gone now, this was the Emma he had fallen in love with. For the first time since they had come on honeymoon he could see a bright future stretching ahead of them.

Back in Berkshire, they moved into the little cottage. Emma and Linda were ready to open their dog grooming business and Mark was busy looking for a suitable farm for them to rent. As he helped the girls move the new grooming table into the old stable farmer Hicks arrived. Mark did not miss the lingering looks the older man directed to his wife's cleavage and her tanned legs under the frayed hem of her denim shorts.

God he might just as well lick his lips and rub his hands together! Mark thought. Still he supposed that any red-blooded man would be stirred by Emma's looks. She was stunning, her tan from the honeymoon complimented her dark hair that now had lighter streaks in it, courtesy of the African sun.

"I hear you're on the look out for a small holdin'" he said to Mark while he kept his eyes on Emma's shapely bottom as she manoeuvred the table into position.

"Well yes, I plan to raise and milk Shorthorns!"

"'Ow many acres you lookin' for? The farmer was leaning forward now to see down Emma's teeshirt.

Mark positioned himself in between them. And the farmer looked at him annoyance on his slack jawed face

"About 50 acres I suppose, a bit more maybe, I am planning to have a herd of about 30 to begin with."

"Milkin' or beef?" the farmer said standing on tip-toe to try and see over Mark's shoulder.

"Both" Mark said, relieved as Emma and Linda went out to their van to begin bringing in their grooming tools.

"Might be able to 'elp you there."

"Oh?" Mark said hoping that the farmer would not make him an offer he cold not refuse. He could not imagine anything worse than him hanging around the girls all the time.

In the end Elijah Hicks did make Mark an offer he couldn't refuse. He offered to let him 60 acres around the cottage and have the use of the barns and yard.

"I'm diversifyin'" he said, goin' into chickens and pigs and I got that set up on the north side of the farm. No-one wanted the land and barns without 'ccomodation but you two are already sittin' pretty in the cottage so it should be right convenient for you!" The farmer eyed Mark up and down.

"You two quite comfortable in the cottage? The bed big enough for you?" Mark shuddered at the lascivious look in the farmer's eye, he really was the most unpleasant character that Mark had ever met.

"We are both very comfortable thanks, Emma tells me you used to know her mother, Mary Channing?"

The farmer looked at him sharply.

"I did, but that was a long time gone now." He said.

Elijah Hicks offered him a really good deal on the land. Mark really could not afford to turn it down. He broached the subject with Emma that night as they sat down for supper.

"I know that he is a terrible letch, but the deal he's offering is a great one and we wouldn't have to move, we'd be near your mother." Mark held his breath waiting for her reaction.

"I can put up with farmer Hicks, if it means that we can be working together." Emma put down her knife and fork and patted his hand. "We would be wouldn't we and besides, now that Linda and I have set up the dog grooming, it would make sense. Who knows how far I would have to travel to it if you didn't find a farm locally."

"Ok then we'll go for it!" I'll give the old boy a ring in the morning!"

That night they made love again and Emma was soft and responsive to his touch. Her eyes studied him during their lovemaking almost curiously and although she seemed to enjoy it, her gaze seemed, at times, almost dispassionate to Mark as though she was trying hard to understand his passion and the overwhelming desire he felt for her. It hurt him that despite all his efforts to arouse her and to satisfy her, their lovemaking still seemed like a one sided affair.

But Mark did not think he could afford to spend too much time trying to understand what made Emma tick. She was on the pill now "The doctor said that I might feel sick with these pills. " she said. As a result, she would often tell him that she was not in the mood for sex, more often than not, he thought as he lay back, sated on his pillow. The old cold fist that had been a feature of their honeymoon had made a

Oliver Kaye

comeback now but somehow just when he got to the point that he felt he would have to confront the situation they would share a night like this and his fears would recede a little again.

The deal done with Elijah Hicks, Mark went to the bank again. His loan had been approved and now all he had to do was to go and sign on the dotted line and give John Abbot the details of the herd of Shorthorns that he had ordered, as well as the equipment for the milking parlour that they were having installed in one of the barns.

Emma had gone with Linda to a local dog show to do some marketing and as he sat outside the bank, Mark looked at his watch. He was a bit early. Fishing deep under the seat of his car he took out a battered packet of cigarettes. He had promised Emma that he would give up after they were married, and for the most part he stuck to his promise. But once in a while he could not resist the temptation and today was one of those days. He knew that this marked the beginning of a new chapter of his life, a new chapter for them both. And yet he had a feeling of unease. He lit the cigarette and took a deep drag. It was just the jitters from tying himself up to such a big loan and responsibility. As he put his hand out of the car window to tap the ash off the end of his cigarette he looked up.

On the other side of the road Mary Channing stood looking at him. He pulled his hand in quickly, stubbing the cigarette out in the ashtray. But it was too late she had seen him. Mark studied her face for a moment. As the older woman turned away from him he read, unmistakably, a look of triumph. He felt confused. He would have understood if she had come over and chided him for smoking behind Emma's back but the look of pure delight and triumph was a reaction he had not expected. He knew that whatever Mary Channing's expression meant, it would be nothing good. And he was right.

He shook his head and took a mint out of his pocket. He was behaving like a naughty schoolboy. He had had a cigarette, so what? He was a big boy and it wasn't against the law. He was blowing things out of proportion. To imagine serious repercussions was to be paranoid. He almost smiled to himself as he walked into the bank. He was being ridiculous.

The next twenty-four hours were to prove to him how wrong he was.

Chapter 6

Farming

Mark came back to the cottage with the paper work for the farm and swung in the back door whistling.

"Em, are you here?" he called out striding through the lounge to the foot of the little flight of stairs that led to the upstairs of the cottage.

He was about to go up when something caught his eye. Sitting silently in the chair beside the TV Emma had her arms folded, her eyes were dark as they met his.

"Darling, there you are, didn't you hear . . . ." He tailed off, obviously she had heard him, he had walked right past her!

"I heard you aright, I was just too angry to speak to you"

Mark was nonplussed.

"Angry with me? About what?" he was genuinely mystified.

"Mother came out to see me at the grooming parlour this afternoon, while you were in the bank." Mark immediately realised what had happened. Mary had seen him smoking and knowing of his promise to Emma that he would stop once they had got married she had wasted no time in getting out to the farm to tell her daughter what she had seen.

Mark laughed and sat down opposite her. Was that all? Well how serious could that be? He was about to find out.

Emma flew out of her chair and stood in front of him her hands balled into tight fists at her sides.

"You think it's funny do you?" she shouted. "My mother was right. You are totally unreliable. If you can lie to me about this, then what else are you going to lie to me about? It seems to come so easily to you! You've obviously been smoking all the while behind my back!"

Mark stood up. There was something about her standing over him, looking down at him that agitated him and made him feel uneasy. Now looking down at her he tried to put his arms around her.

"Em, it's just been the odd one, honestly! I can show you that pack I've got in the car, I've had it since before we got married and it's still half full!"

"Get off me!" Emma hissed through clenched teeth.

"Why is it so difficult for you to give up? Don't you care about me at all?"

"Of course I do, but really Em it's just the odd ciggie, I mean you don't smell it on me do you?"

"What does that matter? You are going behind my back, we haven't been married five minutes and you are deceiving me! What does that say for our marriage, for our future?"

Mark stared at her in shock.

"You are getting this completely out of proportion. What does me having the odd ciggie have to do with deceiving you?"

"Because you promised, me, solemnly promised me that you wouldn't smoke after we were married, and I believed you!" her voice was low now, almost a croak and Mark felt the hairs on the back of his neck rise. Her face contorted, her voice deep and tortured, he hardly recognised her. He sat back down on the chair, his legs too weak to support him. She stood over him, her face a mask of . . . . of what? A mask of hate! Unmistakably. Mark felt sick.

"Well Mark" her voice was normal again now, but clipped and dismissive.

"If that's all you think of me, of our marriage, well then, at least I know."

"What does *that* mean?" Mark said. He suddenly felt very tired.

"Well obviously it means less to you than it does to me, much less, so I will have to be prepared and watch you even more closely."

"I won't smoke again, I promise." Mark said wearily

"You promised before." She said

"Well this time I mean it. I'm sorry I had no idea it meant so much to you."

"Well it does, and to think that I have wasted my time trying to convince my mother that you were a good man, she warned me and now she says she will disown me if I stay with you. So that's how much it means Mark, will that do you?" she stalked out of the room.

Mark sighed deeply. He felt exhausted and a wave of dark depression washed over him. He felt the cold fist in his stomach tighten it's grip.

As they lay in bed that night, Mark reached out to her, putting his hand gently on her shoulder. She shrugged his hand off.

"If you touch me again, I will go an sleep in the spare room!" she said her voice cutting through the mellow night air like a knife.

"Don't trouble yourself," he said shortly, "I'll go."

And that was where he stayed for the next three weeks. Although Emma was pleasant to him, even although it was in a detached polite stranger way, any physical contact was repelled immediately. She told him that she was feeling ill, that the pill was having a bad effect on her. That the last thing she felt like was intimacy. Mark could not believe that his marriage was falling apart so soon. He buried himself in his work. He thought about the thrill of expectation he had had before they were married especially after the first time with Emma when he had come back from Saudi. Now, it seemed, that was likely to be the highlight of their love life!

Mark looked into seeing if he could buy the land he was renting from Elijah Hicks. Searches had revealed that it was very difficult to find land to rent to convert to organic status. And he was determined that his herd's milk and meat would be organic. He knew that it took a minimum of two years to convert land used for other purposes to organic status in most instances. Coupled with that he discovered that landowners would only normally give grazing licenses for roughly ten months.

As he read the local farming news, Mark frowned. There was enormous upheaval in the farming industry and the government had announced that it would be introducing milk quotas. This effectively put paid to most young farmers starting small cow dairy businesses without massive or family support. Mark felt as though his world was falling apart. He lay awake at night worrying about what to do. He tried to squash the anger he felt at Emma who lay asleep next door, seemingly content for their marriage to be over, in all but name, before it had even begun.

Boots, the chemist, had lost the photos that they had taken on honeymoon. Mark had all but forgotten them when he got a phone call from the chemist, offering profuse apologies for the delay but giving him the good news that they had found the two wallets of photographs. It seemed ironic that the photos had surfaced now, now that Mark felt that his marriage was all but over and his business ruined before it even started. He had to go into town to see John Abbot at the bank about buying the land. Elijah Hicks had agreed to sell him some, not all he wanted, but just about enough, Mark calculated. Early again for his meeting, he popped into the chemist and leafed through the photos. He hardly recognised the carefree young man smiling in the photos as his new wife clapped her hands in delight at the herd of goats they had come across being tended by a tall and magnificent Masai in the Masai Mara. Mark smiled as he remembered the village they had visited where they had seen the goats being milked along with a couple of strange looking sheep. The ones of Mount Kenya were breathtaking. As he flipped through them Mark suddenly stopped and went back to the ones they had taken of the strong and handsome Masai women milking the goats. An idea was forming in his mind. He had read in the article about milk quotas that goats and sheep for dairy were excluded. At the time he had hardly registered it. It would be something highly unusual and no doubt local farmers would treat it as a joke, but maybe this was the answer. It was something different. He would have to do his homework, was there even a call for organic goat or sheep milk in England? In the two years he would need to establish organic status how would he survive?

His head spinning with the new possibilities Mark went into the bank. John Abbott had become quite a friend, they had even been out for a drink once or twice together.

Mark sat down in the big office and opened his folder.

"Actually I think this is pretty much useless now" he said.

John sat up straight in his chair.

"Looks like you've put a lot of work into that Mark, surely you're not thinking of throwing it in?"

"Not exactly!" Mark said cautiously. Would John Abbott think that he had taken leave of his senses?

"I will need more land to be able to grow organic hay for feed." Mark said. I don't think I will be able to grow enough on the land as it stands at the moment. And as I want this to be an organic operation I will need organic hay to compliment the hay that I grow to organic standards, and I don't think such a thing exists.

John Abbott sat back in his chair.

"It's certainly radical, Mark, are you sure that there is a market for this type of milk?

"No I'm not!" Mark said honestly "the idea only came to me half an hour ago!"

"Well, do your home work and we'll make anther appointment for the day after tomorrow. John leaned back in his chair looking thoughtful then said cautiously "I know a couple of real characters, Isaac and Paul Rogers that to all intents and purposes are still living in the 1940s. They have no electricity or modern plumbing in their farmhouse. Their farming methods are one step above the horse drawn era! I reckon their farming methods might be closest to what you are proposing. If you want to go ahead with this new plan, I could introduce you to them. . They are of a generation that won't do business with strangers, or at least without feedback from the district, but they trust me. If I introduced you . . . ."

"Thanks John!" Mark said, relieved that the young bank manger had not laughed him out of his office.

Mark spent the next day on the phone and quickly established that there was a market for organic goat and sheep's milk. Not a big one but it seemed to be growing and the costings stacked up. He would not need to spend so much on a milking parlour if he was not having cows, so he could spend more on the land.

Back in the bank Mark shook hands with John.

"Looks like it's a goer, economically!" he said.

John smiled

"I made preliminary contact with the family I told you about. It seems that the younger brother Isaac is keen to sell some land that they have. It joins onto the land that you are renting from Elijah Hicks. I've arranged for us to visit this afternoon."

Over the next few weeks Mark visited the brothers, Isaac and Paul several times to get to know them a bit more, first of all with John and then alone. Isaac was keen to sell, but Paul was adamant that they should follow their mother's doctrine never to sell land. The brothers were quite famous locally for their dry cider and sent Mark home with a flagon. Mark had just started to make his own and the three men talked long into the evenings about the various methods of making the perfect cider.

Through the autumn, the apple harvest and cider making time, Mark met the brothers often to discuss the land sale. These meetings took place in the cool cider house, as they sampled ciders, usually after dark and with moonlight filtering through the barn door. The country side had its own etiquette and it was considered bad manners to talk directly about money so the three men would talk about local gossip for an hour before coming round to the subject of selling the land. Mark found it quite difficult to keep a clear head, as the dry cider was strong. Added to that Paul had the habit of taking umbrage at the most unexpected things and would suddenly storm off to return harrumphing half an hour later.

In the end it took about four months to negotiate to the point of instructing solicitors. But finally Mark bought forty-one acres of land with water but no fences or electricity.

Emma was busy too, the grooming parlour had become a big success with waiting times for a clip of up to a month. She and Linda were working flat out 6 days a week. Mark and Emma were back in the little cottage bedroom together now but Mark could count on one hand the times that they had made love since they were married. He was busy and generally managed to stop himself dwelling on the subject but he could not help feeling cheated. Emma was either too tired from the kennels or was feeling sick or tender from the contraceptive pill that she was taking.

"Hardly worth taking the damn thing is it?" Mark said in frustration one night as she pushed him away again, claiming that she felt ill.

"Mark!" she turned her stricken face to him. In the moonlight that filtered through the window from the clear night sky she looked achingly beautiful. She had lost a bit of weight since she and Linda had been so busy at the grooming parlour and it made her cheekbones stand out more, and her beautiful eyes appear bigger.

"Sorry!" Mark was immediately contrite. He held her to him and stroked her hair as her tense muscles relaxed. Soon her breathing deepened and he realised she was asleep. He lay awake for hours holding her in his arms and listening to her breathe. He loved her and he wanted more than anything for her to give herself to him, to let down her barriers both physically and mentally.

The plans for the farm were progressing slowly. Mark felt guilty that they had to rely on the money Emma earned at the grooming parlour while all his money went on equipment for the herd of goats and flock of sheep that he was soon going to have on the farm. Emma was quick to remind him that she was, in effect, the breadwinner and failed to acknowledge even slightly the contribution he was making to their future. At first Mark found this amusing, and was happy for her to take the credit for supporting them. She was rightly proud of her business and she and Linda even had plans to take on another groomer. But as the time went on and she showed barely any interest in his work towards setting the farm up, insisting, instead, in cutting into what he was saying with her own stories about the dogs and owners that she met each day, Mark began to feel uneasy. It was almost as though she did not see the farm as part of her world, her future. Not for the first time he felt completely out of his depth with the complex woman he had married.

Mary Channing rarely visited the cottage but Mark and Emma were expected to make the weekly pilgrimage to her cottage for Sunday lunch. One lovely crisp weekend Mark had suggested that they take off and head for the coast. Emma looked at him incredulously.

"But we got mum's for lunch on Sunday, it would hardly be worth it, we would have to leave really early to get back in time."

"Well" Mark said gently, "I thought that just for once we could miss lunch and take off, it will be fun!" Mark finished lamely

Emma looked at him disdainfully.

"Don't be silly Mark, she's expecting us!" and with that the subject was closed.

At least, Mark thought Mary seemed interested in his plans and questioned him closely each week about how the plans were going. She made no secret of the fact that she thought he had completely taken leave of his senses to be buying goats and sheep rather than the traditional milking herd. But over the weeks as he carefully explained his reasoning and the finances of the venture she appeared to be grasping the concept. Unlike Emma she did show an interest and for that Mark was grateful. He was still annoyed that she had caused so much trouble between him and Emma over the cigarette she had seen him smoke outside the bank. He still smarted to think that she had threatened to disown her daughter if Emma stayed with him. He had never questioned either Emma or her mother over that one, he was not sure he wanted to know the truth; but by and large he supposed they rubbed along OK together.

Elijah Hicks had offered to sell Mark some fencing for his newly acquired land and he also offered some of his workforce to help Mark put it up.

As the two men drove to the out skirts of the land to start the fencing Elijah said.

"'Ow's that mother in law of yours then?"

"Fine, why do you ask?"

"No reason, I s'pose your missus reminds me a lot of her when she was a young'un!"

Mark could not imagine Mary as a 'young'un' and he smiled.

"Did you know her well?"

Elijah gave a chortle

"S'pose you could say that, there was a few of us knew 'er quite well!" he laughed again and Mark looked at him in frank amazement. Was he hinting that Mary had been a bit free with her affections when she was young? Mark said nothing, hoping that Elijah would continue.

"Ah them was the days!" the old farmer said warming to the memory "and that poor bugger lives over at Burghclere, in the old school house. Well, he knew her the best of all!" Mark held his breath.

"Yes, that poor old bugger, 'e'd be delighted to see your missus, 'e would but at that time old Mary weren't 'aving none of it!"

"Was he married to Mary?" Mark asked trying to sound casual

"Yep 'e was for a bit, but once she popped the sprog, your Emma, she saw 'im on 'is way!"

"The marriage broke up?" Mark said

"Well not so much broke as was terminated by 'er, you could say!" Elijah said.

Mark's mind was reeling. He was sure that Emma had no idea where her father was and to think that he was living in a village not five miles away was incredible.

"'Course 'e moved 'iself off to London when she gave 'im the bums rush, 'e was some sort of a book selling type, and 'e used to get them old books and do them up, that sort of thing! So 'e had no trouble getting work up there. Done alright for 'iself as well by all accounts, bought the old school house over in Burghclere, about five years ago."

Mark could hardly believe what he was hearing. The village was a small place and word spread fast. It was inconceivable that neither Mary nor Emma knew that Emma's father was living so close. If Elijah Hicks knew the relationship then others would too and in Mark's experience, nothing travelled faster on the village grapevine than juicy gossip of this type.

That night as they ate cottage pie for supper Mark said.

"Do you ever hear anything about your dad?"

Emma put down her knife and fork and looked at him

"Why on earth would you ask that Mark?"

"Just curious."

"I have no idea whether or not he is even still alive. You know that it is a sensitive subject for my mother and because of that I don't speak about it. He was horrible to her. She doesn't need reminding of him!"

"In what way was he horrible?" Mark asked.

"Well how the hell would I know Mark? What is this?"

"I don't know I just thought you might be curious. You might have wanted to try and find out where he was and maybe meet him."

"Well I don't!" she said.

"You don't want to or you've always been told that you don't want to?" Mark waited for the outburst.

Emma looked at him and for a moment her dark eyes clouded with doubt.

"I don't know. Of course I have often wondered about him, I'm only human"

"You know, the relationship between you and him would have nothing to do with your mothers relationship with him, don't you? It would be alright for you to know him and form your own relationship with him." Mark said gently.

Emma had tears in her eyes now.

"Well it's pretty much a pointless thing to talk about Mark, no-one has any idea where he is, and even if mum did have any idea, I am quite sure she wouldn't be telling me!"

Mark hesitated. Should he tell Emma what Elijah Hicks had said? She was clearing their plates away now and he helped her carry the things through to the little kitchen. When they had finished, she washing and him drying, he took her by the hand and led her to the little lounge.

"Em, sit down with me a minute. There's something I need to tell you."

As Mark told her what Elijah Hicks had said, her eyes got wider and wider. She looked for all the world like a little lost girl and tears sprang to her eyes.

"D'you think mum knows he's living there?"

"I don't know!" Mark said. "And to be fair we have only got the say so of Elijah that this man was your father and even then he only really hinted at it." Mark tailed off, he was beginning to think he had made a mistake telling Emma about the man who might be her father, for the very reasons he was giving her. Elijah was hardly the most reliable of witnesses. The old man often rambled on about this or that. Mark bit his lip. Maybe this had been a mistake. But Emma shook her head and her dark curls tumbled back over her shoulders. Her face was animated.

"No, it makes sense! The little that mum told me, he was from Burghclere originally, so if he moved away and then came back, that would most likely be the place he would go to!"

The next morning Mark rang Isaac Rogers, who lived in Burghclere and asked if he knew the man who had moved into the old school house. He thought about it for a minute and then said.

"Can't say as I do, but, I should contact our postie, 'e's just retired, 'e knows just about all of them as lives round 'ere."

Mark drove around to the postman's house. When he got there, he found him in his garden at the front of his little cottage, in the winter sunshine.

As he asked him for the information the postie eyed Mark suspiciously.

"What d'you wan to to know for? It's not Royal Mail policy to tell anythin' about our customers!" he said pompously and then, obviously thinking that Mark might challenge that he said.

"Just because I've retired, don't mean I don't still go by the rules!"

"Of course not!" Mark said. "It was Isaac Rogers who told me about you, spoke very highly of you he did, and said you might know the name of the old gentleman who bought the old school house?"

The postie scratched his head and looked Mark up and down. He had relaxed slightly at the mention of Isaac Rogers.

"What d'you want to know for?" he repeated

"I am trying to trace a relative, and I think he might be him." Mark said

The postman thought for a moment. This tall young man did not look like he would have nefarious intentions but you could never be too careful.

Mark watched the man as he struggled with the dilemma. Eventually he took a deep breath and said.

"Channing, that's 'im!"

"Thank you, thank you very much indeed!" Mark said running back to the car.

When she came in from the grooming parlour that evening, Mark told her what he had found out. Emma was so excited she could not sleep. With Mark by her side she arrived outside the cottage the next day.

The old school house was a small neat building made of local stone. It had once been the school for the village and as a result had a large front garden that had once been the playground, behind a medium height wall.

Mark almost had to support his wife as they walked up the little garden to the old school house. It's school bell still hanging above the door.

The wait for the door to be answered seemed interminable. Eventually a tall slim elderly man in a pair of smart trousers and a shirt and tie opened the door.

He looked from Mark to Emma and then back to Emma. He let out a sound that was somewhere between a sigh and a gasp of surprise and said.

"Little Emma!"

"Dad?" Emma said, tears streaming down her face.

The man held out his arms and Emma fell into them. Mark felt tears prick his eyelids and turned away to let them have their moment.

Robert Channing showed them into the neat interior of the little schoolhouse that had in its time, had only two classrooms. The conversion had been done well and the interior was sparsely but elegantly furnished. Along one wall there was an impressive display of antique books, testament to Robert Channing's life's work. He saw Mark looking a them and took some down from the shelves for him, placing them carefully on the small dining table that stood next to the book case and obviously doubled as a desk.

"Are you interested in books Mark?" he said while Emma busied herself making them a cup of tea in the kitchen.

"I'm interested in anything as beautiful as this, these are wonderful!" Mark said.

The older man's eyes twinkled with delight.

"Yes, they are, and look, this is an original Dickens, signed by the great man himself!"

An hour later Mark and Emma left the cottage and made for home. Emma was quiet and Mark left her to her own thoughts. But both of them were thinking the same thing, what was Mary going to say when she found out? And find out she would.

Chapter 7

Fall Out

In the days after Emma and her father were reunited Emma talked of little else and as soon as she finished work she rushed over to the Old School House to sit with her father. He was still travelling back and forward to London, involved in various specialist projects. One was restoring the books for the National Museum. Emma was fascinated by the work her father did and by the books that he showed her that he had on the book shelves that lined the wall of his home.

At her insistence he brought out one of the books he had to restore and showed her how it was done.

"When you start" Robert said, delighted that his daughter shared his love of old books "you have to brush dust and blow the book with gas duster. You must always make sure that you have a clean work area that is compleley dry before beginning work with books. Make sure the work area is free of food, and anything that might spill on the books.

Wash your hands before handling valued material because oils and residues can stain or damage pages."

Emma ran to the bathroom and washed her hands, drying them on a small blue towel by the basin. As she returned to the table Robert said

"Wash them often during the time that you are handling this kind of book. Cotton gloves will protect archival material from oily fingerprint transfer. Dust jackets and pages are often very fragile and less flexible and can easily break or crack. Look for corners that are turned down, what we call 'dog-eared' that might break off and carefully turn them straight."

Robert watched as Emma carefully righted a turned down corner on the book they were working on.

"Never eat or drink while you are working. Liquids are easily spilled and will also stain archival materials. These stains are often difficult, if not impossible, to remove."

Robert smiled at the concentration on his daughter's face.

"Sometimes I use individual expansion file folders to give the best support to fragile books or occasionally a very loose rubber band, if necessary, to fasten covers or pages together."

"Couldn't you do with a stronger light?" Emma asked, the light from the angle poised lamp on the desk seemed very dim to her.

Robert smiled.

"We always use low light. Natural light from a window or a light that produces natural light is ideal to use during examination of books but should be kept away from books that you are working on because it causes damage."

Emma looked at him with dark eyes that mirrored his own and he felt a rush of tenderness for this daughter he hardly knew.

"We dust books with a soft brush or canned air and taking a lot of care not to damage pages. We often have to repair torn pages, broken hinges, and loose spines. Books with book jackets can go into mylar wraps and you can use ordinary pencil erasers to clean pages."

"What's this?" Emma said picking up a sheet of rough sandpaper like material. She could not imagine what part it would have to play in such a delicate exercise.

"That is a very fine grit sandpaper that removes ink marks on pages. But still needs to be used with a gentle touch! Also we sometimes use a single edge razorblade and that will remove food, chewing gum and crayon on pages, covers and dust jackets Go on try it, don't be nervous!"

As she tackled the food stains on the book they were working on, they magically disappeared. Emma said delightedly,

"It works!"

Robert laughed and said.

"Then finally, we place the books into 1 gallon snap-and-seal storage bags. You can then place books upright on shelves using bookends. As an alternative they can be put into individual gallon snap-and-seal sacks into larger 10 gallon plastic storage tubs or archival storage boxes. This shields them from the damaging effect of UV rays"

"Wow!" Emma said.

"Well that is just a taster, there are other methods we use, that in fact that I am using at the moment in London

But this is one way that you could do at home, and it is the method I use when I work at home."

Back at home that evening Emma told Mark what she had been doing. Mark was pleased. Emma had thanked him a thousand times for finding her father and seemed to be more loving towards him. He dared to hope that the fact that she had not known her father might have been the thing that was keeping her from living her life to the full, from giving herself wholeheartedly to their marriage.

That night as they lay in bed Mark felt a familiar stirring as they lay on their sides together, he with his arm around her waist. He felt Emma tense and he knew that she had registered the physical manifestation of his desire for her. He held his breath waiting for her to pull away. She did not and instead lifted the hand that was around her waist to her breast over her thin nightie. He could feel the hard nub of her nipple on his palm and he groaned with pent up desire for her. She turned onto her back and his hand cupped her swelling breast. She kissed him on the lips and soon their kisses and fevered exploration of each other's bodies had them gasping for breath. Mark felt tears prick the back of his eyes as his wife, for the first time since they had been married, abandoned herself to the most intense orgasm.

The next morning Mark felt as though he was walking on air. At breakfast he kissed Emma gently on the back of her neck as he came to sit down.

"Good morning darling" he said. She smiled up at him and he noticed that she had a slight rash around her mouth, a beard rash, the result of their passionate kissing. He felt as though he could make love to her again right here at the breakfast table.

"We'll have to tell mother this weekend." Emma said.

It was like a bucket of cold water being thrown over Mark. The mention of Mary Channing was still the biggest turn off he could imagine.

"About dad" Emma continued when he did not reply.

"Must we?" Mark said "I mean can't we just wait a bit? She is bound to be affected badly and at the moment it seems a shame to spoil the moment with your dad."

"Well that's just it, it's not going to be a moment is it?" Emma said and he noticed sadly that the clipped and dismissive tone to her voice was back.

"Well *of course* I know that, but can't you just put if off a while? I mean can't we have a little time to adjust to the new situation ourselves before the shit hits the fan?"

"Why do you have to use expressions like that Mark? You know I hate crudeness"

"Sorry" he said putting his hand over hers over the breakfast table. She pulled her hand away. Mark felt the cold fist that had been banished in the heat and passion of the night, re-establish its grip.

"We are going to tell her on Sunday, when we go for lunch." She said shortly and Mark knew that it was pointless to argue.

As she poured his coffee he tried to get back something of the mood of the night before by patting her backside. For a moment she thought he saw a ghost of a smile and emboldened ran his hand up the inside of her thigh over her jeans.

"Mark!" she sounded annoyed and Mark withdrew his hand immediately.

"Well at least my mother was right about one thing!" she said frowning. "Sex is really all that motivates men, just because we had an OK time in bed last night doesn't mean that you can take liberties; time and a place Mark, time and a place!"

Mark was speechless. An 'OK' time in bed? He had thought it was their finest hour!

And all he was motivated by was sex? He could not let that go.

"Emma, after all the hard work that I have put in for our future, putting up with your mother and putting you back in touch with your father, all that was just because I wanted sex was it?"

Emma shrugged.

"Well you got what you wanted last night didn't you, wasn't that the pay off for finding dad for me?"

"Emma!" Mark stood up so violently that his chair crashed backwards and skittered across the kitchen floor.

For a moment she looked frightened but then an unmistakable glint of triumph shone in her dark eyes and Mark was shocked to the core. It was as though she had been goading him on purpose, seeing how far she could push him. Mark stumbled out of the back door. His stomach was in knots, the fist had become a clenching and twisting thing that made him feel physically sick.

Inside Emma smiled to herself. She was sorry she had upset Mark but she needed to do that to let him know that he had not got the upper hand. That was a dangerous thing to let a man believe, her mother had warned her of that. But still she felt confused and a bit sorry. She thought about their love making the night before and how she had been taken by surprise at the intensity of the orgasm she had had, something far deeper and more nerve tingling than any of the orgasms she had given herself. Not that there had been many. She thought masturbation was a bit grubby somehow, but still sometimes it had happened when she was half awake in the mornings. What she had experienced last night was something that had made her see stars, literally. She had been out of control, completely at the mercy of Mark's dangerous ministrations. Now that she thought about it, it was a bit scary; maybe that sort of lack of control was what her mother had tried to warn her about. She shook her head; she did not like to think about discussing anything so intimate with her mother and she was heartily glad that now that she was married her mother seemed to have nothing more to say on the subject. Now the talk was always of starting a family. Emma thought about the time when she and her mother and father were a family. Now that Emma had spent a lot of time with her father and although she and not questioned him about his life with her mother, Emma could barely imagine that this softly spoken gentle man with the long tapered fingers of an artist could raise his hand in anger to anyone, let alone her mother who, it seemed to Emma was far the more dominant character.

As she mechanically put the breakfast things away washing and drying the dishes herself Emma thought about her mother and how she was going to react to the fact that she was seeing her father. As she had been growing up her mother had been very careful not to condemn her father outright, rather hinting darkly at violence and some vague deviance that Emma could not and would not guess at, especially now that she knew Robert Channing. Could it be that the picture her mother had painted of her father was false? No, she could not believe that. Her mother had always said that he had died when she was about six months old. So far she had not broached the subject of his leaving with Robert Channing but she could not imagine he did not want to see her. He had been so pleased to see her, his delight and love for her so obvious.

Emma sighed. She wondered where Mark had gone. He would normally go upstairs and brush his teeth after breakfast but he had run out and left the back door open. Emma tutted. She hated waste and the little cottage seemed to cool down so quickly once the heating was off.

Outside Mark had walked down the lane, not going anywhere in particular, just needing to cool off. As he walked the cold of the winter day began to penetrate his shirt and as he started shivering in the cold. He turned wearily and began to walk back to the cottage. At the back door he met Emma who was just closing it.

"For goodness sake, Mark!" she chided. "As if it doesn't cost enough to heat this place, without you leaving the door open, come in and get a coat, you'll perish in this cold!" Mark stared at his wife. It was as though the harsh words they had exchanged had never happened. He shook his head slightly, it almost felt as though he was in a dream. But as he did not see any good place that a conclusion or continuation of their argument could arrive at, he decided that he would play along with the 'pretend it never happened' approach.

"Yes, I'm going to go over and hang a gate in the far field today, I had better take a double layer, that snow we had is still lying there!" he said and Emma shot him an approving look.

"Well good luck with it, don't get too cold!" she said cheerily going up on tiptoes to kiss him goodbye. Mark kissed her back. That should be the end of it but he could not shake the feeling of gloom that was pervading everything he did these days, it seemed.

Then finally as the spring arrived so did the livestock for the new small holding. As Mark walked all the livestock to their new fields he smiled with pride. He was aware that the locals considered him a bit of a joke but with his 100 goats and fifty sheep but he felt that he had finally achieved what he set out to do. As the goats filed into the new pasture, some with little kids gambolling along beside them, Mark smiled with pride.

With the help of John Abbot from the bank they set up a new generator. John had become a close friend now and enjoyed working on the farm at the weekends.

"Makes a nice change from sitting behind that old desk!" he said to Mark. Mark was grateful of the company. The two men fixed up a generator and Mark spent his days looking after his new flock, trying to sort out a new routine with the new parlour. He had done his homework and had identified several buyers for his goat and sheep milk. To keep up with the deliveries he had to work overnight and all the while he continued to make the yoghurts. Mark and Emma did up the remaining old animal sheds they had bought from Elijah Hicks to store the milk bottles and yoghurt pots. The old stone buildings proved perfect for keeping the milk and yoghurt cool.

Using egg incubating cabinets to make the yoghurts set, and a couple of gas rings to heat the pails of milk and sterilise the milk churns they had a punishing schedule to make yoghurts ready for Tuesday and Wednesday deliveries. Mark had no choice but to make the yoghurts at night while Emma took care of them during the day, the new dog groomer taking up the slack in the parlour. Mark and John Abbot had had to put a new water supply up from the village to the parlour and the eventual site for the processing building. Over the months they had run telephone and electricity cables up in the same trench, so that Emma could have a phone in the parlour as well as another in the dairy. Mark worked for seventy hours without sleep to keep the business running.

When Mark finally slept it was a deep and dreamless sleep, his fatigue and the sheer amount of work that he did kept him from thinking too much about his marriage. He saw Emma in his peripheral vision and they exchanged pleasantries but Mark had no energy for anything else. Emma, however, seemed quite self-contained and if he thought about it at all Mark realised that she seemed rather to like their unavoidable separation by work. But as the weeks went by it finally began to get better and easier.

The processing building was built with a corrugated iron extension for the industrial fridge and freezer storage. After a few months Mark got the electricity supply connected to the old animal sheds. The generator could not supply the milking parlour and bulk tank at the same time as the fridges and freezers so it had always been a juggling act. Added to that there was no shelter for the goats, so putting up a barn was also a priority. Goats, Mark found out, were habitual escape artists and he had to use electric fencing to keep them in.

By the time that their first wedding anniversary approached the main barn was up and between him and John Abbott they had finished the feed store and milking parlour.

Two of the fields Mark had bought from the Rogers brothers were fenced now and Mark managed to get a government grant to pay for the fencing of two of the fields that had been designated Sites of Special Scientific Interest. Because of the two SSSI fields and the flower rich meadows Mark was granted immediate conversion for organic status. He also supplied testimonies from the previous owners testifying that he had not used chemicals on the land.

The lunches on Sunday with Mary Channing had all but been abandoned with all the hours that both Mark and Emma were putting in and the old woman was not pleased about it. Mark was not sorry, he did not think he could cope with the inevitable fall out when Mary Channing realised Emma had been seeing her father. But Mary had now taken to arriving unannounced at the farm and 'helping' with the yoghurt production. Then one day with Emma on a short fuse from tiredness she made one criticism too many.

Mark could hear the screaming from the milking shed and hurried to see what was happening.

"Well I don't care if you don't come here again mother, drop dead for all I care! All you do is nit pick!"

"I am trying to give you the benefit of my experience, you ungrateful girl!" Mary shouted back. Mark stood in amazement. He knew his wife more as a sulker than a scrapper and he certainly had never expected to hear Mary raise her voice.

"How dare you speak to your mother like that?" Mary continued.

"How dare you interfere all the time? Just leave me alone, leave us alone!"

"Oh don't worry I will!" Mary said getting ready to leave. "You are just like your father, nasty and coarse and hurtful!" Mary shouted as her parting shot.

"Oh really? Well, I'll have you know I have met daddy and he is a hell of a lot nicer than you, a hell of a lot!"

The silence that followed was almost palpable.

"You've seen your father?"

"Yes and I *love* spending time with him, I just find it difficult to imagine what a lovely man like him ever saw in a witch like you. You come here dripping your poison in my ear about Mark!" Emma threw her arm open in his direction "And all he does is work hard and long to make a future for us. Well no more mother!"

"You've seen your father?" Mary repeated. Her voice was low now.

"Yes, I've seen him!"

"Where?"

Emma hesitated for a moment, as if wondering whether telling her mother where her father was living would be a betrayal, would visit her mother's fury on him as well

"Burghclere!" she said

Mary nodded and sighed, a ragged sound.

"How long?" her voice sounded strangled

"Long enough to know the truth about you!" Emma spat the words out.

Mary seemed to crumple slightly, all the fight had gone out of her. Turning her back she walked off down the farm path and Emma watched her go, her face contorted.

"Emma?" Mark stepped forward. Linda and Suzy, the college leaver they had hired, stood eyes wide, a poodle trembling on the grooming table between them. Mark took Emma by the arm and led her outside.

"Oh Mark!" she collapsed sobbing in his arms.

That evening Emma went to visit her father. Having him to talk to helped deal with the trauma of the terrible fall out with her mother. Until now Robert Channing had not talked much about the past; he thought things past were best left in the past. Emma cried and told him about the fight with her mother, and as father and daughter sat together in the light of the setting sun, Robert told her in as dispassionate a way as he could manage of how her mother had systematically set out to prevent him from having any contact or say in Emma's life. He showed Emma a trunk full of letters that he had had from her mother and letters and birthday cards and countless gifts neatly bound in size order in elastic bands that he had sent and that had been 'returned to sender'. Emma handled the cards and the presents with tears running down her face. The cards that graduated from ones with fluffy pink bunnies for a three year old to a picture of a horse for a seventeen year old all had the same wording after the printed verse.

To my darling Emma, with all my love always, Daddy.

"Can I have them Daddy?" she asked and with tears in his own eyes, Robert nodded.

"Well they were for you, my darling!"

That evening when Emma got home with the box full of cards and presents, she showed them to Mark.

Mark held her while she cried and that night they made love. It was not the explosive union they had had previously, rather a tender and loving coming together of their hearts and bodies. Mark felt a kernel of hope. Maybe with Mary Channing out of the picture, things would be better for them. He hardly dared hope.

As the first light of dawn lit their bedroom the next morning Mark got up quietly and went out into the summer morning. His heart felt light. He had slept better than he had in months and had woken up with Emma in his arms. He felt the love for her that he had tried to suppress burgeon anew. Something in him knew that without the malignant presence of her mother, Emma would be a different girl.

Just when things seemed to be going well Mark found an annoyed Elijah Hicks waiting for him. Despite the fact that he had sold the land and the barns and house to Mark and Emma he still felt free to wander around at any time he felt like it and had blocked off access to one of the fields that he used to own.

Mark was taken aback. He had got on well with Elijah Hicks and apart from the fact that he annoyed the girls by hanging around the grooming parlour, until this point he had been managable. Now however he was not interested in discussing the matter, and used language that would make a sailor blush to tell Mark what he thought of him. Mark decided that he had no choice but to block his access across his fields.

During the time that he had dealt with Hicks Mark had heard a lot of talk around the village of how he was the local village bully and all round neighbourhood nuisance. Mark had always found him fine to deal with, a bit nosey perhaps but generally helpful, so he had not taken much notice of the gossip.

Now though, Mark reflected, Elijah had been quick enough to make mischief telling Emma about her father, and hinting at a dubious moral past for Mary. That could have been a huge problem. It hadn't been but Hicks was not to know that.

Now on one fine summer morning Mark found that the old farmer had tried to use his JCB digger to open up the access that Mark had blocked. As Mark saw him coming, he stood his ground trying to reason with him.

"Come on Elijah, we can sort this out!"

Elijah Hicks shook his head."

"Fuckin' upstart, think you owns the place! get out the fuckin' way! Elijah shouted revving the engine of the JCB

"Come on Elijah, this is my land, you know you have no right . . . ." That was as far as Mark got. With surprising agility for a man of his age Elijah Hicks jumped down from the JCB and lunged at Mark fists flying

Mark blocked the punch his strength arresting Elijah's fist in mid flight. The old man swore again and climbed back in the JCB this time driving the digger straight at Mark.

Hardly able to believe his eyes, Mark picked up a metal fencing bar he had hidden in the hedge and rammed it through the radiator grill of the tractor. Swearing profusely Elijah realised he did not have long before his radiator leaked all it's fluid and the engine would overheat. He drove back to his farmyard and called the police.

Mark returned to the cottage shaking. He could hardly believe what had just happened. The police came out but did not seem keen to get involved, saying as it was a civil matter it was for the courts to sort out.

"Mr. 'icks, 'e can be a bit, er, difficult!" the young constable said, "Bit set in 'is ways."

Mark assured the young officer that there would be no more trouble and went out do the milking. But despite giving similar assurances, before the constable had even got down the drive of his farm house, Elijah Hicks had rung a contractor to bulldoze the obstruction.

After milking Mark went to check the damage. Emma had gone ahead, taking with her one of her canine customers to be dropped off.

As Mark arrived over the field he saw that Elijah Hicks had driven up the short cut right of way.

Emma was holding the gate shut so he could not get back out. He would have to go round the long way. Horrified Mark saw Elijah Hicks approach Emma and knock her to the ground. Running at full tilt Mark arrived shouting to confront him.

Laughing Elijah Hicks leapt into his Land Rover and drove off.

"Leave it Mark!" Emma shouted after him as he ran after the speeding Land Rover

"It's not worth it, I'm not hurt, look!" She stood up and brushed herself down "besides if you hit him or worse who is going to milk the goats?"

Somewhere in Mark's blind fury Emma's words registered. He was needed.

"Fuck you!" he shouted down the road before returning to his wife and holding her in his arms.

Was this how it was going to be? Just when things seemed to be going well for him and Emma, everything else was falling apart. Was it not possible for all areas of his life to go well at the same time?

Chapter 8

Babies

A few days later Mark received a summons and eventually after lots of delays by Elijah Hicks the day came when they were due in court to sort the matter.

At the farm that morning, he had found Emma in tears. Two of the newly hatched chicks had been killed.

"Was it the fox?" Mark asked holding her to him.

"No, they've been stabbed!" Emma sobbed.

Mark set his jaw. He and Emma had had to endure petty vandalism from Hicks and his grandchildren, two very rough looking boys who looked like they never washed.

"Well maybe today will be an end to it." Mark said with more optimism than he felt. Emma sobbed softly holding the two limp little bodies. They had found out that their neighbour had had court cases with two other neighbouring farmers and nearly every resident in the hamlet had at some point exchanged solicitor's letters over some petty matter.

One of Elijah Hicks favourite tricks to annoy residents was to spill cow slurry around their boundaries or driveways. Mark and Emma had been treated to sprayed slurry across the hedge alongside the processing building. Mark had involved the local environmental health department, who had intervened to caution Elijah. The attack on the chicks was obviously retaliation for that. Although things around them seemed to be going into melt down, each month Mark hoped that Emma would tell him the news they both were hoping for; that she was pregnant. When months after month went by with no happy news, Mark and Emma decided to see the doctor.

The results of the tests were devastating, Mark was not producing enough sperm and the only way that they were likely to conceive would be by donor insemination or IVF. Emma looked at him with undisguised triumph in her eyes.

"I knew it would be your fault!" she said. Mark was crushed, he felt useless. He soon realised that one of the reasons that Emma had been eager to make love was that she had hoped to be pregnant. Now that this was not an option and until they started fertility treatment she moved Mark into the spare room.

Mark felt the misery of the early days of their marriage resurface. Despite the trouble they were having with Elijah and the pressures of the farm they had been at their happiest without the malignant presence of Mary Channing hanging over them and with the kind and gentle influence of Emma's father, whom Mark had come to admire greatly.

Once the treatment for fertility started Mark found himself being called to perform on demand. There was nothing tender or loving about the mechanical act Emma had him perform when she was fertile and Mark felt depression overwhelming him. And then one month, long after he had stopped asking, Emma announced she was pregnant.

Mark was stunned by the great news but love for his wife overwhelmed him and he held her to him for a long time stroking her hair and murmuring how much he loved her. Emma smiled up at him with tears in her eyes.

Mark was getting very stressed by the vandalism still being visited on them by Elijah Hicks and on one evening when he found, for the fourth time that week, all the gates open and great swathes of fencing cut he knew he could take no more. After spending hours rounding up the goats and sheep, Mark stormed into the cottage

"That bloody man! I am going to give Hicks a taste of his own medicine." Mark snatched up the bolt cutters that were leaning against the wall of the kitchen.

"No Mark!" Emma said "Think about all the trouble we had with the courts over the JCB incident, do you really want that again, or worse?"

"But Emma, I just can't fucking stand it any more!" Mark winced as she saw the look of dismay on Emma's face. She hated him swearing.

"Look Mark, your parents have even warned you not to do this. For God's sake, I'm pregnant, I can't stand all this upset" Emma sank onto the kitchen chair and started sobbing. Mark was instantly contrite.

"Oh Emma darling, I'm so sorry, I've been so selfish! Of course I won't do anything, I would never do anything to make you unhappy!" He soothed her and that night they fell asleep in each other's arms.

The phone ringing very early the next morning wakened them. The goats were out again, liberated by Elijah Hicks, and heading towards the railway line.

Mark was out of bed and into his jeans in a flash. Hours later when he returned, exhausted, the blood of three of the goats that had been hit by a train on his clothes he broke down.

"I can't take it any more Emma, I've got to get away!" Emma was shocked. She had never seen her husband like this. She felt fear make her go cold, was he having some sort of breakdown?

"Ok darling, you go. Linda and I can manage, with Steve." Steve was a young lad from the village who was home from college and keen to help on the farm. "We know what to do by now, Steve especially!"

Mark arrived at his father's house in Millbrook in Cornwall and immediately felt the tension leave him. In the clean sea air of the little fishing village he slept the clock around and ate the first decent meal he had had in months.

Two days later he felt renewed and rested and was packing up ready to head back to Berkshire when the phone rang. It was Linda, crying so hard that Mark could barely understand what she was saying.

"Its' Emma, she's had a miscarriage. Oh Mark I'm so sorry!" she wailed.

Mark threw the phone down and ran out to the car not even stopping to tell his father what had happened.

He broke all speed limits getting back to Emma and by the time he drew up at the little cottage she was back from the hospital. He found her sitting in her favourite chair in the little lounge.

"This is all your fault!" she said her voice flat and expressionless "I begged you not to make a fuss, to stay calm, but no you couldn't do it, not for me and not for our poor dead baby."

Mark collapsed, devastated, his sobs wracking his body until Emma finally came to his side and they clung together. After so much effort with the fertility treatment to loose the baby at the end of the first trimester was shattering.

Emma recovered physically within a couple of days but Mark could see that she was becoming seriously depressed. Mark was still in shock and Emma's words kept haunting him. He made an appointment to see his GP and then the fertility specialist to see what he could do to help Emma and to see if her accusations about his stress causing her to miscarry were plausible. Emma was now under the care of the mental health team. She had lost a lot of weight and it broke Mark's heart to see her dragging herself to her counselling sessions. He attended a joint session and he hoped that Emma would be happy to hear that neither the specialist nor the doctor thought it was likely that his stress had caused the miscarriage.

As they left the session Emma turned to him and hissed.

"You just had to have the last word didn't you? Parading me there like a neurotic female, to prove that you were right and I was wrong!"

"Emma, it wasn't like that!" Mark said dismayed, "you heard the doctor, there are many unexplained reasons for miscarrying in the first trimester, including something going wrong with the development of the foetus!"

"Blah blah blah!" Emma said. "I know what I know, so you can shut up!"

As the summer turned to autumn Emma, to all intents and purposes ceased to function. She would sit about all day in a daze and Linda had to shoulder the responsibility of the grooming parlour on her own.

A few years later Elijah Hicks developed cancer and died. It was a very unpleasant slow and painful death and although Mark was not a naturally vindictive person he could not help lean towards the commonly expressed sentiment in the hamlet that Elijah Hicks got natural justice for a life spent tormenting his neighbours.

In a cruel twist of fate it was another crisis that finally helped Emma to recover from the deep depression she was suffering from. Her father had a stroke.

Robert Channing had been working on a rare St James bible at the little table in front of the bookcase in the Old School House. That Emma had managed to rouse herself enough to visit him that day was amazing in itself, that she had made that visit only moments after her father had had the stroke was nothing short of a miracle

For days he lay moribund in hospital and Emma felt sickened that she found the misery of worrying about her father a relief from the misery of losing her child. Mark felt helpless to do anything for his wife but sat with her at her father's bed side for as long as he could.

Slowly Robert Channing recovered but his speech and his left arm were badly affected. He would never be able to work on his precious books again. Eventually he was allowed home and between them Emma and Social services provided support for a while but it soon became obvious that Robert could not cope on his own.

During the time that her father had been ill Emma had found that she had two half sisters, quiet studious girls who looked just like their father and whom Mark hoped would be a support to Emma. But it seemed they had all but lost touch with their father and in a quiet censorious way managed to convey to Emma that they resented her suddenly appearing so late in their father's life. Their concern, it seemed was for the implications that Emma appearing and living so close to her father would have on their inheritance.

As they sat over the table in their little cottage kitchen one evening Emma said

"We are going to have to think of something for dad, Mark, he really is not coping, yesterday he nearly burned the place down trying to light the gas cooker."

"Mmm, well I would say that he could come here, but he would never manage the stairs!" Mark said.

"I know." Emma said. "But I can't bear to think of him in a home!"

Mark took her hand.

"But darling you have to think about him. In the right place he could get expert help and have company. I think he really gets quite lonely over there!"

"Well I do my best, but I can't be there 24/7!" Emma snapped

"Emma, I'm not criticising, I want him to be happy and safe and you said yourself, that is not happening where he is now. Lets look at what he would get for the house and then what that would buy him in terms of care."

Over the next week Emma spoke to Ellen and Anna her half sisters but they made it plain that they wanted their father to go into the cheapest local residential home Emma could find. Emma was heartbroken. She could not understand the callous attitude of her half sisters.

Mark sat with a lump in his throat as Emma gently spoke to her father and told him what they thought would be best for him. Then helping the frail old man to his car Mark drove them both to the home that they had picked out for him. As Robert Channing looked around the bright and friendly nursing home tears ran unchecked down his face. Emma was crying too, holding on tight to his hand.

When the tour was over the motherly nursing home owner showed them into a private room so that they could talk together.

"I'm sorry dad, did you hate it?" Emma sobbed.

His speech slurred and laboured Robert patted her hand and told her it would be fine. He thanked her and Mark for finding it for him.

Back at The Old School House, Robert told them that he wanted to leave £50,000 to Emma before he splitting the estate equally. He felt that he had been excluded from all aspects of Emma's life and he wanted to make up for her childhood.

Emma arranged the sale of the house. Apart from a few possessions he would take to his new home, Emma organised the auction of everything else. She spent days laying everything out for the auctioneers to catalogue and removal to the salerooms.

Mark was just coming home one lunchtime when Ellen and Anna turned up at the cottage.

As he looked at them Mark realised that the looks that made Robert Channing look refined and elegant in his daughters made them looked pinched and mean.

"We want to visit the old house before it's sold!" Ellen announced shortly

Emma had done her first morning in the grooming parlour since she had had her miscarriage and came in on the end of the exchange.

"Of course! You will want to go and see dad too I suppose, I can take you over after lunch, will you come back and join us for a bite?"

The women exchanged glances. Mark thought they looked very shifty.

"No sorry we don't have much time, if we could just have the key please?" Anna held her hand out and Emma took the key for The Old School House down from a hook by the door.

As the women walked primly to their car Mark said.

"Don't you think you should go with them?"

"And what would they say to that, d'you think? I'm trying to build bridges here!"

An hour later the women returned and posted the key through the front door. Mark and Emma heard it land on the mat and looked at each other.

Jumping into Mark's Land Rover they raced over to Burghclere. Ellen and Anna had stolen whatever they thought was valuable and could get into their large estate car. After a few heated 'phone calls to the sisters explaining that what they had taken had been entered into the sale and that their father needed all the money he could raise for his care, it became obvious that they were not going to budge, they had no remorse. Mark and Emma contacted the police and they recorded the crime. Robert Channing was very upset, but he did not want to charge his daughters with stealing.

When her father died, a few months later, Emma was at his bedside. She called her sisters in tears with the funeral arrangements.

On the day of the funeral Mark went to the nursing home with Emma to ask them to keep the door of her father's room locked.

As they stood at the graveside Mark felt Emma clutch at his arm. There, all in black and defiant was Mary Channing. It was the first time that Emma had seen her mother to talk to since that awful day at the cottage when Emma had told Mary Channing that she was back in touch with her father. Mark could not imagine what the woman was doing here. He put his arm protectively around Emma, his heart was full of love for his wife. It seemed he had to protect her from everyone.

He noticed that Ellen had left the funeral and smiled to himself. She would not get very far! And, sure enough, while they were at the funeral, Ellen had, they learned later, gone to the home and demanded entry to Robert's room. She left only when the staff threatened to call the police. Ellen phoned Emma later full of vitriol and threatening her with every curse under the sun if the will was not as the sisters expected it to be.

That night as Mark lay in bed with Emma sobbing softly into his shoulder she said.

"Why is all this happening to me? What have I done? Why is everything against me?"

Mark sighed. It was hard to argue with anything that Emma said. They seemed to be fighting one battle after another. And no doubt her sisters would contest the will. As he waited for sleep, Mark thought, that something good had come out of this sad time, and that was that Emma seemed to have been able to come to terms with the miscarriage and was ready to try again.

As the months passed and life on the farm fell into a hectic routine Mark felt sometimes that the prospect of having a child was the only thing holding him and Emma together. She was still suffering serious depression over a year following the miscarriage and her father's death. Despite the closeness that their tribulations had temporarily given them, Emma had now it seemed, decided Mark was to blame.

As he walked around the farm carrying out his tasks mechanically, Mark could sometimes barely see for the tears that seemed to come constantly and unbidden to his eyes. Finally, exhausted and feeling as though he was in danger of losing his mind, Mark went to see Lynn Bond, his GP.

"I'm trying to be patient, I really am, but Emma seems unable to move on and unable to get over the fact that she blames me for her miscarriage."

Lyn Bond smiled sympathetically.

"It's a very difficult time for you both. How is the fertility treatment going? She looked through his notes.

"This is the third attempt?"

"Fourth" Mark said miserably

"Right well I am going to put you on some anti depressants, just for the time being, just to get you over the hump!" she aid scribbling out a prescription.

That evening Mark looked at Emma, her sour face casting accusing glances at him as he passed her sitting in her favourite chair.

"Look Em, I'm sorry you lost the baby! I'm sorry your father died and that your sisters and your mother are such cows, but I am not the bad guy here! You need to pull yourself together! I don't see any point in doing all this fertility treatment if this is going to be your attitude, it can't help, anyway! I am sick of seeing you sitting there in that chair staring into the blue. You've got to pull yourself together!"

Emma got up quietly from her chair and went upstairs slamming the door behind her.

One morning two weeks later Mark awoke to the stunning news that the country was in the midst of a B.S.E. crisis.

As beef and dairy farmers all around him lost their herds Mark thanked his lucky stars that for once he had made the right decision and gone with goats and sheep, animals that were not susceptible to the disease.

His organic goat and sheep dairy business was about to go through the stratosphere. In fifteen months his business had almost quadrupled.

At the end of an exhausting 70 hours of work with little sleep Mark realised that he was going to have to get help. He was going to have to employ people. John Abbott came out to see what he could do for Mark and the two men agreed that the current sad state of affairs had advanced his business plan by about five years.

Mark found himself delivering to more and more shops choosing his milk over the traditional cows milk.

The evening after John had visited Mark sat Emma down at the kitchen table. They had barely spoken since his last outburst.

"Look Em, I can't do this alone. You know what the BSE crisis has done to our business. I can't do it alone, I'm going to take on staff, but I need you beside me. I need you to face up to the challenge or else we just give up."

Mark's stark warning seemed to reach something in Emma and for the first time in months she emerged from her depression as the new challenge gave her focus and kept them both busy working long hours.

Mark began to relax, despite his exhaustion and stopped taking his antidepressants.

But Emma, despite her new sense of purpose, never stopped blaming him for the miscarriage.

Mark and Emma had been advised to join the fertility programme at a local clinic. And for that they had to attend counselling sessions. As they drove to their first session Mark felt apprehensive. Their marriage had always been fairly stormy and now that Emma was so obsessed with having her own child rather than adopting, things were no easier. Her depressions seemed to have been replaced by a vicious resentment.

"When we get there, Mark" Emma said "Leave the talking to me."

"Well I don't know if it really works like that!" Mark laughed trying to lighten the mood.

"And there we have it, you think the whole thing's a joke, don't you?" Emma spat at him. "I wouldn't be surprised if you were pleased when I had that miscarriage."

Mark said nothing. He was used to the cruellest of jibes from Emma and had learned it was better to stay quiet.

In the event although there were a few sticky moments in the counselling sessions, they passed muster.

The pleasant blonde haired woman who took the counselling session aimed to examine their attitudes to when and if to tell a child of its biological beginnings. As the session progressed Mark found that his position that it would be best not to tell a child; at least until they become a mature adult began to shift slightly.

"The earlier that a child knows these important details about him or herself the less disrupting and undermining of the relationship that knowledge will be."

On the way home Mark and Emma talked over what had been said. Mark was relieved to find Emma animated and soft, unlike the brittle person that she seemed to be more and more often these days.

Now amongst the dizzying round of jobs around the farm Mark was immersed in an alien world of cycles and embryo donations. He learned that the donated embryo procedure depends entirely on the availability of frozen embryos.

Mark felt strangely awed as he learned that the tiny embryo that would be his and Emma's future child would be donated by other couples who were having different fertility treatments. If these couples were having I.V.F. treatment and were successful early on there would be an excess of embryos stored, and they would be asked to donate these to other couples like Mark and Emma.

Mark and Emma were assessed for inheritable characteristics. These, Mark learned were the traits and characteristics that you would expect to see in a natural child. For example, he and Emma were both tall with dark hair.

Mark and Emma listened in amazement as the team produced a list of characteristics with a surprising level of detail.

"Well this is a pretty popular profile!" the fertility specialist told them. "If you were both short and fat with ginger hair it might be easier!"

"Not for us!" Emma laughed and Mark tried to remember the last time he had seen his wife smile, let alone laugh.

Mark and Emma slept in the same bed that night, excitedly talking about the baby they would have. Mark felt love for Emma overwhelm him as she lay her animated face lit up in the moonlight. He just knew that everything would be all right once their longed for baby arrived.

The next morning Mark called the three men he had employed together to explain that he and Emma might need to be away. Steven had left college now and was doing very well in the foreman role. He knew the farm and the animals almost as well as Mark did and Mark was happy to leave him in charge.

Dan and Matt two young lads from the village were learning the ropes, but seemed to be keen enough. All of them nodded sagely as Mark told them he would be relying on them to run the place in his absence.

"You can rely on us Mark!" Steven said looking sternly at his two charges.

"Right lads?"

"Right," they chorused.

Linda and the college leaver Suzy were running the dog grooming now and Emma had her time taken up with the yoghurt production side of the business. Mark was kept busy with deliveries of their yoghurt and milk to customers who were finding it difficult to get organic cows milk. As he drove out of the farm on delivery that day Mark sighed to himself. They had come a long way in a relatively short time. They had had their share of ups and downs. It was a major effort for both of them to attend the clinic together and sometimes Emma had to go alone. Mark thought how nice it would be if Emma had been able to rely on her mother for support. But Emma's mother, when she learned of the money that her father had left her daughter, had disowned her. Still despite it all, Mark felt a sense of optimism as he surveyed his herds, his home and the business he had built up.

And then, against all the odds Emma was pregnant.

As they sat together at the kitchen table hopeful and fearful in equal measure Mark took Emma's hands.

"This is going to be the making of us darling."

Emma nodded her eyes were wet with tears.

Once again Mark felt the bond that so often seemed to escape them, tighten. He wanted to protect his wife and unborn child. He would protect them, provide for them and keep them as happy as it was possible to keep them. He would make sure that Emma took it easy this time, there could be no more risk of miscarriage. He knew that she and more importantly their marriage would not stand another blow like that. And Emma herself? Well, everything would be different now that she was going to be a mother. In the months and years to come Mark was often going to look back on this day and wonder how he ever have been so naïve.

Chapter 9

Charlie

As Mark and Emma held their breath, both so desperate for this to be the time when they had the baby they longed for, Emma battled through an uncomfortable pregnancy. She felt ill and sick much of the time. Mark, full of concern for her and their unborn child said that she should not work, especially with the heavy lifting she had to do in the yoghurt room.

"But Mark how will we manage?" Emma asked as they sat at the little kitchen table pouring over the figures for the farm.

"Look Emma darling, I know you want to help but now that we have got to this point we do not want to take any chances." Emma did not take much persuading, there had been a couple of scares over spotting and more bleeding but they had passed. Neither of them said it but both of them knew that Emma would not be able to cope with another miscarriage.

"I think we should take on a production manager to cover you in the dairy." Mark said. He watched as Emma struggled with a mixture of emotions. She had taken to her role in the dairy well and was proud of what she achieved there, but on the other hand she knew that working there could be a threat to the baby. In the end there was no contest and to make her feel better Mark left it to Emma to interview and appoint someone suitable. Mark was rushed off his feet with all the other many duties of the thriving farm and with Steve, Matt and Dan had his days filled with animal husbandry, milking and the thousand and one other jobs that always seemed to need to be done.

After much interviewing Emma announced she had decided on a very large woman named Josie. As Emma introduced her to Mark, Mark almost gagged on the stale cigarette smoke that emanated from her. The fact that she obviously smoked heavily and was grossly overweight made her wheeze when she spoke. Mark was immediately worried about the woman's fitness. Working in the dairy required standing for long periods, lifting heavy pails of milk and rolling heavy milk churns around, as well as a serious attitude to hygiene. Mark had thought he had smelled a slight odour of sweat from Josie mingled with the stale smoke. Not what they needed in the diary!

As Emma saw Josie out of their cottage Mark said.

"Are you sure she is the right one for the job Em? I mean she smells a bit doesn't she?"

"Mark how can you be so rude, you are just prejudiced against fat people, typical of a man! Not interested unless a woman is 36 24 36! She will be a great help, she's worked on farms before. Besides, I don't want the boys distracted by some dolly bird!"

Mark was speechless. Emma had always been very neat and tidy and clean, even to the point of fastidiousness, and the fact that she wanted this woman who, he would have put money on the fact she would cross the road to avoid, baffled him.

As it was Josie lasted about two months before she admitted she could not cope with the physical nature of the job. She left. Gritting his teeth against the overwhelming desire to say "I told you so" Mark had to step in to take over.

Mark took on a new stockman, Greg, and although he seemed a bit odd and eccentric in a dark and mysterious way, Mark had to admit he knew his stuff and seemed to thrive on working long hours. He was happy to have the responsibility of the farm to himself during the week as long as Mark covered the weekends.

As they sat after a particular long day in front of the fire Mark said.

"Emma, I think it is probably best that I cover your job whilst you are pregnant and then for maybe 6 months after the birth? Greg has got a handle on things at the farm and he's doing a really good job. I thought Steve might resent him but he doesn't seem to. Between them I think things are running well but it is important that things run well in the dairy too!" Emma nodded.

"Ok but I want to get back to running things as soon as possible after the baby is born!" she patted her bump and Mark felt an overwhelming love for his wife and their unborn child. He was not sure he could physically do it all, but he knew he would just have to get on with it.

So Mark embarked on a punishing regimen in which a quiet week was 90 hours. It became a pattern to work, eat and sleep: usually working till 11 or 12 pm and then up again at 5 am. About once a fortnight Mark would have to work through the night, usually Fridays, to catch up on the backlog. In the haze of sleep deprivation in which he operated it was actually a rest to do the milking and farm work at weekends. As the end of Emma's pregnancy approached it was decided that she would be taken in for a Caesarean section. This was no ordinary pregnancy and Emma had been monitored carefully all along the way. But before the date of the caesarean however Emma wakened Mark from a dreamless sleep.

"It's started Mark, the baby's coming!"

At the hospital it was decided to let her have a go at the labour on her own for a while. After a few hours though it was clear that she was making no headway and that the planned Caesarean should now go ahead. As Mark sat in a gown and surgical cap at Emma's side in the operating theatre, he held Emma's hand tightly as the surgeon drew the scalpel across her lower belly. As the blood welled up through the brown disinfectant that had been brushed over her skin, the surgeon looked over at him and enquired "you're not going to faint at the sight of blood are you, Mr. Richards?" Mark smiled, amused by the implication that he was squeamish. He replied, "don't worry about me. I have aided at C-sections on my sheep. After several thousand births I am not fazed by blood and mess!" The woman surgeon's expression registered surprise. She smiled and Mark suddenly felt the enormity of what was about to happen hit him. The two of them were about to become three. How were they going to cope? How would they find the time? How would he manage financially to provide for them all? Emma, her eyes wide, was awake and asking Mark what was happening. There was a low green curtain across her body preventing her from seeing the operation. Normally fathers would avoid looking beyond this curtain but Mark watched fascinated and surprised at how roughly the surgeon pulled the two sides of the cut apart to get her hands into the womb to locate the baby. No wonder Emma had been told that she would feel sore and bruised afterwards Mark thought that when he and the vet were delivering lambs by caesarean they were a lot more gentle.

Then with a triumphant "here we are" as the surgeon held their baby up "Congratulations it's a boy!" Mark was immediately concerned with his son's dark purple colour and surprised at how thick the umbilical cord was. All of a sudden the delivery team was galvanised into action. Charlie was assessed and was breathing fine. After the cord was tied off he was wiped down and placed on the scales and then measured. The surgeon explained that he was a funny colour because he had got stuck in labour as a breach which was why they had had to go for the c-section. One of the team asked Emma what we were going to call our baby. "Charles", she said. I was then asked what other name I wanted for Charlie. "Robert", I replied, after your dad,

Emma," Mark squeezed her hand, "he will be called Charles Robert Richards."

Emma smiled up at him with tears in her eyes. As Charlie was placed gently on his mother's chest Mark felt tears well up in his own eyes. He felt a rush of love come over him as he looked into Emma's face glowing with love for their child. He thought about all the happy times they would have together and his heart swelled with love and pride.

Although he knew that Charlie was the beautiful, wonderful and the desperately wanted result of fertility treatment, Mark could hardly believe that this perfect child had started his biological life as a donated embryo.

The maternity hospital was only a mile from the farm, so each evening Mark would visit Emma and Charlie. The mid-wives and staff bent over backwards to help Emma and insisted she stay longer than normal because of the difficult domestic situation, Mark was working very long hours and the building work that they had started to extend the cottage was not yet completed.

Mark had found Emma in tears when he came in the day after their son was born. She wanted desperately to breast feed Charlie, but was having a lot of difficulty. But under the kind and patient guidance of the nurses, the early difficulties were soon overcome and mother and baby were doing very well.

Mark was glad that he and Emma had similar attitudes to living and health. Both of them were very cautious about taking any medicines, preferring always to rely on natural remedies. As a farmer Mark had seen first hand the benefits of mother's milk over formula. He had always believed that some decisions, namely abortion and breast feeding, should be considered to be almost entirely up to the mother. Mark held his breath in those early days, wanting to urge Emma to breast feed but believing it had to be her decision. In the end Charlie had the breast till he was about 15 months old. And as if to repay his parents beliefs, Charlie was an easy baby, who slept well and was rarely difficult.

As the first few months of their son's life passed in a whirl of work and snatching a few hours to spend with his new son, Mark thought that the fact that Charlie was such a good baby had to do in no small part because Emma was so happy and confident as a new mother. In the months ahead Mark was to look back on this time and wonder if they had ever been so happy because unfortunately for Charlie the idyllic days of his first few months were not to last.

As the months passed and he watched his son grow more wonderful every day, a bouncing healthy baby who smiled all the time now, it became obvious to Mark that Emma had no intention of coming back to work as Christmas, the busiest time on the farm, approached. He had thought she would return to work at about 6 months after Charlie was born, as they had planned. One day over breakfast he tackled her about it.

"Mark! I can't believe that you are trying to force me back to work!"

"I'm not trying to force you, you said that you wanted to go back to work! We have our busy time coming up now and

I don't think I can cope with the stock and with the dairy, don't you think you could just do a few hours?"

"No" Emma said flatly, and that was that.

Mark thought about it. Really he supposed he was quite happy for her not to return if that was what she wanted. She was almost entirely occupied with Charlie and seemed even to resent the small amount of time that Mark could spend with his son. But Mark knew that he and the staff could not cope any longer without more help. Mark was mentally and physically exhausted and he sometimes thought it was the few snatched minutes here and there that he managed to spend with Charlie that kept him going. But even those moments seemed to be getting fewer. Mark was on his knees. He begged Emma to let him take on a diary manager but she refused.

"Look Emma, you say you don't want to go back to work, and that's fine, but I really can't manage all this on my own. Let me take on a manager, please!"

"Well you were scathing enough about poor Josie, no wonder she left, no I'm not letting you persecute another poor soul!"

"Persecute?" Mark spluttered "I rarely even spoke to the woman, she smelled foul and she made my stomach turn!"

"Ha! So now we see your old prejudices surface and if we took on a new manager what would you find to pick on about them?" Emma said triumphantly as though the point had won her the argument.

Mark shook his head, and stumbled outside, his head spinning from Emma's unreasonable and totally incomprehensible stance and the total fatigue that seemed to permanently weigh him down.

Greg, the stockman, had approached him in October to say he needed more help on the farm, especially before the new-year kidding season started. Mark knew he was right. The tall swarthy man, who wore an earring in his right ear and reminded Mark of Heathcliff from Wuthering Heights, eyed Mark speculatively. Mark sometimes felt a bit uneasy under the other man's gaze. It often seemed to him that the dark brooding man was weighing him up and finding him wanting!

As each sleep-deprived day merged into another Mark felt despair overtake him. He could not understand Emma's stubbornness and hostility.

One dark day in November after pleading with Emma to appoint another dairy manager had failed Mark felt the misery that had dogged him finally close like a wave over a drowning man's head. She had slammed the bedroom door in his face and turned off the light refusing to talk to him any more. In his exhausted and desperate state Mark went downstairs and picked up his gun and stumbled outside. He could not bear it anymore. There just seemed to be no way to get through to Emma. He walked up and down the garden tears coursing down his face and watched as Emma turned the bedroom light off. He felt fury and despair. He was fucking dying and she could not care less! Maybe if she thought he had committed suicide she would have to admit that he was seriously unable to cope because she certainly ignored all rational arguments. Lately even the brief sane moments he shared with Charlie seemed always to be sabotaged by Emma insisting that he had to have a bath or a change or a feed or anything else that would keep the infant from being with his father for a few precious moments.

Crying with the complete futility of everything and the utter feeling of helplessness and hopelessness Mark looked up at the starry sky above him and fired the shotgun into the air. Crying harder now disgusted with himself that he could not go through with the reality of suicide.

For a long moment the sound of the shot echoed in the still night. Mark could see his breath standing out on the frigid air. He was standing facing the cottage where the lights were out. The light of the spare bedroom that he had occupied since Charlie's birth could not be seen from this side of the cottage but the light in the room that Emma slept in with Charlie in the newly extended master bedroom suite remained off.

There was no way she could not have heard the shot. Mark fell to his knees sobbing. She was not even sufficiently interested to find out whether he had shot himself or not. Finally as he watched the light came on, and Emma appeared at the back door. She was, Mark noticed with surprise, fully dressed; her hair brushed and put up in a loose bun. Had she, then, expected to find his lifeless body outside and got herself ready to greet the emergency services and the police who would need to be called? Had she already made the call?

As her eyes adjusted to the dark and Emma made out Mark standing his gun in his hand she said.

"What the hell are you doing Mark?"

"I've had enough!" Mark croaked.

"Well I've had enough too, of your ridiculous attention seeking behaviour, what on earth do you think you're doing making such a ridiculous scene when I'm trying to get Charlie off to sleep?"

Mark drew his breath in. He felt as though he had been slapped. Was he now completely paranoid or could he hear a note of disappointment in Emma's voice?

"Now come in and stop being such a drama queen. You're not impressing anyone!" Emma said coldly. "All this because I won't let you take on a dairy manager, anyone would think we were made of money! You have absolutely no idea, obviously!" Emma shook her head as one would over a naughty child and held the back door open for him.

"Come on Mark, all the heat is getting out, like I said, obviously no appreciation of the value of money!"

Mark walked back into the cottage. He felt numb. He followed Emma up the stairs and watched her disappear into the master suite without a backward glance. For a moment he stood looking at the closed door. Then he walked quietly into the spare room and closed the door. He lay down on the bed fully clothed and fell into a deep sleep.

But if Mark had been shocked by Emma's uncaring attitude the night before he was to be rendered completely speechless by her behaviour when he attended the appointment she had made for him with their GP. As she explained to the doctor that Mark had been in such a state he had nearly shot himself she held tight to his hand and wiped a tear from her eye with a crisp white hanky. What truly shocked Mark was the contrast between the indifferent attitude she had displayed to him privately, and this concerned face she was now putting on as she talked about the incident. He sat stunned in front of the doctor wanting to scream that it was all an act, that Emma could not care less whether he lived or died, and as he did the thought dawned on him that he rather suspected that she would rather he did die. That would mean that she had Charlie all to herself.

Mark continued to work, his days a welter of exhaustion and confusion. He felt as though he was losing his mind. Coming in mid morning for a cup of coffee to keep him awake, he found Charlie alone in the lounge in his carrycot. Emma was obviously planning to take him out. As he looked down into his son's face he watched a tiny frown crease the tiny forehead as though the child was trying to place him. Mark felt a lump come to his throat. His own son was wondering who he was! Mark sat wearily beside the cot very aware of his dirty overalls next to the pristine neatness of the lounge and the sweet smelling newly washed baby. He put his finger out to the boy and Charlie clasped it in a strong little fist. For a moment Charlie seemed to be thinking about it and then kicked his legs in his baby-grow and smiled a gummy smile. Mark wept openly at the pressure from the tiny fist around his finger, the most precious touch his skin had ever felt. The tiny fingers seemed to leave an indelible soft impression on him that Mark knew he would be able to feel even when his son had been snatched away from him; as he knew he would be as soon as Emma discovered their touching tableau. But in these stolen moments Mark looked down at the promise that his son represented, the future stretching before both of them like an uncharted adventure that they should be able to travel together. In his mind's eye Mark could imagine his son first holding his hand as they walked together then walking shoulder to shoulder as the boy grew into a man. Charlie's strength gaining as his own waned. Facing life's up and downs together, working and planning together, laughing and crying and experiencing all that life had in store for them as father and son. And as his eyes held those of his infant son's Mark realised that he saw no sign of Emma in the picture he was painting in his mind. The cold fist that had become such a feature of his being that he barely noticed it these days tightened in a solid knot in his stomach and in that moment he realised that there would be no future for the three of them together and if that was the case he knew that he would be the one left out of the equation. But now as love for his infant son welled up inside him and the flawless face with its piercing hazel eyes stared up at him unblinking, he knew he could not bear that, could not let that happen. Whatever happened he could not give up the chance to be with his son, to be part of his life, to be his teacher and his comforter and the father that he wanted; no, needed so desperately to be.

"Mark!" Emma's voice had such an intonation of horror that anyone watching would have thought she had come down the stairs and found Mark throttling their son.

"What are you doing in here, at this time? Look at the sate of you, bringing the dirt of those filthy animals in here to my son? Have you lost your mind?"

The fact that she had said 'my son' was not lost on Mark. He jumped away from the carry cot as though he had been electrocuted and Charlie, sensing the change in atmosphere began to grizzle softly, his tiny face crumpling and a single tear escaping from his eye and running down his flushed cheek.

Emma strode over to him and snatched him up in her arms looking at him intently as thought for any damage that contact with his father had inflicted on him. Seeing a tiny smudge of dirt on his palm where he had held his Marks finger she took out one of the baby wipes and rubbed it so hard that little Charlie yelped in surprise.

To Mark watching her it looked as though she was trying to expunge any trace of him from the child's skin and as she held Charlie's palm up to inspect it Mark noticed it was quite red from her rubbing.

"For God's sake Emma, the boy lives on a farm, he will have to get used to a bit of dirt!"

"Oh and that's it is it? Let him get used to it, get every nasty disease going just because he happens to live on a filthy farm?"

"The farm is not filthy, but it is a farm!" Mark tried to keep his voice level "and children have grown up on farms for generations without ill effect, you are being too fussy with him!"

"My God, this is so typical of you Mark!" she spat at him. "You just cant' bear to be wrong can you? I wouldn't put it past you to take Charlie outside and throw him in the slurry pit just to prove your point!" The image of such an horrendous act stunned Mark into silence for a moment. Emma was standing in front of him with undisguised hate in her eyes. He could not ignore it any more. She hated him having anything to do with Charlie. But was that all she hated. Did she actually hate him as well? He could not believe that she did, or maybe he just could not bear to believe that she did, and if she did, why? He had done nothing but support her and Charlie, allowed her to stay off work and acceded to her demand that he take on no more staff. Any mention of this produced outright hostility from Emma and she became unreasonable about everything; especially in agreeing to any measures to reduce Mark's own work load. Time and time again Mark asked for agreement. He always wanted consensus over business decisions, to take on extra workers. Time and time again Emma refused and was even hostile to the overtime that the staff were doing. The workers on the farm were close to breaking point. Mark tried to fob them off saying that they did not have the money for more staff but Matt's mother Caroline did the books for the farm and so he at least knew that this was not true. Since Charlie's birth the pressure on the staff and Mark had been immense. Mark was having to work such long hours that he hardly saw Charlie. Occasionally he would think that Emma was doing this on purpose, keeping him so busy that he did not have any time to spend with Charlie. At first Mark had thought this was just a jealous phase for her and that she was concentrating on bonding with Charlie. For the first few months he had let it pass rather than cause friction over it. But now as the possessiveness became so obvious that the staff were commenting on it Mark knew that he could stay silent no longer.

"Look Emma," he said in a low voice. "I am Charlie's father and I *will* be seeing him, picking him up, playing with him, and taking him out, wherever and whenever I want!" Emma went pale as she recognised the dangerous tone in Mark's voice. "We'll see about that!" she said but her voice wavered as she spoke. She held Charlie to her as though she expected mark to pounce on the infant. "So what are you saying, that you are actively going to stop me seeing Charlie?" Mark's voice was low, his gaze level and his tone deadly serious. Emma hesitated. "I'm saying, I know what is good for our son! Are you saying I don't?"

Mark was wrong footed for a moment. If he agreed with her then he was casting severe doubt on her as a mother, if he said that he thought she was a good mother then how could he argue against what she thought best for their son?

As he hesitated he saw triumph light up her eyes. She had him and she knew it. Furious and unable to trust his actions Mark turned and strode to the back door.

"Shut the door on your way out, there's a dear!" Emma's voice called after him."

Chapter 10

The Split

As day followed relentless exhausting day Mark found it almost a relief to be so tired that he could not think, and therefore did not need to think about his and Emma's relationship. But occasionally he would feel as though he was going to boil over, fuelled by lack of sleep and frustration and this morning's huge row with Emma, when she had found him on his own with Charlie. He had been able to tell at lunchtime, by the tense set of her shoulders, that she was still furious with him. He thought about talking to her about it in the evening. But he had an appointment with a hypnotherapist that the doctor had recommended he see after his shotgun episode and in his already drained physical state, he was likely to be completely wiped out at the end of the session. Mark could not believe that any kind of talking therapy let alone what he considered mumbo jumbo hypnotism could help the deep and corrosive anger that he had inside him. But on his first session Mark sat dumbfounded wondering at how extraordinary it was that a simple sentence could impact so much on him and sum up the life he was leading so succinctly. In the very first session with Moira, a quiet, gentle looking woman, after she had listened intently to the background information he gave she said calmly;

"You have every right to be angry. Anger is a useful, normal emotion. It is what you do with your anger that is sometimes unacceptable". Mark proved a relatively easy patient to hypnotise. They made tapes for him to use to relax and calm himself over the sessions that followed. The sceptic in Mark had been completely vanquished, and as the sessions progressed he thought that he could best describe the benefit he felt after a session or after listening to the tape as having the threshold of anger so reduced in his mind and body that he became far more patient and was able to deal with Emma's unreasonable and erratic behaviour better. Mark reflected that he had only reached that explosive moment of anger a handful of times in his life, and never yet with Emma. He had learned that whenever he got near that stage, when he started to tremble or shake with anger, or sometimes even before that he should just walk away from the situation.

He knew that this behaviour, even the most innocuous or innocent behaviour was like a red rag to a bull to Emma, even driving her to physically attack him in frustrated rage. As he drove to his therapy session with Moira, Mark thought of how the sessions had given him a boost and the strength to stand up to Emma. As though she sensed that Mark had found an ally, Emma was almost immediately hostile and pressed Mark almost every time they spoke to end the sessions.

"For God's sake Mark, everyone gets stressed in their work and their life, you just need to be a man about it, you need to grow a backbone!"

Now as he drove through the country lanes Mark realised that in his mental and physical exhaustion with the incident with the shotgun, Emma had come close to destroying him. He knew that he was on the verge of or having a physical and mental breakdown.

After several sessions with Moira she had offered Mark free counselling sessions if he would be a case study for her counselling course. Mark agreed eagerly, free sessions would remove one of Emma's objections to his therapy. Through the spring and summer he had over 40 sessions with Moira and as they progressed the softly spoken therapist opened his eyes to the possible reasons why Emma might be acting the way she did.

As Mark poured out the deepest, darkest secrets of their marriage, times when Emma had turned really nasty, Moira cautioned Mark never to turn his back on Emma or to sleep without his bedroom door locked.

As the implication of the therapists words sunk in Mark felt the cold fist tighten in his stomach again. How could it have got to this, that a third party thought his own wife might try to . . . . what? Kill him? Even in the horrific and daily hell that living with Emma had turned into, could he really think that she would try to kill him? Mark thought back to the night in the garden when he had fired his shotgun; hadn't she come to the back door fully dressed, as though ready for visitors? What kind of a wife, thinking her husband was dead would take the time to dress and tidy herself up before she even came out to see what had happened?

Mark did not know it then but there was to come a time later when he did fear for his life, and Moira, it would turn out, would not be the only professional to give him that advice.

As winter released its iron grip on the land and spring began to show promise of new life to come Emma had Matt, the young farm hand, in her sights. Matt had come across them arguing in the dairy one morning and with Emma's vitriol hanging in the air like a malignant all pervading mist, he had walked off muttering "cow"

Emma heard him and shouted at Mark

"Are you just going to let him say that? God you're not even man enough to stand up for your own wife! You are pathetic, worse than pathetic, you're a spineless excuse for a man!"

A week later Emma was waiting for Mark, her hands on her hips as he walked home for a sandwich at lunchtime. In her hand she had a box of nails.

"Guess where I found these?" she said a note of triumph in her voice.

Drawing on the training he had had from Moira, Mark stayed calm, resisting the urge to say anything that would antagonise Emma further.

"I found them in Matt's pocket!" she said.

"How did you find them in his pocket?"

"He took his jacket off while he was bringing the churns into the dairy and I moved it—the nails fell out.

"He had probably put them in there to use later." Mark said reasonably.

"Is he due to be working on anything that needs nailing today?" Emma said, her voice low.

"Well no, not that I know of, but you know how things are on the farm."

"Then he's stealing from us!" she said triumphantly

"Don't be ridiculous Emma, Matt would never steal from us. Hell, if he asked for the damn nails I'd give them to him anyway, they cost pence!"

"That is not the point!" Emma shrieked "We can't trust him, today nails, tomorrow money, who knows? No, he's got to go! And don't you *dare* call me ridiculous, you are the ridiculous one, not able to see what is right under your nose. You are a soft touch and an idiot, all the staff know that. They make a mug of you. I grant you, you *may* have taken them in with your mister nice guy act but not me matey, Oh no, not me!" There was a hysterical note to her voice that made Mark think immediately and with alarm about Charlie. He had to try to calm her down; the child was in the kitchen in his high chair, Weetabix smeared all around his face. Mark could hear him beginning to cry, all this hostility could be no good for him, and the boy was probably terrified.

Mark went to take Emma's arm, "Come on let's go inside and make a cup of tea shall we?"

"DON'T TOUCH ME!" she screamed and behind her Charlie began to wail in earnest.

Mark snatched his hand away from her arm immediately and recoiled from the naked hatred he saw in her eyes.

"You sort this out Mark, we can't afford to have people stealing from us!"

"I'll sort it out don't worry, I'll go right now and speak to Matt, you're right, we do need to get to the bottom of this." Mark said and to his immense relief saw Emma begin to relax slightly. As though suddenly aware of her child crying she turned her back and through the kitchen window Mark saw her scoop Charlie out of his high chair and cradle him to her.

The conversation with Matt could not have gone worse. At first Matt thought he was joking but then realising that a serious complaint had been made against him he stared at Mark in disbelief.

"And you believe that mad cow do you?"

"No, look Matt, of course I trust you completely but Emma . . . ." he tailed off miserably.

"But Emma wants me out of here, because I can see her for what she is—a fucking vindictive evil bitch!" Matt was pulling off his overalls. Mark's head was pounding. He knew he should defend his wife, but suddenly all the energy had been drained out of him. Matt was walking out of the milking parlour now. He turned back to Mark as he got to the door.

"And I'm not the only one who thinks she is evil, Mark, you need to watch your back mate, seriously, she is one disturbed lady!"

"Matt, wait!"

"Look mate, I'm sorry that you have lost your balls to that witch, really I am but, I'm out of here, I'm not staying anywhere that someone calls me a thief!" And with that Matt walked off the farm for good.

With Matt gone, Emma found herself forced to help out. After a week of this enforced labour she finally agreed to let Mark appoint another member of staff to support her and Dot, a woman from the village who had been the mainstay of the dairy and was their most senior staff member on that side of the operation

This time Mark interviewed and chose a local village girl, Kerry, young and newly married. She was fascinated with Charlie and Kerry almost immediately ended up looking after Charlie for long periods in the house. To Mark's amazement the short return to her duties seemed to have stirred in Emma some of the original enthusiasm she had for the farm and her duties in the dairy. She even found time to spend with her old partner Linda in the dog grooming parlour and Mark dared to hope that things might have taken a turn for the better. He had read a lot about post-natal depression and thought that Emma might have been suffering from it to some degree. Mixing with the farm staff and Linda, seemed to be giving her back a little of her previous perspective.

Kerry's cheerful presence in the house and her new child minding duties offered Mark occasional times when he could see Charlie unhindered.

One day as Emma returned unexpectedly to the house she found Mark with Charlie on a blanket on the grass outside the back door.

"What the hell do you think you're doing?" she shouted and Mark's heart broke as his son jumped, his face immediately crumpling, fear in his wide eyes,

"You are a man down on the farm and you've got the time to loll about on a blanket, disturbing Charlie's routine?" How long has this been going on?" she demanded. Kerry appeared at the door, her freckled face a picture of shock. She had not seen Emma like this before.

"HOW LONG HAS THIS BEEN GOING ON?" she shouted, this time at Kerry, who almost at the same moment as Charlie, burst into tears .

Mark jumped up, and almost ran away from the cottage. His only thought was to save his son any more suffering and distress. He knew that he was the catalyst for Emma's anger and now he had only one thought, and that was to get away from the scene as quickly as he could. He felt guilty that he had left Kerry to face the wrath of Emma alone, but he knew he had to go.

In one of the outside sheds where a goat kid had been put to be seen by the vet later for a suspected infected foot, Mark sunk onto the sweet smelling hay. The kid hobbled over to him curious, bleating softly. Mark gathered up the little animal and cried bitterly into its soft coat.

The unrelenting work of the farm continued and now as summer approached staff were taking holidays. Back in the thick of it, this time Emma did not object to Mark's suggestion that they take on yet another member of staff. And so a cousin of Kerry's, Sheena, started part time. Emma remained in the dairy but now she had Kerry in there with her along with Charlie in a playpen. Mark felt misery close over him like a suffocating blanket. He now rarely saw his son, Emma made sure of that.

Mark was fighting on all fronts. Greg, the stockman had started to indicate that unless big changes were made he was going to leave. In front of the doctor, Emma had paid lip service at least to the notion that Mark needed to reduce his stress level and work load.

On one stifling evening when Mark felt that he could take the relentless exhaustion no longer. He sat opposite Emma in the airless little lounge knowing that unless she agreed to help him relieve the work load, he did not think he could go on.

"Emma you remember when were at the doctors and you said that you could see that I needed to take things a bit more easy?" Emma did not reply, but she shot him a look of barely disguised contempt.

Mark pressed on,

"I am thinking of selling some of the rare breed cattle or maybe the sheep or the pigs. That way I can reduce Greg's workload; either that, or we can get someone else to work in the yoghurt room in my place so that I can help him."

"No, Mark, it was only a couple of weeks ago I found you stretched out on a blanket in the middle of the day with Charlie, you can't have it both ways, either you're busy or you have time to stop work and butt in where you're not wanted, which is it?" Her voice had the hard brittle note of triumph he had heard so often. He knew it was fruitless to argue.

He ended up doing more until one day in June he knew that he could go on no longer.

He confronted Emma in the dairy, trying not to register the inquisitive look his son was giving him, as though trying to decide who he was.

"Emma, I can't go on. I have take a break to recharge my batteries. I'm taking a week off!"

Charlie's birthday was a couple of days away and Emma had arranged for them to drive five hours to her cousin's house for a barbeque. Mark had protested but Emma would brook no argument.

For a moment Emma said nothing. Mark held his breath for the outburst but it didn't come. Instead Emma left the dairy leaving Mark staring after her.

Mark crossed the room to where Charlie was standing up against the rails of his playpen. As Mark reached out to him, Charlie turned away holding his arms out to Kerry who hurried over to him. The look on her face was one of sympathy and embarrassment and Mark turned away to hide his tears.

That Saturday Emma took Charlie and left the farm at six in the morning. By the time that Mark had got up at 7 am the van was missing.

Emma had known he wanted to go and visit his father for the week, her act had been purely vindictive. Mark swore and got out the cash box, He would have to take money from the float and hire a car. When he opened the box he could barely believe what he was seeing. The chequebook and credit card had gone. Instead of the usual fifteen hundred pounds, all there was about one hundred pounds.

He could go nowhere. That night he walked down to the pub determined to get away from the farm. John Abbott was propping up the bar and looked up as he came in.

"Mark, mate!" As Mark emerged into the light of the bar John's face fell.

"God Mark what the hell has happened to you?"

"Nothing, I'm fine." Mark thought he sounded like an old man, his voice was weak, quavering and full of tears.

John was looking very concerned now. He led Mark to one of the window seats and said.

"God man are you ill?"

"No, I'm fine, really." Mark put his hands on the table, they were shaking.

"You've lost so much weight, what does the doctor say?"

"Nothing, I haven't been." Mark said weakly.

The concern in his friends' eyes touched something in him that was ready to burst and he broke down in tears. John looked around the bar. Two other couples were at tables on the other side of the room and both looked up as Mark's wracking sobs filled the room.

"Right, we're getting out of here." John said taking Mark by the arm.

Outside, Mark stood swaying, and caught a glimpse of himself in the shiny brass plate that bore the pubs name on the wall of the old building. He saw a stooped man whose trousers hung off him and looked about 60.

"Right you're coming back home with me!" John said and every fibre of Mark wanted to do that but he couldn't let

John know what was happening. He couldn't let anyone know. He pulled himself up and gave a hollow laugh.

"I'm fine John mate, don't you worry about me. You know us farmers at this time of year, not enough time to scratch our arses".

John looked doubtful, but Mark was walking away.

"Catch you for a pint soon!" he said.

"Mark!" John called after him, but Mark did not stop until he reached home and in the quiet of the house collapsed on his bed and cried until sleep claimed him. In his dreams he dreamt he had died and the elation that he felt to be free of the pain he was going through allowed him to wake up feeling briefly happy for the first time in years, until the realisation of his wretched life brought him back to reality.

Mark waited for Emma to return and she did on Sunday afternoon. But far from being sheepish about what she had done she was actually angry to find that he was still on the farm.

Mark confronted her.

"Yes, I did take the van and the money, so what? In any case my solicitor advised me to do that!"

Mark felt the cold fist take hold of his gut again. Her solicitor, what the hell was going on?

As the summer wore on Greg said he would do the milking over the weekends to give Mark a bit of a break.

Looking at Mark with his impenetrable dark eyes the swarthy man said.

"I'll help, God knows you need all the help you can get." His steady gaze always had the power to make Mark feel that he was entirely to blame for any and all shortcomings on the farm.

"Thank you Greg mate," Mark said, "I really want to get out this weekend and try to regroup a bit, I think if I don't get a break soon I'm going to turn into a bloody goat!"

"Hmm" Greg looked at him thoughtfully, then shrugging his shoulders sauntered off, tossing an "OK" over his shoulder.

As it happened the weather was right for hay making on the first weekend that Greg and Mark were going to put their plan into action. The hay was ready to bale and bring into the barns. Mark steeled himself, trying to push his disappointment at not getting his well deserved break to the back of his mind. He was bitterly disappointed. He even found himself wiping tears of frustration from his eyes, but haymaking was the single most stressful time on the farm and it was every hand to the pump. He could not be absent at this time of all times. He never fed silage to the milking goats and sheep because of the danger of bacterial contamination. The winter feed was based entirely on hay and straw for roughage. With 300 goats, 30 sheep, 45 Short Horn cattle and 4 Gloucester Old Spot sows the farm used a lot of hay and straw. Mark tried not to let the unending relentless cycle overwhelm him but as he thought of the months turning to years in this living hell, he felt something in him was going to snap, to break and to leave him crumpled and helpless unable to move, speak or even think. And as his fevered over taxed brain considered an immobilised future, a future of nothingness, he found the thought of being unable to function, to be what . . . . .? dead? a most acceptable even desired option.

Contractors were hired and rowed up and baled the hay in big half-ton bales. The weather was forecast to change to rain by the end of the weekend and everyone was working flat out, desperate not to miss the window of opportunity.

Exhausted to the point that he did not know how he was still standing Mark got back from his dairy deliveries on the Friday of the haymaking weekend to be told by Emma that Greg had walked out.

"Why, why has he walked out?" Mark asked. "I've got to find him and talk to him!"

"I wouldn't do that if I were you!" Emma said barely disguised pleasure in her voice, "he is refusing to talk to you apparently because he says he can't trust himself not to knock you out cold if he sees you!"

Mark was completely at a loss to imagine what had gone wrong but with no explanation, and Greg not answering his phone, he had no option but to accept that Greg had gone. Mark had got used to the fact that Greg often behaved strangely and that the strange dark man was prone to telling extremely tall tales. But he could not understand it. The chat he had had with Greg had given him no indication that there was a problem, Greg would know that this was the most difficult time possible to walk out, in the middle of haymaking and if his grievances had been so serious that he felt he would hit Mark if he saw him, why had he not come to him, talked to him? As Mark stood stunned in the milking parlour trying to get his thoughts together he realised that the week ahead of him, with staff on leave and without Greg, was going to be pure hell. He was not disappointed.

Mark came home as the sun set that evening, forcing his protesting body upstairs to get ready for his therapy session. Although he would happily have fallen into bed, his sessions were the one bright point in his life and he truly believed that without them he would not be able to cope.

As he looked across the little lounge on his way down the stairs he saw that Emma was sitting there, waves of a cold fury seeming to emanate from her. Charlie was already upstairs in bed, Mark had dared a few stolen moments next to the child as he slept, listening out for Emma's footstep on the stairs. Now he wondered if somehow she had known he was up there with Charlie, maybe from the creak of the old floor boards of the cottage, or did she have a spy camera? In his exhaustion he could feel his mind spinning out of control and a feeling of panic beginning to overwhelm him. Emma sat rigid in her favourite chair, the one that she always sat in, with its view through the trellis on the patio down the garden that Mark had planted for her when they were first married. He often thought it was an enigma that at the times she was her most disturbed or angry with him she would sit there staring out at something he had made for her, with love.

Her eyes flashed dangerously as she glanced at him. She never quite made eye contact these days, and for a moment Mark thought that he might be able to leave the cottage and go without saying anything to her but then as he stood, his hand on the front door and speaking through clenched teeth she said

"It's over, Mark, there is no future for us, I've known that for a long time and I want a divorce!"

Mark stepped back as though she had hit him. It wasn't a complete surprise, their relationship had been moribund for a long time. It was the vehemence of her words and the hostility in her voice that made him go cold. He swallowed hard and tried to keep his voice even.

"OK Emma, of course I don't want to be with someone who doesn't want to be with me, but I am sure that you want things to be as amicable as they can be, for Charlie's sake?"

Emma flashed him a hate filled look that said that she could not care less how unpleasant things got. She made a sort of unconscious movement as though she were holding Charlie to her before her hands fell into her lap again, clenched into tight fists, her knuckles white.

The unconscious clasping movement had an electrifying effect on Mark. He already knew that Emma made either conscious or unconscious efforts to keep him away from

Charlie, the infant had often slept in their bed in the early days, but on the rare occasions Mark was allowed to be in the master suite Emma had always held their son in her arms on her side of the bed, her back to Mark. If the boy was ever in the middle of the bed, Mark would breathe in Charlie's baby smell and watch his tiny perfect features in the half light of the bedroom, nudging his sleeping son's hand so that the pudgy fingers would open and curl around his thumb. A love that he had never known possible overwhelming him as tears of joy and pride rolled unchecked down his cheeks. But now something in Emma's impulsive movement sent a cold shiver down Marks' spine as in that moment he realised that she had already decided that he would never again find it easy to be with his son, he had served his purpose and was now dismissed.

Chapter 11

Living apart together.

Mark tried to come to terms with his new circumstances, married but separated from a wife who made it clear that he was only being allowed to stay out of necessity and his contribution to the farm. Then one day when he was dragging himself back to the farm his eyes drooping from exhaustion, he saw something that made his blood run cold. As he drove past the cottage making for the yard where he would park the van he saw Emma, Charlie on her hip, kissing an older woman at the door. For a moment Mark thought that his eyes must be playing tricks on him. It couldn't possibly be, could it? It was. Mary Channing was offering up her cheek for her daughter to kiss while she held the podgy little hand of her grandson. Mark felt bile rise in his throat and realised he was going to be sick. Stumbling from the van he vomited up the half a cup of coffee that he had managed to snatch earlier.

The only thing that had kept him sane and had given him a glimmer of hope that he might be able to bring things back around was the fact that Mary Channing was out of the picture. With her in the picture he knew that he had little hope. Her warped and poisonous influence on Emma would be the final nail in the coffin of what had been their marriage. As he leaned against the wall of the dairy Mark closed his eyes. He felt hot tears sting the back of his eyelids.

The next morning Emma drove off early with Charlie. It emerged that Charlie had been taken to the village day nursery, Little Ted's. Mark felt helpless and very angry that he had not been included in this milestone decision about Charlie. As Emma arrived back at the farm without their son he confronted her. In the background, Kerry who had told Mark where Emma had gone looked anxious and unhappy.

"Why didn't you tell me you were taking Charlie to nursery?"

Emma shrugged

"Why should I?"

"Because he's my son as well as yours!"

"And if I had told you, would you have objected?"

"Well no, but that's not the point!"

"I think it's very much the point Mark, you are just so stupid and so ridiculous you pick fights over nothing, what does it matter if I tell you or not, if it is something I know you would not object to? " Emma's lip was curled and her eyes were dark. Naked contempt lit her face and made her look ugly.

"I want to be involved in all decisions about Charlie, whether I support them or not, I want to know every detail of his life, God knows second hand information seems to be the most I can hope for, and now that your mother is involved, I suppose I can hope for even less. It's not fair Emma; it's just not fair! I have done nothing wrong, and just because you have fallen out of love with me does not mean you have the right to keep Charlie away from me.

"Its' not fair, it's not fair!" Emma mimicked in a whining tone of voice, mocking him. "Oh grow up Mark, you've got your precious goats, just be content with that and let the rest of us worry about Charlie!"

"I will not!" Mark was furious now, how dare she dismiss him in such a callous and uncaring manner? "You are a class A bitch Emma and I can see that you learned that from your equally vile mother. You are not fit to have the care of a young and vulnerable mind that you can twist and infect with your evil. I am the only chance that boy has of turning out in any way normal!"

"Normal?" Emma said incredulously "You normal? You must be joking, you are underhand and a liar and my mother was right all along. I should never have married you and definitely never should have trusted you!"

Mark was stunned into silence. The sense of injustice seemed to be about to overwhelm him. Before he could answer, Emma had gone inside and slammed the door behind her.

Mark looked at his watch. His run in with Emma now meant that the produce was going to be late for afternoon delivery. He would now have to fit them in after morning milking the next day. The wholesaler's lorries came on Tuesdays for their deliveries for the rest of the week and above all he had to be ready for that. Mark threw himself into his work trying to ignore the pain that seemed almost to paralyse him.

As he sat in his bedroom that night fighting sleep, he wrote out an ultimatum for Emma. Something had to be sorted. He asked for an answer within two days. The suggestion was that he stop working on the processing side completely and no longer do the deliveries.

Mark offered to milk four days a week, employing a relief milker for the other three days. He would do all the farm work but, Mark proposed they sell all the cattle, sheep and pigs and give up the rented land. Mark concluded his proposal with the fact that doing as he proposed would reduce his stress level and leave him time to finish the house and sort out the garden. Mark also suggested as an alternative that he could be a 'house husband' and just advise on the farm. Mark thought about what life had been like before Charlie had been born when he had done about a third of the cooking and most of the housework. He knew he would make a good job of it.

When he handed Emma his carefully written proposal she took it and said.

"Ok, I'll have a look at it and get back to you."

She never did.

Mark started milking at 4am next morning. He took the milk up to the yoghurt room to be frozen down. Emma refused to deal with it,

"That's your job *Mark*" she said emphasising his name, her voice dripping disdain.

"Emma, I have to be out on deliveries! Are you saying you are not going to process the milk?" Mark could feel white-hot rage burn the back of his throat.

"As I said, Mark, that's your job!"

"Right!" He tuned on his heel and in full view of Emma and the rest of the dairy staff poured the 130 gallons of milk over the field beside the dairy.

Mark rushed off to do the deliveries. He had arranged a special meeting between Emma, their GP, Dr. Bond and Moira his hypnotherapist to talk about their marriage and the problems they were having. Mark knew that this meeting was the last chance they had to get things back on track although he half expected Emma not to turn up. To his surprise as he turned up 10 minutes late, she was already there.

Moira took charge of the meeting and asked Mark to describe how he felt about Emma and what he wanted in the future.

Mark cleared his throat and said,

"I still love Emma and I want us to be together. I trust her implicitly. Now that we have Charlie I want to be involved, hands on, with his upbringing. If we cannot work together then I am prepared to sell up and get a job and be like other people. I feel that all this stress is destroying us."

Moira smiled at him encouragingly.

"Do you still find Emma attractive?" Mark tried to ignore the looks of disgust that passed fleetingly over Emma's face and said

"Yes, I still find Emma very attractive physically." Mark looked at Emma. She looked away. " I want, more than anything to have a proper physical relationship but I don't think that is what Emma wants" he said sadly.

"Stick to the positives, Mark" Moira said gently. Mark sighed.

"I love the way Emma is so practical and capable and when she shows her caring side it is very attractive. I like the way we still think about how to live economically and healthily with a united approach." Moira nodded her encouragement and asked Emma the same question. Emma favoured Moira with her most disarming smile and started to catalogue the things she wanted for Charlie.

After a few minutes Moira interrupted her.

"Emma do you realise that you have not mentioned Mark once, not even with respect to the future?"

Emma's façade slipped for a moment and a look of irritation came over her face.

"Well obviously it is taken for granted that he is included in the future!" Her disarming smile was back now but when Moira asked her again what she felt about Mark, Emma evaded the question and Moira had to press her several times.

Suddenly Emma burst into tears and rushed out of the room. Dr Bond leapt up and said he would go to her. Moira turned to Mark

"What do you make of that?"

"Well, she has never done that before" Mark said. "I have never known Emma to burst into tears. When she gets emotional the tears come slowly. Emma always likes to be in control. She can argue and argue with a calm voice, when she raises her voice or shouts I know she is on the verge of loosing it. I ought to go to her."

"No Mark leave it to Dr. Bond. I am afraid that I think that what we have just seen was an act and the tears do not convince me either. I am pretty sure that her outburst was a way to escape answering the questions that she did not want to answer. There was a lot more going on here than is obvious. Look you've got an appointment for tomorrow, lets leave it there for today."

Mark had no choice but to agree, When he got out to the car park Emma's car had gone.

That weekend Mark had all the stacked hay to bring into the barns before he could return to the problems of the next week. Thankfully Dot was back from her holiday so the dairy was functioning at full staffing levels again. Mark saw Moira on the Saturday morning and had a session of hypnotherapy. Slightly relieved of his stress after his visit to Moira Mark decided to tackle Emma that evening after Charlie had gone to bed.

Emma had made it clear that she did not expect him to sit with her in the lounge and if he ever had the energy or the time to watch any TV he did so in the kitchen sitting beside the aga. This evening, feeling ridiculous, he knocked on the door of the lounge. Getting no reply he went in.

"What do *you* want?" Emma did not bother to hide the irritation in her voice.

I want to know if you have an answer for me?"

"An answer, about what?" Her irritation had turned to contempt, as she looked him up and down.

"My proposal, the one I gave you, about the future of the farm."

"Oh that, no I haven't got an answer for you, in case you haven't notice I have better things to do that to bother myself with your whining little complaints and 'oh poor me' ramblings."

Mark tried to stop the anger building inside him. He kept his voice calm and asked Emma again to respond to the ultimatum and the questions Moira had asked her. For one and a half hours Emma evaded answering his questions. Mark felt exhaustion wash over him as he tried for the hundredth times to get Emma to reply to his question and to say what she wanted to happen on the farm.

"Emma, for pity's sake just answer me straight, what do you think about my proposals for the farm,? You can see it's killing me, I don't know how much longer I can carry on at this pace, with Greg gone."

Emma looked at him with defiant eyes.

"Look Mark, I've told you before but obviously I am going to have to tell you again, "there is no future between us . . . . "

"Does that mean that there is no future for the farm either? Is that why you have been procrastinating, because you want to see the farm die along with our marriage?" Mark could not keep the bitterness out of his voice.

Emma looked down at her hands.

"Look Mark, I'm tired of talking about this and if you are going to raise your voice . . . . !"

Mark could not believe his ears, the queen of vitriol was accusing him of raising his voice!

He stood up without another word and went up to his bedroom. On the way he paused at the door to the master bedroom. He could see Charlie's little outline under the sheets on the king sized bed. He was about to go in and kiss his son goodnight when he heard Emma's footsteps on the stairs. His heart breaking he opened the door of his room. He did not have the strength for any more of her viciousness that night.

The next day Mark managed to get all the hay into the barns. In the evening he returned wearily to the cottage, determined to get an answer to the ultimatum. As he came in through the back door he came face to face with Mary Channing.

"Hello Mark." She said. Behind her Emma was feeding Charlie and the older women stood between Mark and his wife and child like a guard.

"Mary, how are you?" Mark managed.

"Very well thank you, and Charlie, isn't he a delight?" she smiled a smile that did not quite reach her eyes.

"He is." Mark said fighting the urge to say that he barely got a chance to be with the boy.

"These long evenings are wonderful for working later aren't they?" she said cheerily "No need to worry about Emma and Charlie, I'm here helping them if you want to get on with more things on the farm, Emma has told me about how busy you have been." With that Mary took his arm and tried to manoeuvre him out of the back door that stood open behind him. He pulled his arm free and saw the startled look on Mary's face.

"I've finished work for the day thank you Mary, and I am sure you have a lot to do at home, so don't worry , *I'm* here now to help *my* wife and child, let me walk you to your car."

Mary sat down hard on one of the chairs at the kitchen table.

"I've hardly been here 10 minutes, Mark, you're surely not going to throw an old lady out on the street before she's even been offered a cup of tea?" Her voice was wheedling with a steel undertone that made Mark's blood run cold.

He crossed to the kettle, unplugged it, filled it with water and slammed it down so hard on the work top that some of the water spilled out. He took a mug from the cupboard above the kettle and slammed that down too.

"How do you take it Mary? It's been *so long* I've forgotten."

"Just milk please Mark, but if it's too much trouble . . . ."

Mark glanced at Emma; she was standing with a spoon of food just in front to Charlie's face. The child was ignoring the food and was watching the scene with wide eyes. As the child's eyes flickered over to him Mark thought he saw fear in them and immediately regretted slamming the kettle and mug down on the work surface. He felt rage bubble up inside him; the only person he cared about here was Charlie, and he was frightening the child.

He pushed past Mary and ran upstairs, leaving mother and daughter alone. In his room he paced up and down, he felt helpless and impotent to do anything to end the horrible situation he found himself in. As tears ran unchecked down his cheeks he thought back to the early days of his marriage to Emma, how they had been together when they were in love. But unbidden into his reverie came stark reminders of how she had always been one step away from unreasonable and often completely over the line. Had he been a fool? Had he ignored the obvious? He thought about his old friend Tony whom he had not heard from in years. The last time he had seen him was in Kenya, newly married to Tilly. The thought of Tilly, lovely freethinking, free wheeling Tilly, brought on a fresh bout of tears. Emma could not be more different. He had thought at one time that that was a good thing but now when he felt his head might explode with the frustrating complexity of his life, he longed for someone uncomplicated and uninhibited. Tony had warned him, God lots of people had made noises, but Tony had been blunt. He could hear his friends voice in his head as clear as though he had been in the room:

Seriously Mark mate you need to be bloody careful!"

"What?"

"Emma, I've seen her type before. Sex kitten one minute and iron maiden the next."

Mark was about to say that Emma and he were saving themselves but thought better of it, Tony would not understand. Instead he said

"Don't know what you're talking about."

Tony leaned forward. "All lovey-dovey, kissey-kissey one minute then bam, frozen out the next! Ring any bells?"

Mark wondered where Tony and Tilly were now? Probably had a brood of kids and enjoying life together. The frustration Mark felt tightened a band around his head. He rubbed his temples. All of a sudden he had an overwhelming urge to see his friend. He realised that he had no friends any more. Even John Abbott never came around any more. Emma did not like him and had made it clear.

His stomach was rumbling now, he realised he had not eaten all day. He went to the top of the stairs and listened. He could hear Emma talking to Charlie but he could not hear Mary's voice. He went to the front of the house. Her car had gone. Now he could hear Emma gather Charlie up to bring him up to bed. He ducked back into his room and waited for Emma to go downstairs again. Quietly he tiptoed into the master bedroom and stood beside Charlie. Charlie looked at him doubtfully, he clearly felt unsure. Mark put his hand out to his son and Charlie's face began to crumple. Mark beat a hasty retreat fighting back his own tears. Emma was back downstairs now. He was going to have it out with her once and for all.

As she stood her arms folded in front of her in the kitchen Emma denied all of the discussion they had had the night before, as well as what had happened at the meeting with Dr Bond and Moira on the Friday, including her repeated demand for a divorce.

Mark lost control

"Emma, in all the years I have known you despite our ups and downs I have trusted you fully because I felt you had never knowingly lied to me, that is until Charlie was born! Now there are so many lies, I have no idea what you are becoming! You seem to emanate hate, and having your mother's renewed input is bound to be part of that!"

Mark stopped shouting, had he gone too far? He could not help it. Emma stared at him dispassionately. Mark continued. "Emma if you can't discuss the problems addressed in the ultimatum about my work on the farm, then I'll make the decisions necessary myself!"

Emma's gaze faltered for a moment and Mark continued, buoyed by this perceived moment of uncertainty.

"From now on, with Dot back, I am not going to work on the processing side. I will do the farm work and deliveries." Mark said with more confidence than he felt

The look of confusion on Emma's face was reward enough for Mark and as she ranted back at him accusing him of everything to being useless at farm management to actual cruelty to animals. He clung on to the thin thread of triumph he had felt at seeing her rattled.

As Mark stuck to his new working schedule Emma retreated into a sulk. She was a sulker by nature. If she did not get her way she stonewalled or ignored him for days. She sulked for Monday and Tuesday. The hostility emanating from her was scary although, for Mark, a welcome relief from her constant sniping and sarcastic belittling. On Wednesday evening while he was washing up Emma came into the kitchen and adopting her customary folded arm stance, she said.

"I want you to get out. I'm sick of you and I want you gone!"

"That would be fine Emma if it was not for the was the little problem of milking 200 goats every day." Mark said evenly

Emma turned to Mark a look of triumph in her eyes.

"Oh don't worry about that Mark, you can go anytime. I have arranged with Greg to look after the animals when you have gone. But he won't come to the farm till you have left."

Mark was stunned. He had thought Greg was long gone but he was obviously still in touch with Emma. He tried to hold it together and said.

"OK get him to do the afternoon milking tomorrow. I'll leave in the afternoon and take a month off to think about things and try to get back to some sort of a normal physical and mental state." And before Emma could reply and before he gave into shock Mark ran back upstairs.

The next morning Mark took longer with the animals than usual because there had been torrential rain overnight. One of the sows, called Polly, had had her ark flooded. She was on the point of farrowing. She had scraped a big depression and lined it with straw and twigs but the depression had filled up with rainwater. Sometimes, especially around farrowing, Polly could be very cantankerous and she could move very fast in the mud, so Mark had to be very careful. On one occasion he and Greg had tried to herd her using a heavy metal five-bar gate. She turned to attack them and flipped the gate over Mark's head! At other times she would happily stand and have her ears scratched.

She was in a foul mood after the thunderstorm. As Mark could not trust Greg to move her, he stayed on to move her farrowing hut to drier ground.

"Are you still here?" Emma challenged him furiously as she spotted him in the shed.

Mark said nothing and by lunchtime was ready to leave.

"Can I have the car keys please?" Mark said putting his bag down on the kitchen floor. The car keys that were usually kept on key rack by the door were not there. "No I'll need the car and the van." Emma said shortly.

"Emma even you can't drive them both at once!" Mark said. He had taken the van keys as a possible bargaining chip. He had been expecting trouble.

"No Mark, I said NO!"

Mark shrugged. "Ok then, I'll take the van and you can hire a van to do the deliveries."

"I wouldn't advise it Mark I've cancelled your insurance as a named driver and if you insist I will ring the police!" She waved her phone at him.

"Well I don't suppose they would be interested in a domestic dispute of this nature, but go ahead if you want to!" Mark said heading for the door. He heard Emma speaking to the police and could not help a smile as she obviously was being told that the police would not be coming out.

"Wait there!" she shouted after him and Mark hesitated while she spoke to someone on the phone. From the conversation, Mark gathered that it was her solicitor. She had left the phone on speakerphone obviously hoping to stop Mark in his tracks but instead he heard her solicitor advise her to reinstate the insurance and swap the keys over. Emma was nearly apoplectic. Mark could barely suppress the feeling of elation that for once he had come out on top. After reinstating the insurance Emma threw the car keys at Mark, while he put the van keys down on the worktop.

"I've taken £250 from the cash box, Emma." He said as a parting shot.

"Well you're not having any more and I'll make sure you NEVER see Charlie again.!" There was an hysterical tinge to her voice now "And I will change all the locks on the house."

Emma stormed off with Charlie, the child's face creased with a mixture of fear and confusion. Mark felt an overwhelming sadness come over him. He knew that Emma was railing at him out of frustration at being outfoxed. He had no idea how serious she was.

As Mark did the rounds to say goodbye to the staff, Dot shook her head. "No-one can tell 'er nothing these days, it seems" she said. "Tell you what boss, unless Emma gets 'er act together, can't see none of us bein' around much longer.

At 4.00 pm Mark drove off, Dot's words ringing in his ears. He had been unable to contact his mother but drove to her house in Bath anyway. It turned out that she had gone away for a few nights, so Mark drove to his uncle's house in Corsham to find out where she had gone.

"She's visiting friend in Yorkshire, Mark lad, but you come on in and stay here till she gets back. Are you all right son? You've lost a lot of weight haven't you, is Emma not feeding you?"

Mark collapsed into a chair, his head in his hands.

The next morning, as Mark came downstairs after a long and dreamless nights sleep his aunt Beth said, "Now then, come and see who the wind's blown in!"

Mark walked bleary eyed after his aunt to the hall.

His sister Laurie had just arrived, en route to her home in Devon. Her smile of delight at finding him there turned to one of horror as she took in his emaciated form and dishevelled appearance.

"Oh my God Mark, what the hell has happened to you?" She put her hands to her face as tears welled up in her eyes.

Mark looked down at himself. His shirt looked about five sizes too big for him and his trousers were hanging off him. His belt tied around his waist. He looked back at his sister.

"God sis, I don't know I really don't!" she opened her arms and he clung to her as they cried together.

Chapter 12

Conflict

Mark's sister Laurie had a key to their mother's house and stayed with Mark there until Jenny Richards got back. His sister's caring and loving concern for him had him in tears for most of the day as the sad story of what his life with Emma was like, came out. As he heard himself telling his sister about the life he was leading he realised that most of it she must find almost unbelievable hell. As he recounted the stories even he found the catalogue of abuse and bizarre behaviour fantastical. So unused was Mark to anyone being gentle and compassionate to him that he could not stop the tears. And it was true, Laurie could barely believe what she was hearing; but one look at her brother convinced her that he was not exaggerating. She cried with him as he told of his treatment on the farm and the fact that his own son often barely seemed to recognise him. By the time that their mother arrived the pair had a severely edited version of events ready. Even so, the edited version upset Jenny Richards tremendously. She had only met Emma a couple of times and had found it difficult to understand her daughter in law's reluctance to get involved in any family gatherings.

She knew that the farm was demanding for them both but still she had the definite feeling that her son's wife used it as an excuse not to mix with her husband's side of the family. She had refused each and every invitation to Richards' 'clan' dos. Jenny did not make a big thing of it. She could see that Mark worked hard and did not want to make his life any more difficult. She could also see that Emma was a complex person, and suspected that things between her and Mark were not always easy. She had decided that it would be better to keep her distance, however hard that was, rather than make any trouble for Mark. Now what she was hearing made sense of things for her. Mark was obviously under tremendous pressure and the thought that Emma was keeping Charlie from him was heartbreaking.

Unknown to Mark his mother had called several times asking to visit young Charlie, but Emma who had taken the calls, had always had an excuse as to why that would not be possible. Jenny had stopped short at ringing Mark directly. She knew he was on the farm and if she were to visit, Emma would be the one who would be there to receive her.

After the month away Mark returned to the farm to a barrage of verbal abuse

"What the hell is the point arriving here at midday when the goats have been waiting to be milked since 6 am?" Emma shrieked at him stabbing at her wristwatch.

"Emma when I said I was coming back today I assumed that you would expect me later in the day not at the crack of dawn. I would have had to leave Bath at 4 30 to get here in time for milking!"

"Then that's what you should have done!" Emma said through gritted teeth.

"I have told you over and over again how I don't think you treat the animals well, in fact you are downright cruel to them. You won't have it, but this just proves it. Mark comes first. God forbid we should put you out!" Emma's voice dripped venom.

"I'll go to the milking shed right now and then I'll come and see Charlie."

"Don't bother, just get on with your work, I am so sick of your attitude Mark. I can't tell you how nice it was when you weren't here, without your whining and complaining and trying to get other people to do your work for you!" Mark was hurt but his break had given him renewed strength.

"That's not fair Emma, but I am going to do the milking now and I *will* be seeing Charlie when I finish.

Mark tried several times after milking to see Charlie. Every time he tried to see the boy, Emma blocked him, physically standing between him and his son. Rather than cause a scene in front of Charlie, Mark waited patiently. When Charlie was having his supper the lorry arrived for its collection and Mark thought he would at last be able to grab a few minutes with Charlie.

But Emma picked Charlie up and grabbing a large piece of cheese rushed off with Charlie to load the lorry. Mark could not believe it. The child was put precariously on the side of the drive while the loading took place. It seemed that

Emma was determined to keep him from his son despite any detriment to the child.

As the lorry rolled off down the drive Emma carried Charlie in and in a nonchalant tone threw over her shoulder.

"Oh by the way, my bedroom is now out of out of bounds to you, I have taken all the stuff you had in and put it in your room, so you don't need to go in there again." Mark thought sadly that what had once been their bedroom' was now 'her bedroom'. It was hardly a surprise, he supposed.

"Oh and that goes for Charlie's room as well."

Charlie's bedroom had been finished and decorated shortly after Charlie was born. It was a light shade of blue with Thomas the Tank Engine transfers all over the walls. Because of Emma's over—possessive attitude Charlie had never slept in his cot in his bedroom.

The second room, that Emma had called 'Mark's bedroom' was full of furniture and storage boxes. Mark had made a space for a mattress on the floor and, it seemed, that was where he was going to remain.

The next morning after milking Mark steeled himself to go up to the house. He felt very vulnerable, as though one by one the rugs were being pulled out from under his feet. He felt as though he was being manoeuvred closer to the front door every day. If it was possible, over the next few days, Emma's bullying got nastier. Mark refused to put the milk in the formers for freezing in bulk blocks, despite her repeated and ever more forceful demands.

"Emma I told you I was not going to work in the processing side."

She made a sound of pure frustration.

"Look Mark I can't take much more of your attitude, I have had it with you. I think that the best thing we can do is split the house, I can't bear the sight of you!"

Mark gritted his teeth. He would not be drawn.

"That's fine Emma but I will need that secondary credit card you said you would arrange, and I need to buy a mobile phone."

"Yes yes, Mark it's all I, I, I with you isn't it? Look I will deduct housekeeping from your wages."

As it turned out Mark never did receive money from her for work he did in the business.

For the first few days after his return, Mark faced a constant barrage of how nasty and unpleasant he was, and how everyone thought he was nasty and "mental".

Mark could feel tension building in him again. The cold fist had hold of his guts and he felt permanently sick. Returning from the fields, Mark thought how he not seen Charlie since he got back for more than a couple of moments, snatched whilst Emma and the staff were pasteurising and bottling the milk. Mark went into the processing room to finally get to pick up and hold his son. Emma tried to physically block

Mark but he pushed her gently but forcefully to one side and picked Charlie up to cuddle him.

Emma stormed out, leaving the staff to manage.

As she stormed back to the cottage the staff cheered. Mark looked around at them incredulously.

"'Bout time you stood your ground mate!" Dot said, smiling at me.

"I know but I feel I'm in a difficult position with Charlie. Even if Emma doesn't care what she does in front of Charlie I don't want to be responsible for any upset to him.

"You're a good man Mark!" Dot nodded sadly.

"You're right though, the missus don't care about the young un as long as she gets what her wants."

A few days later Emma left to make yoghurt deliveries, taking Charlie with her. Mark could not believe that she would drag the child around with her, leaving him for frequent periods alone in the car while she unloaded the van. Was it really preferable to drag their son around belted into his car seat rather than risk him spending a few moments with his father?

Mark spent an anxious day on the farm and when Emma had not returned at the time she was expected he felt a sick feeling in his stomach. What if there had been an accident? Mark phoned Dot at home to find out if they had heard from Emma. Dot told him Emma had a mobile 'phone and that the number was posted on the board in yoghurt room. Mark rang the number but it went to voicemail.

Mark's heart was racing now. He rang a mechanic friend to see if he had been called out to a breakdown. No, he had heard nothing. Mark rang the owner of the last shop on the route at his house. He told Mark that Emma had only left the shop at 7.45pm. Mark relaxed. If that was the case she was not due back yet. Mark ran a bath and sank into it exhausted. He was still in the bath when Emma and Charlie returned.

Jumping out and putting on his dressing gown Mark met them on the landing as Emma carried a sleeping Charlie to bed. She kicked the door to her bedroom shut in his face, and Mark got dressed. He felt silly putting his clothes on again, after all he would be going to bed soon but somehow he felt vulnerable in his dressing gown.

When Emma emerged from the bedroom she laid into him.

"How dare you ring up all and sundry to check up on me? Oh yes, don't worry they all let me know, I think they feel quite sorry for me, being married to such an idiot! My God anyone would think I was a naughty child!"

Mark was stunned by the ferocity of the attack.

"I was worried about you, you were so late . . ."

"Did it ever occur to you that it would take me longer with Charlie? Changing, feeding etc? No of course it didn't, you're such a control freak, and you have to have everything your own way, don't you?"

Mark literally felt that the wind had been knocked out of him. The irony of what she was saying, *he* was a control freak? My God he thought, she is clearly losing her marbles.

"Well why did you take him? You never have before, and Kerry is here, she could have looked after him, instead of having him stuck in the van all day in that car seat. I can't see the point!"

"The point is that I got him away from here and from you. I don't need you interfering with him, confusing him, in fact I wish you would just stay out of both our way!" Emma shrieked and Mark thought he heard Charlie whimper in the bedroom.

Mark could see that Emma was close to losing it now, and decided, for Charlie's sake that he should go to bed.

On Saturday Mark had decided to go fishing to try and relax. After breakfast in the kitchen he was cleaning the crumbs around the bread bin and moved it to clean and shake it out the back door. There, behind the bread bin, was a letter from the bank, dated almost a month previously stating that his signatory and mandate had been duly removed as requested by Mrs Richards. In future the bank would honour no cheques that were signed by Mark Richards.

Mark stood staring at the letter. The enormity of it sinking in. The bank was the one that Emma had used before they were married that she had insisted they move their accounts to when she saw Mark getting friendly with John Abbott.

Mark was thunderstruck at such duplicity, and then keeping it secret for a month. Mark was appalled that the bank could do such a thing without consulting him first. Later when his solicitor challenged the bank they responded that they were prepared to defend their legal actions in court if necessary. But Mark was never to find anyone who was aware that this could happen, that a joint account signatory could be removed by one joint account holders without a word to the other.

A cold sick feeling now followed Mark most of the time, every day now. The penny had finally dropped. Emma was going to fight, no holds barred, to get what she wanted. But the final realisation of what he was up against became clear when he was away on holiday. Mark had come back from his mother's home in Bath to have a hypnotherapy session with Moira. After the session and feeling ridiculous for feeling so nervous, Mark called in at the farm hoping to see Charlie. There was no one in, so Mark went for a walk around the fields to see the animals. When he got back he found Emma and Charlie with Jane Taylor. Mark had a frosty reception from Emma and Jane. Jane was married to one of Emma's cousins, and they hosted a family get together every year on August Bank Holiday. Mark and Emma had been to several. Of all his in-laws Jane was the only person who had gone out of her way to welcome Mark to the family. She used to joke that she used to be an outsider once too. She always struck Mark as a balanced, sensible lady. Charlie was teething and Jane was occupied soothing him when Mark arrived.

Without so much as a hello Emma demanded that Mark help her deliver a beef carcass to the butcher. When they returned from a torturous, silent journey during which Mark could feel the resentment and hostility coming in waves from Emma, Mark followed her into the living room.

"I want to talk about this whole situation Emma." Mark said.

"Right, well I am going to record whatever you say!" Emma said waving a small Dictaphone triumphantly.

"I need a cheque, Emma so I can engage a solicitor to respond to your divorce proceedings."

"Well I'd be pretty crazy to give you what you need to fight me now, wouldn't I?" she snorted.

"Ok then I need the company cheque book, I have to have access to money from somewhere!" Mark said trying to hold his temper in check. Out of the corner of his eye he saw the spare chequebook under a pile of papers on a corner table.

Emma followed his eyes and realised what he had seen. But Mark was too quick for her and crossed the room snatching up the spare cheque book holding it above his head so that she could not grab it from him.

"You really are the most immature, irresponsible and childish man I ever had the misfortune to meet!" Emma shouted in her frustration. As he sat down the cheque book safely in the back pocket of his jeans, Emma launched herself at him.

He caught her fists before they could make contact with him and thought how sad it was that this was the closest he had got to his wife in months.

"Right I'm calling the police!" Emma's voice was shaking with fury

"Go ahead, you know what they are going to say!" Mark said.

Mark could see that Emma was out of control. His thoughts immediately went to his son. He would be leaving the farm shortly but Charlie would not. He would have to do something to calm Emma down, if only for Charlie's sake.

"Ok look I'll just take the one cheque I need for the solicitor and some cash, I need about £200."

Emma went to the cash box, took out the money and threw it at Mark. But the mad look in her eyes had gone and he felt able to leave his son and the farm.

Mark was housesitting for his sister whilst she went on holiday to France. With time on his hands he rang Emma to say that he wanted to see Charlie that week, and left it to her to say when it would be convenient.

The curt reply cut Mark to the quick.

"It won't be convenient for you to see Charlie anytime in the week nor the following weekend, we're going away."

Mark was due back on the farm the following week so basically the message was that he would not be able to spend any of his holiday time with his son. Mark was so taken aback by Emma's attitude that he phoned Jane Taylor.

Jane had been to stay for days at a time after Charlie was born to help Emma. Rather in the role that her mother would normally have done, had they been speaking at the time. During those visits Emma had asked Jane to mediate and give some marriage guidance for them so as a result she knew quite a lot of their problems.

Mark spoke to her for twenty minutes but it was as if a curtain had come down between them. Mark was being stonewalled. Mark felt a deep depression settle over him.

Back at work, Mark was surprised by a visit from Greg, the stockman. He appeared whilst Mark was milking to ask if there was any work available.

As Mark watched the man favour him with his customary searching look he felt suspicious.

"I'm surprised to see you Greg. Last I heard you would rather not see me for fear that you might 'smash my face in?' Was that the expression? That and the fact that you have not replied to any of my messages . . ."

Greg fixed Mark with a questioning look.

"I don't know what you are talking about man, I've never had a problem, the missus told me that you can be a bit paranoid at times." He said with his customary bluntness.

Mark felt anger building and tried his best to quash it. He needed a milker and Greg, whatever else he was, was a good stockman.

"Well I'm looking for a relief milker for two days a week. You will have to square it with Emma, Greg. She now controls the company money and she will pay you."

Greg raised his eyebrows and looked at Mark, giving him one of his more appraising looks, and nodded.

"Right." And he was gone.

Mark was very busy on the farm. While he had been away the farm had become disorganised. The grazing routine had collapsed, and the sheep and cattle had been neglected, to such an extent that the sheep were on a neighbouring farm and the Short Horn bull had gone walkabout. Mark eventually found him at the end of the valley about 3km away. A cow was missing and he eventually found her in a neighbour's wood with a newborn calf. The pigs all needed to be moved on to fresh ground. It took Mark almost a fortnight to get things back on track. Meanwhile other tasks were piling up. So Mark gave Greg extra jobs such as cleaning out the dung from the barns, and preparing the animal housing for winter. Just as Mark was getting used to the extra support on the farm Greg went off sick claiming that the stress had brought on his M.E This was the first that Mark had heard that Greg had M.E. Mark had made an appointment to see his solicitor; one that his mother had recommended in Bath. Greg insisted he would be OK to cover. But then in the middle of milking, Greg rushed off to the doctor in great pain. Mark finished off and did the other stock. Greg re-appeared later saying he had had an injection of painkiller, and insisted Mark go.

Full of misgivings, Mark gave him his mobile number and said he could return anytime. When Mark returned on Friday evening he rang to say he needed the weekend off to recuperate. Mark had not expected him to work then, but as he came in that evening he found Emma waiting for him, arms crossed, a triumphant look on her face.

"Well looks like you've done it again, Greg has gone, he says he can't work with you anymore!"

Mark was stunned, he had no idea what the problem was. On Saturday morning Greg reappeared and said that if he was asked nicely he would cover days off.

Mark felt anger well up inside him, this was obviously an attempt to play with his head. Greg had taken him in enough, and, Mark suspected, was very much under the thrall of Emma.

"Don't worry Greg" he said shortly, "I'll make other arrangements."

As the end of the summer approached and while Mark was preparing the farm for winter, Emma took Charlie to stay with Jane.

As he sat in the house on his own that evening, Mark fought between missing Charlie's little noises around the place, and the relief at not having Emma's volatility to deal with. As he made his way upstairs past Charlie's room, Mark stopped.

He set his jaw. He was going to do it, he was going to move into Charlie's room.

Charlie was still sleeping in a cot in Emma's room and it was obvious that he would not be moving into the room that Mark had decorated with so much care and anticipation all those months ago. There was no reason that Mark should remain in the cramped and stuffy spare room amongst all the boxes and storage bags. Mark was already in bed when Emma returned in the late evening of the bank holiday Monday. She went ballistic when she discovered what Mark had done.

"What the hell do you think you are doing?" she shrieked dumping a wailing Charlie in his cot in her bedroom.

"What does it look like?" Mark said feeling vulnerable in the bed he had bought and erected in the place where the cot had once stood.

"My God, some father you are, stealing your child's room from under him!" she said.

"Emma, he never sleeps in here, tell me that he is going to and I will be out of here like a shot, you know that!"

"Oh yes, you'd like that wouldn't you, then you'd wait until I was asleep and come in waking him up and disturbing him, I'm not that stupid Mark!"

Emma looked around the room and said.

"Well you're not having the chest of drawers,!" Mark shrugged.

"Fine, take what you want, I am tired of sleeping on the floor Emma, and since Charlie is not using the room, I am!"

Emma stormed off taking Charlie into the bathroom to bath him. As Mark lay his eyes squeezed shut and his teeth clenched, Charlie was subjected to a torrent of abuse and a catalogue of criticism of Mark: how nasty Daddy was, a very spiteful man, a liar, a horrible man, and a dangerous man.

Mark wanted to cover his ears, but he felt in some way that he had to listen, had to go through the torment with his son, who was grizzling quietly. The fear he felt obvious.

It was not till several years later that Mark learnt just how damaging it was to tell very young children repeatedly untrue and unpleasant things. These would become imprinted in Charlie's subconscious memory. Even though he could not understand the words, those almost daily mantras delivered with such venom and hate would become deeply ingrained so that later it became easy to alienate Charlie from his father.

Mark relaxed his shoulders as he heard Emma singing a lullaby to Charlie. The boy would be asleep in no time now. He was about to turn over and try to sleep himself when Emma threw the door of his room open.

"Well Mark it seems that you are determined to make life as unpleasant for me and your son as you can!"

Mark sighed wearily

"No Emma, I just think that I should be able to sleep in comfort in my own house."

Emma went into the storage bedroom that Mark had vacated and started to throw large empty boxes into the doorway of his bedroom.

"Emma! What the bloody hell do you think you're doing? For Christ's sake, just go to bed!" Mark shouted

Emma smiled a thin-lipped smile that owed nothing to humour and continued to throw boxes into his bedroom. Mark jumped out of bed and shouted at Emma again. There were boxes all over the landing and in both bedroom doorways. Charlie started screaming behind the barricade in Emma's bedroom doorway. Mark pulled the boxes aside and strode into the room snatching his son up in his arms to sooth him.

Emma came bounding out of the second bedroom.

"Give him to me Mark!" she screamed "GIVE HIM TO ME!"

"Emma, for God's sake calm down, can't you see what you're doing to Charlie?"

"SHUTUP MARK, GIVE HIM TO ME!" Emma screamed launching herself at him, hitting and slapping him on his shoulders. Charlie was crying in earnest now clinging terrified to Marks pyjama top.

Mark realised that Emma was hysterical and was not going to stop until he handed Charlie over. He handed Charlie to her. She flew back into her room slamming the door behind her. As his son's wails subsided Mark cleared the boxes that had been thrown into his room. Emma reappeared carrying Charlie and went downstairs. Mark could hear her speaking in a voice intentionally loud enough for him to hear. She was speaking to the police.

They arrived quite quickly in two cars, Mark stayed in bed. He could hear lots of laughing downstairs as Emma spoke to the officers.

Eventually Mark got up and halfway downstairs was met by a policeman.

"How long are you planning to stay in our house, officer, only I am very tired and it is very late?"

There were four policemen. PC Ball, a young officer who still had a face dotted with acne listened to Mark's side of the story and went with him while he showed him the scene.

The reason that the police had come mob handed Mark discovered, was that Emma had told them that he had two shotguns, although both were legally held. The police impounded the guns together with Emma's air gun. PC Ball said he would have had Mark locked up too if Emma had not pleaded with them to leave him to milk the goats.

Mark was shocked to the core. He knew that Emma was never in fear of him using the guns, but she had raised her game to another level, she really did not care how much she lied, or hurt him, obviously. That was to be the first of many visits by the Police; and as Mark's life spiralled out of control it was to be the first of many dark days.

Chapter 13

The Law

As the end of August approached, Dot had a bad fall on the farm and was going to be off for some time. Without consulting Mark, Emma asked Greg to help out in the processing room. Greg then announced that he would like to milk and feed the animals for the following two days. When he came up for his pay on Saturday Mark was clipped in his interaction with the surly stockman. As Emma stood by Mark said.

"Do you think you'll want any work next week?"

"Well whether he does or not, I can't afford to pay Greg anything next week!" with that Emma turned tail and went back to the cottage.

Secretly quite pleased that Emma had knocked Greg back, Mark suppressed a smile and shrugged.

"Sorry, looks like it's a no-go, unless of course you want to work for nothing?"

Greg looked at Mark with undisguised disdain and left.

The following Saturday Greg came to see Mark when he was milking to say that he needed to earn a wage. To Mark's surprise he said,

"Truth is, I would rather work for you than anyone else 'round here but I can't live with the uncertainty." For once the man did not look so cock sure and smug and Mark thought to himself, you and I both!

"OK, I'll have it out with Emma, Greg but no promises." Greg nodded muttered 'thanks' and left.

In the kitchen that evening while she was preparing Charlie's dinner, Mark put Greg's concerns to Emma.

"The man wants to work for us but he says that he can't live with not knowing from one week to the next what is going on or how much work he has to do. I can see his point." Mark said.

Emma ignored him.

"Right Emma, in that case you leave me no option. I want a proper agreement by the end of work tomorrow, in writing, or else!"

"Or else what?" Emma said.

"Well, if I do not have an agreement in writing by tomorrow I will not work on the farm anymore, especially as I am not getting paid either!"

The next morning, waking with his stomach in knots, knowing that today was going to be make or break, Mark came downstairs to hear Emma on the phone. It was very early, but she was already speaking to Greg. The warmth of her tone and the note of triumph in her voice told Mark all he needed to know. He had been set up! He had played right into her hands.

Emma was asking Greg to come in and look after the farm full time.

As a cold wave of fear engulfed him Mark realised he had been too stupid to see the trap Emma had set in collusion with Greg. He began to shake uncontrollably. He was out of a job and would soon, no doubt, be out of a home and have even less chance to see Charlie.

Trying to muster a semblance of strength Mark told Emma that as the legal aid board would require up to date accounts to support her request for legal aid he would get the accounts up to date. Mark asked her to clear one of the desks.

"Oh Mark just shut up! I will not clear it, stop trying to boss me about. I'm not clearing that or anything else for you, you are getting on my nerves so much!"

"Fine I'll do it myself then!" Mark said.

As he crossed the room Emma flew across the room and stood between him and the desk.

Mark changed direction and tried to go around her, she jumped over to cause an obstruction. Eventually Mark ran out of patience and pushed her aside.

Emma ran out of the study to the lounge and snatched up the phone.

"Police please!" Mark heard her say, her voice shaking.

They arrived within the hour and a sergeant Towning came in to speak to Mark.

Far from the hostile reception he had expected, the sergeant was very helpful and gave Mark some advice.

Speaking softly with the study door shut, the sergeant, a man who was about the same age as Mark said,

"Look, I've been there, done that, got the T-shirt. Sorry to say Mark, I don't think you can win this, it is stacked against you. Maybe if you do the books out of Emma's way, go somewhere out of the house, like the library?"

Mark nodded. He felt close to tears, he had been prepared to put up a fight, he had not been prepared for the understanding that the police sergeant was showing him.

"Thing is Mark" the sergeant continued "Incidents like this will be used by Emma to fight your access to your son" There was a tap on the door and a woman police constable came in.

" Mrs. Richards says that she feels very nervous with her husband here." The Sergeant looked at Mark, his eyebrows raised.

"Thanks constable." He said and she went out of the study and closed the door.

"Ok Mark I'm going to level with you, it's probably going to be best if you leave for a few days. " the sergeant said.

Mark nodded still unable to trust himself to speak. He called Laurie, his voice breaking.

"Of course, Mark, come straight here. Stay as long as you need to!"

So Mark packed his stuff feeling like some kind of monster while the police waited for him to leave. He felt like a criminal as he got into his car, the Police sergeant and two constables standing on the doorstep. As he drove off he looked in the rear view mirror. Emma was standing at the window of the cottage. She was smiling.

Mark returned home a few days later ready for their first court hearing. As he got ready he realised that both Emma and Charlie were still in their pyjamas. He wondered briefly why Emma was not getting herself and Charlie ready and had a moment of foreboding. But Mark had arranged to meet his barrister Ms. Davies, a pleasant motherly looking lady from the local chambers before the hearing and he had to go.

223

The case was to be heard before District Judge Williams. Far from the motherly style of his barrister the judge reminded Mark very much of Betty Boothroyd, the former Speaker of the House of Commons. She was a very forceful, no nonsense type of lady.

After some time, the judge realised that Emma was not going to appear. Mark wanted to say something, and put his hand up feeling every inch the naughty schoolboy to ask if he could speak.

"No Mr Richards, you will only speak when you are spoken to", was the sharp reply. Even Mark's barrister was finding it hard to get a word in.

Mark watched in frustrated silence as the judge flicked through the documents. Suddenly her demeanour changed visibly.

"I see that the police have been involved." She said. Her expression, not the warmest at the best of times, changed; it was as though the shutters had come down in front of Mark's eyes.

As he sat deflated in his solicitors office after the court hearing, Andres Sims, the young solicitor who Mark had instantly liked, agreed with Mark that Emma's petition for divorce seemed to be moving at a deliberately slow pace. It was explained that in order to see Charlie, Mark had to apply for a contact order.

"That's just mad, I'm still living in the same house, how is that supposed to work?" Mark said

Andres smiled apologetically and cleared his throat.

"Also Mark, you will not be able to apply for an order until the divorce action is formally started."

"What? But the way things are going that could be this year, next year, sometime never!" Mark said in dismay.

"Yes, it's true, Emma could easily delay things. I would advise you to petition for divorce yourself Mark."

"Right then that is what I will do!"

"I should also add" Andres said "that it will not be possible to add new parts to the petition later; so if you might at some point in the future feel it necessary to ask the court for Charlie to come and live with you, then really you will have to have it on the documents from the beginning."

Mark sat thinking. Although he knew her behaviour at the moment was far from satisfactory he clung to the hope that at some stage Emma would calm down and act reasonably for Charlie's benefit. He did not really think Charlie would be better off with him. Like most people he thought a young child would be better off with their mother unless there was a danger of serious abuse. But one thing Mark was sure of was that he wanted considerable contact. Mark was to look back on that day in the solicitor's office often in the months to come. If he had ever imagined that Emma would go on to abuse Charlie the way she did, his reaction to the custody issue might have been very different.

His head spinning Mark left the solicitors office and spent the next few days with his family asking for advice. His father was so angry at the way that his son was being treated that he could barely trust himself to speak. Jenny Richards wept quietly. It was obvious that there was going to be no easy fix to this. She ached to hold her grandson. Laurie tried to stay strong for Mark but was never far from tears as she looked at her brother, reduced to skin and bone from the stress he was under. Mark eventually set off for the farm on Sunday afternoon.

As he drove home from his sister's in Devon, Greg rang to tell him he had had enough and could not work for him anymore.

"Greg, we've been through this, it's not my problem. Emma is the one you need to speak to!" Greg hung up.

Mark arrived home to a dark house. Wearily, he wrote out a note for Emma about Greg's decision and went to bed.

By the time that he woke the next morning Emma was already up and form the moment she set eyes on Mark was extremely unpleasant and abusive.

"Are you going to do the milking then?" she asked hands on hips, her eyes flashing hate.

"No, but I will feed the stock until you can make other arrangements, look Emma you can't just throw me out and take Greg on and then expect me to pick up the slack when you two fall out! I don't want the animals to suffer so I will feed them. But you can't expect to make it clear I have no place on the farm and then expect me to pitch in. I am not going back to work unless the basic terms for working that I laid out in that earlier ultimatum, that you ignored, are agreed and documented! Let me know if you need a copy!" And with that Mark left the cottage to feed the animals, feeling a small ember of triumph.

Now that Mark was in the house most of the time, Emma barricaded Charlie in the master bedroom and took him to the processing room all day.

All offers from Mark to look after Charlie were rebuffed.

One day Emma said

"I have to defend a summons for non-payment of a bill in Reading. I'm going to be gone most of the day."

"I see", Mark said, resisting the urge to ask for the details." Well I can look after Charlie, take him to the nursery and pick him up later." Emma looked at him as though he had lost his mind.

"Leave Charlie with you? I don't think so, I don't trust you and in my opinion you are dangerous! And I don't want you interfering with any farm work either, in fact keep away from us and the farm!" Mark was shocked to his core. Surely Emma did not really believe what she was saying?

An agency milker turned up at 7.30pm to milk the goats. He did not leave till midnight. Mark felt miserable and wanted with every fibre of his being to pitch in and help with the animals he had so diligently cared for over the years. He was angry at Emma for destroying his long reputation for always paying his bills on time, making it a point to always treat other small companies as he himself would like to be treated.

In the middle of the week, Mark went to the library to do some paperwork only to discover that it was closed in the afternoon. As he wandered through the town, which was ghost like on early closing day, he bumped into John Abbott coming out of the bank.

"Mark, how are you?" Mark felt relief flood over him. He had dreaded bumping into his old friend; afraid of what the banker would think of the summary closing of their accounts with the bank. He had not had the courage to come and tell him that it had been all Emma's doing. He did not want to open himself up to the kind of ridicule that other men would no doubt heap on a man who could not control his own wife!

But John had put his arm around his shoulders and was walking him towards the pub.

"Time for a quick one?" John said.

Mark nodded. Any kindness these days was likely to bring him to tears and he could not trust his voice.

"So how have you been mate?" John said, loosening his tie and putting it in his pocket as they sat down in the garden of the pub in the warm autumn sunshine.

Mark shrugged. Tears were choking him now. John Abbott seemed to realise this and left the table saying

"Still drinking cider?"

Mark nodded gratefully and composed himself while John fetched their drinks.

When he got back to the table, Mark poured his heart out to John. The banker sat, his drink untouched before him as he heard what Mark had to say. If he did not know Mark so well he would have thought he was making it up; but he clearly wasn't. John could barely believe what he was hearing. He had no idea what to say. But just being able to talk to someone who was not legally representing him or attacking him proved a huge boost to Mark. They agreed to meet again for a drink.

On his return Mark found Greg putting up an electric fence and feeding the pigs.

"Greg, surprised to see you here, I thought you were never setting foot on the farm again?" Mark asked him.

"I don't have much choice do I?" Greg's eyes flashed dangerously and Mark was immediately aware of his aggressive reputation and the fact that he was prone to lose his temper quickly.

"The way you treat these poor bloody animals is a disgrace!" he shouted at Mark.

"Look Greg you are hardly the last word in reliability yourself. How am I supposed to keep up with your love hate relationship with the farm?"

"You fucking wanker!" Greg shouted. "You complete arsehole! I am just about ready to flatten you!"

"You know what Greg? Feel free!" Mark squared up to the man.

"You're not fucking worth it!" Greg shouted and turning on his heel stormed off "You are pitiful, a nothing, a has been, I work for Emma now!" As Greg strode off Mark realised he was shaking. He remembered that when Greg had first worked for him on the farm he had given him a two-week trial period. Greg was an experienced stockman and not afraid of hard work. In his third week he was chatting to Mark and Mark remembered him saying that he done time in prison for GBH. Mark had asked him for details but he had been a bit vague.

Mark did not know what to make of the comment and thought it might have been just the stockman's attempt to make himself out to be a hard man. Greg had said that it was because he used to drink excessively. But now he never touched a drop of the hard stuff.

Mark had thanked the stockman for his candour and added that he believed people should be given another chance. When Mark had told Emma, she demanded that he got rid of him straight away.

Mark had partially comforted Emma by saying that any signs of violence or drinking and Greg would be out on his ear. Over the next few months Greg seemed to be fairly depressed. Mark listened to hours of his moaning about how his wife had left him, taking his son. It transpired that his wife had met another man. She was apparently asking Greg to declare he had no objection to them adopting his son. Mark remembered being startled by Greg's attitude. Greg said he did not care, and if his little boy wanted to find him later in his life, that was up to the boy. Greg would be pleased to go back to being a bachelor with no responsibilities. He told Mark that his particular interest was married women. Mark had not thought much of it at the time. Greg thought he was God's gift to women. He certainly had a silver tongue.

It amused Mark now in this later stage of his separation from Emma to see Greg simmer with the expectation that when Mark left he would move in. In their working relationship Mark and Greg had got on well at first but Mark soon realised that Greg hated any authority. If Mark wanted him to do something it involved quite a rigmarole of making him believe it was his idea. If Mark told him to do something straight, he would never quite do it properly or would leave it unfinished. The stockman kept coming up with little stories, especially about how people feared his reputation for violence. He often boasted of his criminal past, even describing some of the details of counterfeiting scams with mates in the Reading underworld. Occasionally he would say that if he did not turn up some day it would be because he had to run as he was still hunted by some vague 'Asian gang' from Reading. Mark did not relay this to Emma as he no longer cared whether it was true or not.

After a year he told Mark how his business with his father, as a cattle dealer, had gone bankrupt during the BSE crisis. He then claimed he had ME. A lot of the time he worked for him Mark had thought he had been supportive and had given advice if he was asked for it.

Things between Emma and Mark worsened and things were getting nasty with Emma frequently washing their dirty linen in public or at least in front of whatever staff were present. After one particularly vicious attack on Mark obstructing him from seeing Charlie, Greg said

"Don't be a mug man, the woman's as mad as a box of frogs, walk away and leave them."

"Oh yes? Well I can tell you Greg I have no intention whatsoever of walking away and abandoning my son."

Greg looked Mark up and down, his contempt obvious. Over the next few days Mark noticed a change in his attitude. Mark felt a pang of regret as he wondered if Greg assumed he had been trying to make him feel guilty for abandoning his own child. Mark was to be extremely hurt by all the lies and scheming Greg entered into with Emma but as yet he had not realised the extent of their duplicity.

Since his father had stopped working on the farm Charlie had been barricaded in Emma's bedroom in the mornings if he was not at nursery, until Emma went over to the dairy taking Charlie with her. If Mark was downstairs sometimes Emma would move the barricade to the top of the stairs, to allow Charlie the run of all the upper floor of the cottage.

Mark had just collected the post from the doormat when he heard Charlie crying. Mark waited for Emma to come through from the kitchen. She did not. Mark sprinted up stairs to Charlie who was hanging over the barricade, to comfort him.

Emma was in fact in the bathroom and when she realised what Mark was doing she shouted.

"Mark leave the child alone, for God's sake, don't interfere! You know nothing about toddlers. I'm warning you Mark!" Her voice was so menacing that Mark thought Emma was about to get violent. He put Charlie down and Emma appeared scooping Charlie up none too gently repeating like some kind of hateful mantra that Daddy was a nasty, sick, dangerous and spiteful man.

As Mark struggled to control his temper and hurt he listened as Emma continued to rant at their son, even returning to the staircase several times to shout the abuse up at him. Mark scrabbled for a small dictaphone he had bought and took it to the top of the stairs waving it at Emma indicating that he was taping her diatribe. This was the only effective way Mark found to lessen her hurtful and unjustified rants. And although he never recorded anything, he often waved the little machine at her. As long day followed long day and Mark found his enforced inactivity almost unbearable, he did his best to keep out of Emma's way and her demand that he not go into her bedroom.

However if Mark ever did go out he would often return to find that his bedroom had been rifled through. Emma would claim that it was Charlie, but on occasions Mark would find things like his reading glasses that had gone missing, in places that Charlie, at his age, simply could not open or access.

On a bright autumn morning when the next contact hearing came up, two weeks after the adjourned first hearing, Mark dressed carefully, stopping short of a suit but taking Andres's advice dressed smartly, a jumper over a crisp shirt. At the court a detailed schedule of contact was drawn up, with provision for Mark to have contact for an hour or more every day. Mark glanced at Emma across the courtroom. She was sitting apparently impassively staring ahead of her. She gave no indication of how she felt about the ruling.

Mark was soon to find out how Emma felt about his contact order. The next day Emma was very abusive and obnoxious ranting at him in front of Charlie and then continuing to heap abuse on him as she warned the toddler about his father, making the most vile accusations about him, which, whilst Mark knew the child would not understand the words, he would certainly understand his mother's vicious tone. Emma denied Mark his court ordered contact for several days.

Although they lived together in the same house Mark and Emma lived separately. Mark usually waited to use the kitchen until after Emma had finished. Emma was always ordering him to clean up after her and do her shopping and other chores.

For the most part Mark ignored her. He would be told when he could use the washing machine or cook. The constant pettiness was designed to wind Mark up and although some days it was as much as Mark could do to stay in the house, his solicitor advised him early on not to become violent, whatever the provocation, as that would completely destroy any court action.

It soon became obvious that Emma's objective was to get Mark so wound up that he lashed out. She tried very hard every day with her snide remarks and unreasonable ramblings to their son. Mark gritted his teeth. The only chance he had to be close to Charlie was if he stayed in the house and he knew that if he lost control there would be no question of that. It was in Mark's nature, when he got angry, to walk away and he had to continue to hold on with all his strength to this trait.

Emma's spiteful behaviour and need to control knew no bounds. In an effort to fill his time and to offer him a much-needed distraction, Mark had enrolled for evening classes to learn about computers. Emma refused to give him the password for the computer in the office so that he could practise on it. He had also signed up for courses with Business Link. Mark knew that if she could she would disrupt these with her strategic undermining of anything that he wanted to do. Similarly if she knew he had an appointment with Moira the hypnotherapist she would suddenly dump Charlie on Mark for half an hour.

This put Mark in a terrible position. Andres, his solicitor had said that he must not refuse to look after Charlie, however inconvenient, as this would give Emma the chance to argue that Mark was not interested in having Charlie. Mark realised that he must never write down appointments and always enjoyed the time that he had Charlie.

As day followed gruelling day Mark did find it very difficult to endure the constant verbal abuse and petty actions, simply because there was no effective way of combating them or getting them stopped, short of moving out. He could not afford to move out as Emma never gave him any money from the business.

Mark spent a lot of time on the phone to his sister and borrowed money from Laurie. She was a Godsend and a rock of support, especially in the early years. Laurie was a professional counsellor, so she was able to give Mark lots of good advice as well.

"Mark you've got to see the doctor, you can't go on not sleeping and losing weight like this. I can see why you want to stay in the house but I really think it is the worse thing for you." Laurie said.

"Laurie, I know that but if I leave there is no chance at all that I will be able to see Charlie."

"Well you might be able to, and the court order for one hour a day would still stand, maybe things would be easier if you two were not in the same house and . . ."

Laurie drew her breath in and Mark thought she was about to say something. She hesitated and then said. "Ok look, keep strong and I'll see you soon. Lots of love."

Had Laurie been going to suggest that he give up trying to see Charlie? Give in to Emma? Mark felt she might have been, but whatever else he had doubts about seeing and being a father to his son was not one of them. Throughout all the abuse and in the face of the insults and hurtful remarks that rained down on him on a daily basis there was one thing that Mark never had any doubt about. He was going to do everything in his power to make sure that his son grew up knowing him.

Chapter 14

Battles

Mark's misery continued. Although they lived under the same roof, Charlie was kept away from him, except when there was some petty spiteful motive to disrupt something he had planned to do. One evening Mark took a call from his mother.

"Hi mum"

"Hello son, how are you?"

"Oh not bad" Mark looked into the kitchen; there was no sign of Emma.

"Mark, I was wondering if you could do me a favour. I know it's a lot to ask, I know you are up to your eyes with . . . well one thing and another, but I have to go to the hospital tomorrow for a cataract op."

"Mum you didn't say!"

"It's no big deal these days Mark, a quick in and out job, but I won't be able to drive afterwards."

"Of course Mum what time do you need me there?"

"About 10?"

"What time is the op?"

"Midday, they ask you to be there an hour and a half ahead of time."

"Great, then I'll be there at 10."

In the kitchen Emma was standing still in the pantry. Mark had not seen her in there. She smiled to herself.

Later that day as Mark was washing the car in front of the house she came out.

"Good news! I've got to go to Reading tomorrow, so you can have Charlie all day!" Mark drew his breath in. Did she know? No, he had looked into the kitchen and she wasn't there when he had spoken to his mother.

"That OK?" Emma asked brightly, her forced smile brittle.

Mark set his jaw.

"Of course!" he smiled back. He saw her smile waver, a slight frown crease her brow. She had known, he could swear it!

Right I'll be off about 11 is that OK?" The triumphal look was back.

"Fine." Mark said. The frown deepened. Emma turned on her heel.

Game to me! Mark smiled to himself.

The contact periods ordered by the court were regularly broken and abused. Mark had started with the certainty that if the court had ruled it then Emma had to abide with what they said, but now he found it increasingly frustrating that the judges simply refused to deal with the problem practically. Emma, whatever else she was, was an intelligent and gutsy person who had realised early on that there was a strong prejudice in her favour. Unsurprisingly she went on to wreck contact order after contact order, without fearing the consequences.

The next day, Emma showed no sign of dressing for what Mark presumed was another court hearing. From what he could see Emma was treating people very badly completely eschewing Mark's determination to always be fair in business, in favour of a haphazard payment lottery as far as their suppliers were concerned.

As ten 'o'clock approached he saw Emma looking at him. He was sitting in the lounge watching the BBC 24 hour news programme. Emma glanced at her watch again. He must have had a change of plan.

"What time do you leave for Reading?" Mark asked stretching and settling himself down in the chair putting his feet up on a footstool that was an old camel saddle. This brinkmanship was killing him but he was not going to show Emma that.

Emma studied him for a moment.

"I'm not now, so you're not having Charlie."

Mark stood up.

"That's a shame, a real shame but I'll see you both when I get back."

"Where are you going?"

"To take my mother to hospital, see you later!" And with that Mark was out of the door laughing, despite himself at the look on Emma's face. And that, he thought, to himself is game set and match!

Now that Charlie was a toddler there were times when the child came looking for Mark outside the contact times. If Emma's guard was down, usually at weekends when Charlie was not taken to work, if the child did find his way to his father, when Emma discovered them, Charlie was forcibly removed, often traumatically. There were occasions when Charlie came downstairs, when Emma was in the bath or otherwise occupied. Emma would drag Charlie like a rag doll back upstairs by one arm, yelling and screaming abuse at Mark. Many times Charlie was yanked off his feet, crying his eyes out. These scenes nearly killed Mark. His child's outstretched arms in his direction as he was carted off were almost more than he could bear, but he said nothing. He firmly believed that he needed to be in the house to protect Charlie. It could have been argued that Charlie would not have been subject to the abuse that Emma meted out to him if Mark, the catalyst for the outbursts, were not there. But Mark could not afford to take the risk. Emma was volatile, unpredictable, and Mark could not be sure that if he was not there, she would not find other reasons to castigate the child.

As winter drew closer Mark became concerned that Charlie was being kept for large parts of the day in the yoghurt building that was unheated. The days were getting colder and Emma did not seem to care. Mark went to discuss his concerns with Dr. Bond, but, the doctor said, there was nothing he could do.

Mark even raised the matter with the health care visitor, but she did not take the concerns seriously.

"Oh now come on Mr. Richards, I am sure your wife is making sure that Charlie is kept warm!"

"But Charlie is taken out on deliveries for hours at a time, when I am available to look after him! Surely he would be better at home in the warm?"

"Well, I am sure Mrs. Richard's has good reason to take Charlie with her." The woman said in a placatory voice that put Mark's teeth on edge.

"But Charlie is left in the van whilst Emma is in the shops!"

"Well I'm sure that it's not for long, why don't you try and have a quiet word with Mrs. Richards and put your concerns to her?"

Mark looked at the earnest plain face of the woman and almost laughed. He was bashing his head against a brick wall! Have a quiet word with Emma? That would be like saying why didn't a Jew have a quiet word with Hitler!

Even though Mark was not working on the farm or in the business, it did not mean he did not care about what was happening. He regularly inspected the milking parlour, the livestock and the management of the land. Mark was well aware that Greg was simply not competent to manage the farm without guidance. Emma had no knowledge of farming. She had always made it clear that she would never work on the farm. Mark was not going to turn his back on years of investment and very hard work despite Emma's desire that he do so. Emma would get very angry when she saw Mark checking up on the farm. Then one day he found the milking parlour door padlocked. He marched to the yoghurt room.

"Why is the milking parlour door padlocked?" he asked.

"You know why, you have been interfering with the bulk tank and water heater!"

"What?!" Mark shouted, it was such a ridiculous claim; he could hardly take it in. Over Emma's shoulder he saw Dot shaking her head.

Sometimes Emma would follow him around the farm with a clipboard and pen, apparently making notes. Many times she would accompany her stalking with a stream of abuse, hurling constant criticism of Mark's management of the farm. Mark would voice his concerns and give advice, sometimes written, about the problems on the farm and made sure that he did not talk or interfere with the staff, except on one occasion when he found Greg placing big bales of silage by the drive.

"I wouldn't put them there mate." Mark said as pleasantly as he could. "The drive will be a mud bath as the bales are used through the winter."

Greg grunted.

The police had given Mark forms to reclaim his shotguns. When the forms disappeared. Emma blamed Charlie for taking them.

Emma often interfered with Mark's contact time by remaining in the room and keeping up a quiet stream of verbal abuse. This put Mark on edge and Charlie would pick up on this and cast worried glances at his mother. Other common disruptions that Emma employed was arriving with Charlie ten minutes late and taking Charlie away fifteen minutes early from his hour long sessions with Mark. Sometimes Emma would claim that Charlie was asleep in the yoghurt room. She insisted that no other time for the contact would be suitable.

When Mark did get Charlie and the weather was nice he attempted to have the full time by taking Charlie outside for a walk or to see the animals. This resulted in the disappearance of his coat and boots before contact times. They were usually taken over to the yoghurt room or locked in Emma's van. Mark bought duplicate items and kept them locked in his gun cabinet.

Mark would cry with frustration that there was no one to referee the problems. The only thing that Mark could do was to complain to his solicitor and log all the contact disruptions.

When Andreas felt they had logged enough he would apply to the court to complain. The process would take two to three months, sometimes longer. In court Emma would deny the allegations, then she would invent all sorts of excuses, and if the judge seemed bothered by her actions (invariably they appeared completely ambivalent) she would agree to improve in future. Later on as Charlie got older a similar pattern would evolve, denial of breaking the order, excuses and then apparent contrition. When a new order was given she would comply for a few months, then break it completely knowing it would take three to four months to get the matter back into court. The police, Mark discovered, had a very biased role. If Emma contravened the order as the resident parent (the parent looking after the child most if not all the time) they would not get involved. It was a civil matter and had to dealt with by the court. If Mark did anything contravening the contact order, they were quick to threaten him with arrest.

Mark thought back to the police sergeant who had advised him early on in his nightmare that there was no way he could win in this situation. He had made it plain that whatever the personal abuse, the police were not interested.

Now Mark realised that what the police sergeant should have told him was to get in touch with victim support and the local district domestic violence liaison officer and log all the abuse, so they were familiar with the background situation.

Much later Mark was to have some understanding from the local domestic violence liaison officer and eventually an apology for the way the police had treated him.

One day in October Mark was hoovering the living room carpet when Emma pulled the plug. Hand on hips, her lip curled in contempt she said "What sort of pathetic man allows his wife to stop him working? The doctor, the health worker, the solicitor, even the police can't believe the way you treat your wife and leave her to run the business and bring up my son without any help is disgusting!"

Mark flinched but said nothing.

The bullying slowly increased through the week. Mark found a note on his door to say he must work on the farm on Monday, and that he had to get the frozen milk out to defrost for yoghurt making on Sunday.

Mark found Emma. "Emma I've told you before if you have a problem you have to sort it! I no longer work in the business. You've made that very clear, and I will not be working until decent conditions are implemented. I am not going to be your slave. You're on your own Emma!"

Emma refused contact with Charlie. Charlie tried to see Mark himself on Saturday and banged on his bedroom door.

Before Mark could get out of bed he heard Emma dragging Charlie away in floods of tears. Emma stamped downstairs telling Charlie that his father was a nasty, spiteful, sick and dangerous man. On Sunday afternoon Emma said they were going to visit local friends. Mark went to bed before they got back. Dragged from a dreamless sleep something disturbed Mark around 2am the next morning. As he blinked in the harsh brightness of the landing light he realised that all the lights of the house were still on and that there was no sign of Charlie or Emma.

After a sleepless night Mark dressed and went out to see the staff. Shaking, he explained to the staff that he thought Emma had done a runner with Charlie.

"I'm really sorry guys, I am going to have to put you all on a week's notice unless Emma reappears within 24 hours."

The staff left and Mark went down to feed all the livestock. After speaking to Andreas Sims, Mark rang the police and spoke to the child protection unit.

They rang back in 20 minutes to say that Emma's solicitor had assured them that Charlie was well and would be returning later that day. Mark would have his contact later. Breezing in at 4pm, Emma ignored Mark and refused any contact with Charlie.

The next day Mark fed the livestock again. Emma was very aggressive. All through Mark's contact time with Charlie Emma kept coming in and out being verbally abusive.

"Emma, that's ENOUGH!" Mark said eventually, "Can't you see you're upsetting Charlie?"

Charlie was playing on his pulling train and fell off it onto the carpet. He cried out and Emma came rushing over demanding that Mark hand Charlie over to her.

"Emma, just leave us alone!" Mark said through gritted teeth. Mark could see Emma was not going to leave, so scooping Charlie up he rushed into the kitchen and closed the door.

"Mark give that child to me NOW! I'm warning you!" she screamed. She ran out of the front door, round to the back door and tried to come into the kitchen. Mark dashed upstairs with Charlie and locked them both in Mark's bedroom. Charlie chuckled delighted with this high-speed game of hide and seek. Mark felt a lump in his throat, thank God the child did not realise what was going on. Mark and Charlie had the rest of the contact with Emma banging on the door and shouting abuse.

At the end of the contact time, Mark handed Charlie back to his mother. She snatched him and said.

"Think you're very clever don't you? Well I have called the police about your cruelty, let's see if you think you're so clever when they've finished with you!"

As an alternative to solicitors Mark had said that he would be interested in trying mediation. In the early hearing Emma had said she was keen too. But when it came to it, she cancelled the first two appointments, and turned up late to the third one in Reading. It did not last long. She said it was a waste of time and left. Mark was refused contact later that day too.

"Look Mark" she said coldly. "The least I have to do with you the better. If you have to live here then we will have to have separate milk, bread, everything!"

"Don't be ridiculous Emma, that is totally stupid!" Mark said.

"Oh stupid now am I?" she shouted, "Just let me make a note of that, my solicitor has told me to record all your insults and unreasonable behaviour!"

Mark nearly choked. *His* unreasonable behaviour?

But true to her word Emma tried to prevent him having access to the milk. Mark went to the dairy and helped himself from the industrial fridge. Emma then locked the dairy when she could!

Despite Mark's earlier requests to be included in decisions concerning Charlie, Emma decided unilaterally to put their son in the nursery for each week day morning. Mark went to see the nursery and introduce himself to the owner and staff, telling them that from time to time he would be picking Charlie up after nursery.

Mark received a 'phone call later from the owner to say that his name was not on an approved list from Emma and social services had advised the nursery not to release Charlie to him.

"You can't be serious, I'm his father!" Mark protested.

But the woman was adamant. Mark rang the police and Andreas Sims. The police said it was nothing to do with them. Andreas was amazed that people did not respect Mark's parental rights and reassured Mark that they would raise the matter in court next time.

"You know Andreas, let it drop." Mark said wearily

"Really?" the young solicitor said.

"Yes, it will only give Emma the opportunity to make more fuss, and it is important for Charlie that the nursery not become a battle ground. Besides if I do pursue it Charlie will be moved to another nursery or private child minder."

"Well, if you're sure." Andreas said uncertainly

"I'm sure," Mark said.

It was to become a recurring theme: if Mark put Charlie's needs first, very often he had to suppress his own rights and Emma wasted no time in trampling all over them. In any event the explosive pressure of frustration was hard to contain.

Mark continued to meet John Abbott for a drink in the village and often thought it was what kept him sane. Escaping from the pressure cooker atmosphere of the farm was a relief and the fact that he and John talked about all sorts of things but rarely about his situation kept Mark in touch with the real world.

"I met an old friend of yours in here the other night." John said as the two men sat in front of the pubs roaring fire one late October night.

"Oh?"

"Yes, he was here with his wife, Tilly I think she was called, quite a girl! They live in Kenya."

Mark felt his heart beat faster.

"Did you tell them where I lived?"

John frowned. "No, is there a problem? I understood they were good friends.

"In a previous life." Mark said softly. The thought of Tony and Tilly turning up at the farm and being subjected to one of Emma's rants was unimaginable.

"Did they say they were staying long?" Mark asked.

"They didn't say, listen Mark I'm sorry if I put my foot in it, I really thought they were friends. I can see now though that you really don't want to see them."

"No mate, sorry, I didn't mean to come over all paranoid, but Tony tried to warn me off marrying Emma back in the early days and I feel sort of, well I don't know, but I don't think I could bear his 'I told you so's' on top of everything else."

John nodded.

"I understand, but I have to say he didn't strike me as the type to crow."

"No he probably isn't but let's face it, my marriage, my whole life is a joke and the last time I saw him I was on my honeymoon!"

Back at the farm Mark took out his diary that he had started to keep over the past months recording that Charlie had tantrums and cried for long periods at night. On those nights Mark would lie awake in his bed, his fists clenched, his jaw tight, wanting more than anything to comfort his son, but knowing that any move to do so would lead to another scene.

In November Mark went with Andreas to another contact hearing to deal with the breaches from the first order.

Mark was dumbfounded to hear the judge acknowledge that there had been significant breaches, but not once admonish Emma for her behaviour. Emma demanded that Mark could not drive Charlie in a vehicle as she alleged he was a dangerous driver.

Mark sat dumbfounded as that restriction was imposed on him, without any supportive evidence being produced.

Emma also got the judge to agree to all day nursery two days a week. Though Andreas Mark objected pointing out that this move was designed purely to keep Charlie away from him, and meant that he would have less contact time. At 17 months of age, Mark was convinced that Charlie was too young for all day nursery. The judge denied an interim hearing to discuss this. He then asked if violence would be a consideration in the judgement. Emma's solicitor suddenly announced that they would prove that as Mark was cruel to animals, he was a danger to Charlie. In support of that premise Emma's lawyer put forward American research that correlated cruelty to animals would lead on to cruelty to children.

Mark's barrister, and Andreas Sims and Mark himself were incredulous. The judge gave Emma's legal team, enjoying the considerable benefit of legal aid, 21 days to submit allegations and witness statements. Mark asked Andreas if they could appeal to the high court for an interim hearing. But he knew the answer; Mark had been repeatedly told he would be wasting his money.

Mark braced himself for the fallout of the latest hearing when they got home and he did not have to wait long. Emma initiated a new bullying tactic. After cooking she left everything for Mark to clean up. Mark gritted his teeth. There was no way he was going to succumb to this. After a few days the dirty pots and pans began to smell, so he put them outside on the patio. Whatever he needed Mark cleaned, used and left clean.

A tidy kitchen person, Mark had used to smile at the way that Emma was one of those cooks that seems determined to use every pot, pan and utensil for seemingly simple tasks. But this was an entirely different scenario, childish and deliberately antagonistic. Emma tried to make enough mess to get under Mark's skin; and Mark was equally determined not to do her bidding. Mark cleaned the house, except Emma's bedroom. On a couple of occasions contact was refused as when she came over from the yoghurt room with Charlie she found Mark washing the floor, or on another occasion hoovering. She decided that Mark was too busy for contact and took Charlie back to the yoghurt room.

After about a month and after taking almost all the reserves of restraint that Mark had, this particular type of bullying eased off as Emma saw that she was not getting anywhere with it. The verbal abuse also changed tack. As Mark was no longer working on the farm or business, the continuous criticism and abuse about his management of the business changed to more attacks on his supposed ignorance of how to be with little children, to look after children and to feed children. Mark often retorted, that they were both learning together. Emma would rant about what an expert on children she was.

"I've got more idea of how to parent, even in my sleep, than you would have surrounded with a ton of Dr. Spock books!" she crowed.

"I see" Mark said evenly. "Well what do the experts say about children of Charlie's age still sleeping in bed with their parents and not in the perfectly good cot he has?"

"How dare you!" Emma's dark eyes flashed dangerously.

"I'll have you now that I have to have him sleep with me. You have such a bad effect on him that he has nightmares, he needs at least one parent who is there for him!"

"There for him?" Mark shouted back "What the hell do you think I spend all my time and money trying to get proper access to my own child is about? Well let me tell you Emma, it's about being there for him because as much as you believe that you are some kind of superhuman mother who is completely above reproach, I happen to believe that the boy needs both parents"

Emma seemed to falter for a moment. Then she spat.

"Not if his father is a complete waste of space like you! He could well do without that! Whenever you aren't around he is like a different child, no tears or tantrums, sleeps well, *it's you Mark*, accept it!"

Now it was Mark's turn to falter. He had no way of knowing what Charlie was like when he was away from him but he did accept that the malignant hostility that Emma seemed to exude from every pore must have an impact when Mark was around.

"I'm not going to argue with you Emma. Charlie will be awake soon and I don't want him subjected to any more of your hysterical vicious rants." Mark turned his back on Emma.

"Ha, well at least you know when you're beaten!" she shouted triumphantly.

As the days went by Mark did his utmost to get the contact he had been awarded, but at the times when he had contact when Emma was not actually working she developed a new tactic to disrupt Mark's precious contact periods.

The first time she did it, Mark did not realise what she was doing. She was in the kitchen and turned the radio up to full volume. As Cold Play blasted out of the DAB radio Charlie toddled into the kitchen to investigate the noise.

"Hello Charlie boy! Do you want to help mummy make some cakes?"

Mark gritted his teeth as he heard Charlie shout YEAHHH! Contact over.

Mark decided that he would take Charlie upstairs to his bedroom to get uninterrupted contact. But Emma would follow and demand that Mark stay with Charlie in the living room while she was in the kitchen playing her music loudly or doing something else to cause their son to investigate. When Mark refused she followed him upstairs and banged on the bedroom door repeatedly.

Although sometimes she would get enough of a reaction out of Mark to ring the police, later on she would just invent any excuse to ring and complain that Mark was frightening her.

On a cold December day Mark had been splitting logs for the living room fire down at the farm buildings. Looking around for something to carry the logs in Mark saw some builders' buckets to carry the logs from the log store to the house.

"What are you doing?" Emma asked.

"What does it look like?" Mark said shortly.

"Right that's it then you're not seeing Charlie today if you are in that kind of a mood."

Mark followed her back to the house and taking Charlie by the hand he started to play with the child's' train set on the lounge floor.

"I said NO CONTACT!" Emma shouted.

"And I'm saying LEAVE US ALONE" Mark shouted back.

Emma made a grab for Charlie.

Whisking the boy out of her way and sitting him on the couch as he began to wail. Mark caught hold of Emma by both arms and marched her out of the room trying to take Charlie's shoes out of her hands.

"*I* will have to put his shoes on! You really have no idea, Mark how many times do I have to tell you that?"

"Don't be ridiculous, give me the shoes!" Mark shouted back, bending Emma's thumb back till she released the shoes.

Mark was shaking as he heard Emma on the phone to the police.

Holding his sobbing son to him, Mark took Charlie up to his bedroom and locked the door; Emma was in hot pursuit. Amazingly the police only took ten minutes to arrive.

Charlie, already upset, was very nervous of the policemen. Mark spoke to two policemen in his bedroom with Charlie. They seemed unsure what to do, so they left. Mark's feeling of triumph that Emma's call to the police had come to nothing was tempered by the distress he saw on Charlie's face and the fear in his eyes.

Mark knew he would pay for the incident, and he did. In retaliation he did not have contact with Charlie for several days. On two occasions Charlie threw a tantrum when he saw Mark but was whisked away, crying, his arms outstretched to his father. And once again. Mark's heart broke.

Chapter 15

Old Friends

Desperate for a break from the malignant atmosphere of the farm Mark went away to stay with Laurie in early December for a weekend. On his return Mark found Emma had fitted safety chains to the front and back doors. Mark realised that if he was not careful he was in danger of getting locked out. Any benefit he had felt from his time away dissipated as he realised that his battles were only just beginning.

The legal train rumbled on. Statements and papers were being sent in the post, sometimes with a requirement to be filed at court by a deadline. Emma started to intercept Mark's post. Because the farm had a long driveway they had a box for the postman at the entrance gate. Emma started to leave post for Mark locked in her van, sometimes for days before handing it over. By the time that Mark realised this and got his court papers, from a totally unrepentant Emma one deadline had already been missed.

"Emma, don't you know that it is an offence to delay the mail?"

"Me, delay the mail?" Emma looked at him with wide innocent eyes.

"Good luck making that one stick. If a harassed mother left to run a farm and raise a child alone while her husband loafs around the house, sometimes gets overwhelmed and forgets to bring the post in from the van, who is going to blame her?"

"I'm warning you Emma!" Mark said through clenched teeth "If you keep this up I will smash the van window with a hammer. Why don't I get one now and get my post out?" Mark went and got a hammer. As he approached the van Emma opened the door, retrieved the mail then threw it in the mud. Mark felt a small sense of triumph but the next day the post was locked in the van again. He opened a P.O. Box in Newbury sorting office.

As Christmas approached Mark steeled himself for what was always a contact nightmare. Most parents want their children for Christmas so the usual compromise is alternate Christmases and New Year holidays. This was the path the judges took with Charlie. But every year Emma just took Charlie away or arranged for contact orders to break down beforehand. If Mark had done that he knew he would have been arrested. And true to form Emma disappeared with Charlie from the 23rd to 28th December, in direct contravention of the contact order.

She returned on the 28th followed by two police cars. The firearms unit had come to impound Emma's illegally held pistol. She had found the pistol in her father's safe. Mark had refused to allow her to keep the bullets and had disposed of them. Delighted to see his son again, Mark asked the police if he could have Charlie for his contact time. They said they had taken Charlie to his grandmother's house.

"Why the hell did you do that?" Mark tried to control his anger.

"e should be left with me, I'm here and the court have awarded me contact, which incidentally has been broken by his mother, over this Christmas period."

The policeman looked uncomfortable.

"Look Mr. Richards I am sure that the judge would not want me to interfere."

Mark wanted to scream with frustration and wanted to say to him that his job should have been to uphold court orders. But he didn't. The thought of Mary Channing taking care of his precious son made his stomach churn. God knew what poison she would be dripping in his ear! She had made a bang up job of screwing up her daughter; the thought of her influencing his son was unbearable.

In January Mark was served with a summons by a court bailiff. Emma had brought an injunction against him with a hearing on the 10th. The bottom line was that Emma was applying to have Mark evicted from the farmhouse and also looking to impose a non-molestation order.

There was a hearing already booked for contact review. With injunctions there is usually very little time for preparation Mark had found. Emma had removed the fax machine and 'phone to the yoghurt room but Mark needed to send some statements to Andreas Sims quickly.

"Emma" he said as she was leaving for the yoghurt room

I need to use the fax machine in the kitchen, would you bring it back from the yoghurt room please?"

Emma gave him a withering look and ignored his request returning at lunchtime without it. Later in the day while Emma was busy with a delivery, Mark nipped over and brought the machine back with him. He had just plugged it in when Emma flew through the backdoor, and physically tried to snatch the machine from the worktop. Mark pushed her out of the way. He set the machine up and sent his fax. Charlie had been delivered to him for contact and he played happily with his son on the lounge floor while he waited for a response by fax. When Charlie had been taken back to the yoghurt room Mark went to check the fax. It had been sabotaged it's innards spewed across the work surface like a disembowelled animal.

An earnest woman from CAFCASS saw Mark and Charlie for assessment for her report for the court. As it was the hearing turned out to be largely procedural. Emma's cross petition for unreasonable behaviour was ruled out of time by the judge. Mark felt a faint glimmer of hope. But it was, it turned out, a tiny victory as the judge went on to allow Emma to refute Mark's allegations in each hearing. He gave timescales for answers to the questions for the first Ancillary Relief hearing (financial matters) to be filed. Mark was served in court with another summons, to have him evicted from his home.

The judge ruled he would see us again a day and half later. So instead of 14 days to build a defence Mark had just 36 hours! The thrust of Emma's' allegations were that he had interfered with the staff so they had left. Mark was shocked. He was really angry at his legal team firstly for not anticipating such tactics, and secondly for not suggesting a similar non-molestation order against Emma months back. Mark rushed around contacting staff and explained what had happened. Two of them wrote short letters for the court; the others said they did not want to get involved. Greg was already in league with Emma over the divorce.

Predictably after a hearing Emma became more obnoxious and contact with Charlie was withdrawn. When they went back to court a day and a half later Mark's team asked for an adjournment. Mark had to sign undertakings. Emma refused to sign cross-undertakings. Mark was banned from entering the yoghurt building, farm buildings or interfering with the business or management.

Mark set about contacting staff that no longer worked on the farm, as well as current staff that knew him. He managed to contact Matt, who Emma had accused of stealing nails, and met him for a drink at a local pub.

"Look Mark, I feel for you, really I do, Greg has already had a word, and that guy doesn't mess about!"

"I know" Mark said grimly.

"He told me that he was going to take whatever he could and then walk away!"

"Well that doesn't surprise me!" Mark said.

"Would you write a statement?"

"Yes of course!" Matt said.

But when Matt's statement was read out, Mark was told that he had compromised Matt's testimony. At a later meeting Matt said that Greg had warned off other staff from helping Mark. When Mark spoke to Dot she told him that Greg had threatened her and told her that her life would not be very pleasant and she would loose her job if she were to support Mark. Mark was stunned to think that the surly stockman was prepared to go so far.

The CAFCASS officer came to discuss her recommendations for the forth coming child matters hearing. She recommended that Mark look after Charlie when Charlie was not at nursery, and that he should have priority over Mary, the grandmother. Mark should also have a full day at weekends with Charlie. Mark could scarcely believe what he was hearing. He almost floated out of court, a smiling Andreas at his side.

In retaliation, Emma cancelled their joint account to which Mark already had no access. This meant that all direct debits and standing orders Mark now had to fund himself. She also demanded that he pay for the TV license. The personal abuse rose to a peak at the end of January. Emma would make calls from the kitchen speaking so loudly that Mark could not fail to hear, recounting incidents which were what she had done to Mark but saying that it was what Mark had done to her! It was most bizarre. Later in court she would allege that Mark had done this or that, but in reality it was what she had done to him!

In February Mark made a rare stand against Emma's bullying over contact. The previous day while Mark was working on some papers, Emma had breezed in.

"I'm changing contact time to the afternoon tomorrow" she said imperiously. "I've got an appointment with my solicitor in Reading in the morning."

"I see" Mark said evenly "I'm sorry Emma, that is not acceptable and contravenes the contact order."

"Tough!" she said and turned on her heel.

In the morning as she tried to leave, Mark blocked her van with his car. Emma 'phoned her solicitor and then the police. Two policemen arrived. Mark asked if he could tape the interview, they agreed. Mark produced the two court orders that detailed the contact times and the fact that Emma was not to be present at contact. Mark said "I am quite happy for Emma to go to her solicitor's appointment but she will have to leave Charlie with me for the contact period."

As the policemen studied the court orders Emma shrieked

"I am not leaving Charlie with him, he's dangerous!"

"Do you want to say that a bit louder, just so we are sure you've got it on the tape?" Mark said and one of the policemen suppressed a smile.

The police read the documents carefully.

"Mrs. Richards" the officer said carefully "if the judge had thought Mr Richards was dangerous he would have ordered that you remain on the property during contact."

Emma began to sob violently and refused to leave, so missed her appointment.

The police left when the contact period came to an end, and Mark moved his car. He did not see Charlie.

For the next few days Mark smiled in amusement as Emma tried to block his car in with her van. She never succeeded; he always left enough room to manoeuvre.

The next afternoon Mark took Charlie out for a walk in the winter sunshine. When they came back Emma was packing the van with suitcases.

Snatching Charlie from Mark, she shoved him into his car seat and announced that she was moving out to stay with her mother,

"And don't think that you can go whining to the courts Mark, I have been advised to go by my solicitor, the CAFCASS officer and the health visitor!"

Mark stood and watched her speed off down the drive. His brain was in turmoil, what did this new move mean? What was she plotting now?

Because there was so much spite and undisguised hatred from Emma, two counsellors Mark was seeing had advised him to put good locks on his bedroom door and never to turn his back on Emma.

The thought that these people physically feared for his safety made him feel sick. It was surreal, like a bad nightmare. But he certainly felt that Emma was capable of stabbing him in the back at any moment.

Now that he was alone in the house Mark was grateful that she had put the security chains on the outside doors. He would not put it past her to have him beaten up one night.

When Mark was allowed to see Charlie the next day Emma started to remove things from the house. Mark watched he but did not want to make a scene in front of Charlie. The following day she took cooking equipment and the hoover out to the van. Armed with his tape recorder Mark demanded that they discuss and agree what she took.

True to form Emma rang the police, and while she was speaking to them Mark snatched the hoover back. The police arrived but said that disputes over the ownership of joint possessions would have to be sorted out through solicitors. Mark pointed out that Emma was staying with her mother who had a well-appointed house and certainly no need of duplicate electrical goods!

The cottage felt empty without Charlie, quiet and eerie. Mark decided that he needed to keep busy and started to finish the dry lining in the house and started to decorate.

When she came to the farm to work Emma frequently deliberately damaged or ruined the work Mark had done. It made no sense at all! It was very frustrating.

"Emma!" Mark challenged her, finding a piece of wallpaper torn and hanging off the landing wall.

"Why the hell did you do that? Don't you want a nice house to live in? You've gone on about the decorating for long enough!"

"Oh whoops!" Emma looked at him wide eyed, putting a finger to her chin. "Did I do that? Oh naughty, clumsy Emma!" she smacked herself on the hand and went downstairs laughing.

As she was not living in the house she left all the outer doors open, so the house was freezing.

And then, in February, she started to move back in.

Another child matters hearing was scheduled for March. They were before district judge Francis. Mark had nicknamed him the dinosaur. He was a ponderously slow, pompous man. One of his first statements was to tell Mark and Emma that he liked to crack the tough nuts. He would soon sort them out. It was a contact hearing but part way through he suddenly blurted out to Mark's barrister that there was no way Mark would ever get joint residency (custody).

The subject of residency was not being discussed! The judge was completely out of order.

After objecting three times to his comment Marks' legal team were threatened with eviction from the courtroom. Mark's barrister and Mark himself both made formal complaints about his behaviour, but neither had a reply.

The day dragged on with a back-to-back hearing for the divorce finances but now judge Francis had become noticeably biased after the heated exchanges of the contact hearing. Mark's barrister wanted to appeal, but Mark shook his head, sadly, he did not want to delay the divorce process.

While he had been alone at the farm house Mark had got two dogs, Maggie a border terrier and Paddy a cocker spaniel. One evening, Mark was in his bedroom watching television with Paddy. The door was ajar. Emma returned to the house with Charlie at about 8.15pm and put the boy to bed. As usual she carried Charlie to and from the bathroom so he would not see Mark. Emma came back to Mark's room and tried to take Paddy away.

"Come on Paddy, come with me now!" she said as Paddy stared at her from the comfort of his position curled up with Mark on the bed.

"Leave us alone Emma!" Mark said.

"Come on Paddy" she coaxed "You don't want to stay in there with that horrible man!"

"Emma, he is quite happy where he is!" Mark said.

"Come on Paddy, come and have a treat, there's a good boy, what's this then?" she pretended to have something in her hand.

"Fuck off, Emma, just leave us alone!" Emma left but then came back. Jumping off the bed, Mark shut the door in her face.

She came in again and tried to catch hold of Paddy's collar. Mark grabbed her hand and pushed her back out of the room. She stumbled and fell against the bathroom wall. Mark closed his eyes as she went downstairs and 'phoned the police.

As he sat in his bedroom, Paddy curled up licking his hand, as if to say he understood, Mark felt the tears prick the back of his eyelids. He knew what was coming.

A policeman and policewoman arrived and took the stairs two at a time. They arrested Mark in his bedroom at about 10.30pm.

Mark was not allowed to say anything and was driven to Newbury police station. Mark had to wait with the policeman for quite a while until the custody sergeant was ready. He was searched, then booked in. Mark had to sign various forms then taken to a cell with a very bright light and left there with two plastic cups of water. At about 3.15a.m. an officer came to take Mark for interview.

The policewoman seemed very hesitant and inexperienced. Mark gave a long description of the incident on tape and then answered a few questions. At around 5am he was processed for finger prints, photographed and had a swab taken from his mouth for a DNA sample. Mark was then cautioned and told to wait outside the police station. He was then picked up by the policeman and woman and taken home.

Mark was close to tears with the injustice of it all.

Mark asked Emma for the child car seat for their next contact. The judge had ruled that Mark could drive Charlie and leave the property for contact, to get a more peaceful contact.

Emma ignored repeated requests for the car seats throughout the day.

"Mark will you *shut up*! I'm busy, I can't drop everything for you!" she shouted at him.

Mark had tried for days to get hold of the District Domestic Violence Liaison officer (DDVLO) at Newbury police station. Mark went to the Kingsclere police station, but they insisted it was nothing to do with them. Mark pointed out to them that if they or someone in authority could speak to Emma about her behaviour it may prevent a more serious incident when he might finally loose his temper.

Eventually they promised to contact the DDVLO and get her to contact Mark. Nothing happened. Mark had to wait well into his contact period before Emma supplied the car seat. He took Charlie to feed the ducks at the park in Newbury. Later in the day Mark went back into Newbury to buy another car seat. The next day Mark took

Charlie and the dogs for a walk in the Savernake Forest near Marlborough. Charlie thoroughly enjoyed the forest and the rough ground and puddles, frequently doing his little jigs in a circle saying yea yea yea, which he always did when he was happy. Mark felt his heart swell with love and pride.

Singing along to a cassette of nursery rhymes Mark had brought for the car, he and Charlie arrived home. Before Mark could even turn the engine off, Emma yanked open Charlie's door and tried to pull him out. She was so angry that she could not even undo the car seat belt.

"Emma, don't be so ridiculous, can't you see you're frightening Charlie?" Mark said

"Just go and wait for us in the kitchen!"

Emma was screaming and sobbing with frustration yanking Charlie against the seat belt, trying to drag him from the car. Charlie was crying then screaming in pain.

Mark jumped out of the car and forced Emma away, prizing her fingers off the seat belt. Mark calmed Charlie and carried him to the back door, where Emma repeatedly tried to grab him; all the time yelling abuse.

Mark put Charlie down and Emma whisked him away.

Mark stood in shock. Emma's behaviour was disgraceful, shocking, the worst kind of abuse of their child who Mark could now hear wailing inside the house. Emma refused to let Mark into the kitchen, blocking him physically with

Charlie in her arms. She was very abusive, shrieking the most horrible insults and vile threats.

Mark, afraid for what she might do if he provoked her further, backed off and rang the police. He explained the situation and was told a car would be sent. Mark waited but the police 'phoned back and asked questions. Mark asked that the Newbury DDVLO contact him as soon as possible, as the police announced that they had now changed their mind and would not be sending a car. Mark was assured that they would arrange it. They did not.

As he walked through the village a few days later Mark detoured into the bank to see if John Abbott could come for a drink. He was told that John was in a meeting. He left a note saying he would be in the pub and walked over the road to have a drink and wait for him. As he walked into the pub a familiar laugh reached his ears. Before he could place the joyous sound as Tilly's laugh and leave, he had been spotted.

"Mark!" Tony was beside him in two bounds. He still looked athletic and tanned, the picture of health. Beside his old friend Mark thought he must look pretty pitiful, thin and pale and aged from the unrelenting stress of his life. Indeed, Tilly, not as adept at hiding her feelings as Tony, could not disguise the look of shock on her face. Before she could compose herself Mark had read the expression on her face and cringed. For a crazy moment a flashback to their wild lovemaking lit up his brain before Tony was clapping him on the back.

"There you are you old bastard!" he said. "We've been camped out in this pub for a week waiting for you to make an appearance, it's been hell!"

"I can imagine" Mark said with a weak smile. He had no idea that Tony and Tilly were back. He had breathed a sigh of relief when John Abbott told him that they had gone back to Kenya the last time they had been home, the banker tactfully refraining from asking why Mark had not wanted to see his old friends. Mark had assumed it would be years before they visited again.

"Bloody hell mate, no need to ask if you've been working hard, look at you, you're skin and bone!"

In his peripheral vision he could see Tilly trying to compose her face into a smile and trying to signal her husband to shut up. She had realised that Mark's appearance owed more to emotional devastation than hard work; that or a dread disease.

As he sat down with them Mark felt almost too weak to speak.

"So mate what's the gen?" Tony leaned back on two legs of his chair, his right ankle resting on his left knee, in the way that was so familiar to Mark. It brought a lump to his throat, this innocent reminder of a happier time.

"How's Emma?" Tilly said softly. Mark could see that she had been struggling with the question and he cleared his throat.

"Actually we're getting divorced" he glanced at Tony, but there was no sigh of an 'I told you so'. Rather his friend leaned forward returning the front legs of his chair to the floor. His face was full of concern. It was as though the penny had dropped, that Tony was realising that his friend's desperate appearance was not due to hard work.

"Oh, I'm sorry to hear that Mark, you've got a child haven't you?"

Mark nodded,

"Yes Charlie, actually it is difficult at the moment, she is doing her best to keep him away from me."

Tilly was shaking her head sadly.

"Where are you living?" Tony asked.

"Still at the cottage, you remember the one I used to rent? We bought it and did it up."

"Oh I see and where is she?"

"In the cottage."

Tony and Tilly exchanged glances.

"That must be difficult." Tilly said softly and put her hand on Mark's

"It is." Mark said miserably, looking at her from eyes brimming with tears.

As Mark sat with his friends and watched their faces register expressions ranging from horror to heartbreak as he told them the sorry tale, strangely Mark felt himself getting stronger. It felt good to get it all off his chest, to share his pain with friends who truly cared about him. By the time John Abbott arrived they had started to talk about Tony and Tilly's life in Kenya. They were thinking of coming back for good. Mark thought that he would welcome having them close. The kindness and concern in their eyes was hard for Mark to cope with, with his emotions as raw as they were, but by the time they parted, he felt a slight glimmer of optimism. He would have people on his side. That would be good.

Over the next few days Emma, almost as though she knew that he had found some comfort ratcheted up her abuse. She refused to provide Charlie with socks and shoes so that Mark could take him out and his coat was never available. Mark built up the duplicate stash of clothes he had, and over time Charlie ended up with a ghost wardrobe necessary because on occasions Emma had been known to present Charlie for contact in his pyjamas! The injunctions meant Mark could not go into the other buildings on the farm or into Emma's room. Mark thought about a claim for contempt of a court order, but decided he would not give Emma the satisfaction.

As part of the new contact orders Mark had asked that he be allowed to feed Charlie at lunch or supper on occasions. This gave Emma a new topic for verbal abuse.

One lunchtime as Mark was giving Charlie some seedless grapes, Emma came into the kitchen. Charlie looked up warily. She strode over to the table and leant over so that her face was inches from Mark's.

With clenched teeth and hate filled eyes she shouted,

"If you dare to feed Charlie anything other than organic food, so help me Mark I will kill you!"

Charlie began to whimper and then to cry.

"For God's sake Emma, can't you see what you're doing to Charlie, what the hell is the matter with you?"

"What's the matter with me? Hell, Mark *you're* the one trying to poison my baby!"

"Emma, calm down, can't you see, this constant verbal abuse and screaming are the reason why Charlie has tantrums and can't sleep?"

"SHUTUP Mark!" Emma screamed and Charlie clung to his father, his small body trembling.

Mark realised that Emma was close to the edge. He had to calm the situation down.

"Ok, look Emma, You're right, we need to feed Charlie the very best, you let me know what it should be."

Emma looked at him with wild eyes, as though she had hardly heard him. But the hysteria was dissipating, being replaced by hate filled anger—she had stepped back from the edge.

This time.

Chapter 16

Fever Pitch

Mornings followed a similar pattern for Mark at the cottage. Emma would have a bath with Charlie each morning and Mark would often lie in bed listening to his son gurgling with pleasure splashing around in the bath. When Mark got up though, Emma's tone would change, and her voice dripping venom, she would say to Charlie

"Oh listen Charlie, the hermit is leaving his cave!" followed by a mock growl. She would also say—the beast is leaving his cave or the nasty man is leaving his cave. Her tone and the growls and other frightening noises that she attached to her statements would put an end to Charlie's happy gurgles. At the time Mark had no idea of the seriousness of the psychological impact on Charlie of these derogatory mantras. In hindsight he knew he should have raised it with his therapist who had already suggested that he got the court to have Emma psychologically assessed.

Sometimes in answer to much of her criticisms of his care for Charlie, Mark would ask Emma to show him how she wanted things done.

One day in the kitchen as Mark was preparing a drink for Charlie Emma snatched the glass from him tipping the juice out and refilling it using part water. She slammed the beaker down on the counter and some of it spilt over her hand.

"Can't you do anything right?" She said "Even making a simple juice drink seems to be beyond you!"

Mark tried to temper the anger he was feeling.

"OK Emma, you show me how you want things done and I'll make sure I do it that way, I know that you know best with these things."

"Then why not just leave it all to me?" she said.

"Because I want to take care of Charlie too, and, after all, you initially learned from the nurses and midwives in the hospital, why can't you teach me, for Charlie's sake?"

"How dare you?" Emma screamed

"Are you trying to say that I wouldn't have known what to do if it was not for the nurses? Of course I would! Because, unlike you I do have a brain, I can work it out!"

Mark wanted to argue but he bit his tongue. Charlie, in his high chair, was looking from his mother to his father, a frightened look, that was now becoming very familiar, on his face.

One of the small victories of the last court order was the fact that Mark was to be allowed to put Charlie to bed one night a week. Mark loved sitting reading Thomas the Tank Engine to his son but this proved a concession too far for Emma. She sabotaged every attempt and disgracefully used Charlie himself to make the process difficult.

Mark always made sure that even at the times that Emma invaded his and Charlie's contact time he never stopped his son from going to her or being hugged by her. He always put Charlie first even though at times he wanted to yell and scream at Emma. Emma showed no such compunction. She was ruthless in using Charlie to get at Mark.

After many delays and false starts Mark finally had a meeting with WDC Claire Theale, the Newbury district domestic violence liaison officer. Mark found the young woman sympathetic and easy to talk to. Before Mark knew it they had been talking for over an hour. She suggested that Mark approach Social Services and ask them to have a talk with Emma about her behaviour in front of Charlie. Mark also talked to the Citizen's Advice Bureau, and they arranged a meeting with social services in Newbury for him. Mark was nervous about involving Social Services but when he met with the duty social worker she seemed sympathetic to his concerns and promised to have a talk with Emma about her behaviour in front of Charlie.

If Emma wanted to talk about something Mark was usually prepared to listen, unless she timed it to clash with something like computer class. If Mark wanted to discuss something, however, he was always told to do it through her solicitor. Mark thought long and hard about how these things might affect Emma's behaviour but he could not let it go on any longer. A week later he wrote a letter to Emma via her solicitor detailing all his concerns about her behaviour in front of Charlie and how damaging her behaviour was to Charlie.

What Mark was totally unprepared for was that when the final divorce hearing came, his letter would be used as the basis for her accusing Mark of all the bad behaviour outlined in them!

This became a theme over the next few years: Mark was accused of all the things that in actual fact Emma had done to him. Mark's therapist assured him that it was Emma's way of addressing her guilt by transferring all her guilt onto Mark.

Mark did not know what he thought of that. At least it meant that she did realise that what she was doing was wrong. Not that that was likely to stop her doing it!

But, as Mark was to find out, in a court of law it was her word against his. In UK family law courts Mark was to learn the hard way that judges invariably default in favour of mothers unless there is irrefutable evidence to make this unwise. In Mark's case, as in most divorces, there were no witnesses to the family situations. Indeed whenever there were other people around Emma made very sure she behaved reasonably. As it turned out it was going to take years of appeals backed up with opinions from professionals involved with the case to change the perception of the judges. What annoyed Mark so much was that despite the fact that a clear pattern of Emma's behaviour emerged, the prejudice of the judges still gave her the benefit of the doubt time and again, even, it would turn out, after seven years of pleas and explanations proving what she was doing.

Emma had supporters who were prepared to lie in court too. Some like Greg were just opportunists expecting some sort of pay off, but most, like neighbours and her relatives were simply told fabricated stories about Mark's behaviour and simply believed them. Mark overheard Emma on the phone talking to supporters giving a completely spun account of an incident. Mark kept thinking, hoping, praying that she would revert back to upright, moral, honest person that he had fallen in love with.

Mark could not believe that Emma would do to Charlie what her mother had done to her. He remembered the hours she had lain crying in his arms over the pain her mother had caused her. How could she not see that she was laying the same foundations with their son? In the event it was to take Mark about four years for the penny to drop that he was Emma's number one enemy and that she would never change. She would do anything it took to keep Mark from being in Charlie's life, irrespective of the effect on Charlie!

Now that the contact periods that Mark had with Charlie were for several hours at a time Mark often took his son down to Newbury to the park there or for a walk along the Kennet and Avon canal with its brightly coloured narrow boats. There were cygnets and ducklings to watch, it was a great youngster's playground. And there were usually other children around. On one occasion they chatted to some young girls fishing for tiddlers in a shallow area of water at the side of the canal. When they caught some Mark put one into Charlie's cupped hands. The memory of his face completely enthralled by the tiny flapping fish was a memory that Mark knew would be with him forever. Another time a pigeon landed on Charlie's head. He was about to burst into tears, Mark started laughing. His reaction immediately changed to joy and he called out to everyone within earshot to look at him. Charlie would speak of these incidents for months afterwards and Mark loved these special memories being made between father and son.

So that the contact order provision for Mark to put Charlie to bed one evening a week could be upheld, Mark had to have access to Emma's bedroom. Emma really resented this. She kept saying that Mark was preventing Charlie from sleeping in his own room, in his own cot because Mark had made it his bedroom. Worn down by a bitter stream of recriminations from Emma, Mark moved back into the poky second bedroom. He took a lot of the boxes of books and personal stuff down to his sister Laurie's house. Although Mark had been very careful to make sure that none of Emma's belongings were sent by mistake, Emma insisted that Mark had stolen some of her possessions.

As he had known would happen, Charlie never moved into his own room, and continued to sleep mostly in Emma's bed. It was pointless to argue. Mark felt his strength draining from him.

At the end of April the house fridge-freezer packed up. Emma refused to give Mark the 'phone number of the commercial freezer service man, and removed all her food to the big industrial fridge and freezer in the yoghurt building. She refused to allow Mark to store his food there and as he was banned from entry by court order, there was not much he could do.

Mark went away to stay with Laurie for the weekend.

Arriving back at the cottage he let himself in and sat down in the lounge. It was a moment before it hit him, the TV had gone!

He went to find Emma. She was nowhere to be found but there was a note to say that when Mark had paid the television license the set would be returned. The note added that Mark also had to pay the council tax and buy a new fridge-freezer.

Mark shook his head and sat down wearily. He had noticed that Emma had returned a lot of things she had taken when she had moved out to live at her mother's. Some of Charlie's toys and games reappeared. Mark was pleased to see that. But his pleasure was short lived. A few days later he got a letter from Emma's solicitor accusing him of keeping toys in his bedroom away from Charlie! Mark laughed out loud. As if he would do such a thing!

When he saw Emma next Mark asked her if she would agree to them both have a psychological evaluation.

"What?" Emma shouted at him "Well we all *know* you are completely off your head, so what would be the point in your case, but hey, I have nothing to hide, maybe if we have it then other people will see what I have to put up with all the time!"

Mark tried not to show how excited he was by the thought that Emma might at last be diagnosed and get the help she needed.

"Oh, I should say Mark, I'll do it if my solicitor says that it is OK to."

"That's good Emma, can you please repeat that so that I have it on tape?" Mark held his breath.

"Oh I see your little game. No! I won't" Emma said.

Summer was around the corner now and Tony and Tilly were back from Kenya. They had rented a cottage in the next village and Mark spent many a warm afternoon in their garden with Charlie. Tony and Tilly loved his son and Charlie loved them. Mark finally felt that he truly had somewhere he could go and be himself and enjoy being with Charlie without fear of being seen by anyone who might report what he was doing back to Emma.

One warm May afternoon, after lunch with his friends, Mark helped Tilly to weed some of the flower beds they had inherited while Tony drove off for a meeting with John Abbott at the bank, Mark offered to run Tilly to Newbury on his way home so that she could do some shopping and meet up with Tony when he had finished at the bank. As they drove past the farm Mark noticed a car waiting to join the road from the driveway. The driver was looking the other way and Mark slowed to make sure that he had been seen. The driver looked around as Mark brought his car almost to a halt outside the farm. It was Mary Channing.

Her eyes lingered on Mark and then Tilly and then back to Mark again and she nodded slightly, her lips curved into a spiteful smile. Mark felt his heart sink.

Tilly noticing his unease said

"Problem?"

"I expect so" Mark sighed, "that was Emma's mother, she pretty much hates me and will stop at nothing to make sure I am perceived in as bad a light as she can."

"This was kind of a gift then?"

Mark smiled,

"Probably, but it was worth it! Instinctively he put his hand out and patted Tilly on her jean clad knee. It had been so long since he had touched a woman in anything other than anger and he immediately felt fearful. But he need not have worried. Tilly covered his hand with her own and patted it reassuringly.

Mark felt a lump come to his throat. It could have been very different if he and Tilly . . . . Still there was no point in even thinking that way, he was just starved of affection, he knew that.

A few days later Emma cornered him in the kitchen as he was feeding Charlie his supper.

" I hear you've taken up with an old flame, poor cow!" she said. "What was her name now, Milly, Silly, oh no that's right Tilly! Well she's welcome to you, but if I ever find that you have been out with her and taken Charlie with you, then that will be the last time you take Charlie off this farm!" she said.

"Tilly is married to Tony, as you know very well Emma, they live in the area now and I was giving Tilly a lift to meet up with Tony."

"Oh I believe you, thousands wouldn't" she said over her shoulder, as snatching Charlie out of his high chair she stormed upstairs.

Mark looked down at the half finished plate of food. What was the point, Emma would believe what she wanted to believe.

Mark did not have to wait long to find out what his punishment would be. Emma called the police out about an incident over the washing machine. One of Emma's petty bullying tactics was to refuse to give Mark more than one set of sheets for his mattress on the floor. So Mark picked a day when the weather would allow him to wash and dry them before making up the bed again. So, just before Mark was due to have Charlie for contact, while Emma was having breakfast, Mark put the washing machine on for his sheets.

"Oops *so* sorry Mark can't have the machine on, there's a problem with the water supply, and I have to give Charlie a bath and I need to do his nappies before you use it."

"Emma, as I have only one set of sheets, I've got to get them out early so I can go out and so that they will be dry before bed time."

Mark turned the machine back on. Emma flew at him trying to push him away from the machine. Gritting his teeth Mark slowly pushed her away from the machine.

"I will call the police Mark!" she screamed

"Be my guest!" Mark shouted back

As she ran to the phone Mark locked the utility door and chained the back door. Sometime later the police arrived.

Hoping that Emma was paying attention Mark heard the police officer say that social services would not allow this bad situation for Charlie to continue indefinitely.

After the police left and the washing was done Emma came over with a hammer and tried to knock the security chain off the door. Emma did not put any washing on that day but later in the day she started loading some of her belongings into the van. Mark assumed she was going to move out again as she had often threatened.

He gathered things like the kettle, iron and the hoover and locked them in his room. Mark did not see Charlie for several days. Emma said she was going back to court to reduce his contact with Charlie. Mark felt in the depths of despair again. A couple of days later Emma asked for the iron. Mark said she could have the iron or anything else in exchange for the van keys; so she could not remove these things from the property. She refused and locked Charlie in the van so that Mark could not have him for contact. She said that if she could not have the iron, then Mark could not have Charlie.

Emma was still gone and Mark missed Charlie desperately. After Emma moved out Mark got a letter from the district council for council tax and a form for single occupancy rebate. Mark smiled ruefully. Emma had instigated this; she had obviously planned to move out for some time. The abuse and nastiness from Emma reached a crescendo as she turned up each day for work. She was nearly always present during Mark's contact time with Charlie if he stayed in the house. If he went out she would shout out after him that he better not be going to see his tart with Charlie. The personal abuse was very vitriolic with no concern at all that it was all in front of Charlie. Even Mark producing the tape recorder did little to tame Emma's out bursts.

"You would do well to find yourself another woman to keep you, see if tarty Tilly can't shake off her loser of a husband 'cos I ain't going to keep you anymore. Have a word when you see your old whore, there's a dear!"

Now that Emma had moved out again the fight was "anything goes!" If the washing machine was on, she would turn it off. In the evenings she would leave the hot taps running to drain the tank before Mark could have a bath. She would leave the outer doors open, even at night. If Mark was watching television or reading in the living room she would try to wind him up. Sometimes Mark would lock the living room doors to keep her out. Then Emma would go around to the large windows on the outside and bang on them with the sharp edge of a credit card. She would keep this up for ten minutes. She took the water softener tablets. She would damage any plastering or decorating work. She removed food from the new fridge-freezer and put hers in without any discussion. When she came into the kitchen Mark removed all her food from the fridge, explaining that as she had refused to pay for the fridge from the money she owed him and had forced him to buy it with borrowed money.

"Look Emma, as you are obviously incapable of acting in a mature way over the use of the fridge, and as you no longer live in the house then you are not, repeat *not* using it."

Emma ignored him and continued to remove his food: so Mark bought a long chain and padlocked the door to the fridge. As he looked at the new fridge freezer with the chain on it, he felt a sadness engulf him. Something about this, the most ordinary of appliances chained was so bleak that Mark could hardly bear it.

Increasingly worried about how the constant combative atmosphere was affecting Charlie, Mark spoke to a child psychologist. She recommended that Mark go to social services and accuse Emma of emotional abuse and get the whole situation investigated. When Mark contacted social services again, however, they said as the matter was before the courts and because CAFCASS was involved, they would not get involved. Mark later learned that this was more about budgets and less about Charlie's welfare. Mark was beginning to think that his legal advisors were not experienced enough or capable of providing what was needed in the deteriorating situation. Mark knew that he was very naïve and "green" himself but it was too awful to contemplate the fact that the expensive advice he was paying for might not be sound.

As Mark felt his stress levels rise about the situation he found himself in, he knew that he was watching the management of the farm and business slowly coming apart. With the court order banning him from involvement in the running of the farm, Mark could not do anything practical. He tried in vain to give Emma advice on the farm.

Running an organic goat dairy farm takes a lot of skill and some luck with the weather to get the grazing rotation right. Goats, unlike sheep, have no resistance to stomach worms. If they suffer an infestation the lining of the gut can be so damaged that the goat can die or loose condition and be unable to produce milk. Because of that the grazing area has to be kept clean of worm burden, as using chemicals to worm the animals is not permitted in an organic operation. Even if used medically the milk withdrawal time (when milk has to be discarded) for organic regimes is very costly. Greg had never fully grasped this concept and Mark realised that he had put the goats back on to previously grazed pasture with its high worm burden.

Mark found Emma in the dairy.

"Emma, despite all the advice and information I have given both you and Greg, he has put the goats out on the wrong pasture! I will hold you responsible if any of the goats die, and they will, if you do not address this problem!"

"Oh you will will you? Perhaps you could repeat that threat for the tape recorder?"

"No problem!" Mark stormed "I'll go an get my recorder, it would be a very good idea to get this on record!"

When Mark returned Emma had gone down to the farm buildings to talk to Greg. Mark stood outside the barn.

Spotting him Emma came out.

"Right, you explain to Greg what you told me!"

Mark nodded

"Greg, the goats can't go out on the pasture we have just used. It will have a high worm burden. They will catch it and they will die. I thought I had explained this? Hell, I even wrote it down!" Mark struggled to keep his temper.

Greg exploded with rage and rushed up to Mark waving his arms about.

"When you get off your backside and do a sodding day's work *mate* then you can tell me what to do, till then keep you fucking mouth shut or I'll shut it for you!" he roared.

Mark laughed in his face.

"I'm well over worrying about anything you could do Greg, come on then give it your best shot!" Mark spread his arms in invitation

Greg just stood there. Mark turned his back and walked back to the house.

"Getting Paddy and Saffy into the car he took them up to the woods. The bluebells and wild garlic were so beautiful that Mark felt his anger melt away.

The next morning Emma found him.

"You are going to have to work on the farm Greg has left!" she announced.

"Well that would be OK if you hadn't put in place an injunction to keep me off the farm." Mark said evenly. I've told you before Emma, you can't have it both ways, you threw me off the farm and now if you have a problem you will just have to deal with it. I warned you that Greg was unreliable!"

Emma said nothing, and it was not till later, that Mark realised that he had walked straight into a well-laid trap. In retaliation Emma took the dogs to live with her. Greg reappeared at work two days later.

Emma often had to work late at night or very early in the morning, partly due to ongoing staff problems and also because, in the day, she would waste a lot of time interfering with Mark's contact time with Charlie. Emma would come over to the cottage and make a lot of noise at unreasonable hours. After being woken one morning at 5 am by Emma noisily loading the washing machine and the radio in the kitchen blaring, Mark came downstairs.

"This is going to stop Emma, don't think I don't know what you are doing! It amounts to harassment and things can be done about that! And if you leave the back door open you are creating a security problem. If you don't stop I am going to lock the kitchen to utility room door at night. You can have access to the rest of the house during normal hours!"

"Ha! We'll see about that!" Emma shouted back at him

The next day Mark was woken by a policeman at 6.30am.

Mark spoke to the officer and explained about the harassment. The policeman was sympathetic and left after fifteen minutes saying he would take no action.

Mark sat down to write a long letter to the NDDVLO. The dogs, Paddy and Saffy spent most of the days now locked in the van and Charlie was often locked in the van for long periods too.

A week after the visit by the policeman Mark drove up to find Emma outside with the dogs. The organic farm inspector had arrived to do his inspection, Emma was distracted.

The dogs ran over, delighted to see Mark and as he opened the estate car's boot they both jumped in. Laughing at their delight at seeing him, Mark decided he would take them for a long walk.

Realising what was happening Emma left the organic farm inspector standing bemused as she tried to stop Mark.

Mark employed the central locking and began to chuckle to himself.

Yelling abuse that had the organic farm inspector open mouthed, Emma stood in front of the car to prevent Mark from leaving. The drive had a very slight gradient. After staring at each other, and after listening to her call him an evil bastard for the fifteenth time, Mark put the car gear into neutral and took his foot off the brake. The car rolled forward very slowly. Emma tried to stop it but was not strong enough, so she jumped onto the bonnet. Mark applied the brake and Emma slowly slid off the bonnet landing in an ungainly heap on the ground. Mark reversed and drove round her.

As he drove off Mark felt depression settle over him like a black cloud. God knows what she was going to make of this incident. And he was right to be concerned. Later, in the way that seemed to fool so many people Emma would recount the incident, every inch the plausible victim, claiming that Mark had driven the car at her and had run her over.

Chapter 17

Moving Out

After an incident when Emma had tampered with the outside door Mark was forced to dismantle the outer tumbler mechanism. Mark asked for the locating screws to be returned. Predictably she denied all knowledge. She later claimed in her statement that Mark had instigated a double bluff, claiming that he had placed the screws in the yoghurt building so that he could claim she was harassing him. Emma certainly displayed an amazing imagination. She told Mark he could not see Charlie anymore. So Mark retaliated by saying she could not come into the house anymore. Mark kicked himself again, as he realised that he had fallen into another of Emma's traps! In his constant and supreme efforts, despite everything, to keep on an even keel, he had missed the obvious. Emma's newest ultimatum meant Mark would not be able to see Charlie on his birthday or on father's day.

In June there was an ancillary relief hearing, the final directions hearing. The judge ordered certain information to be ready for the final hearing. On that day, there was also a child matters hearing, back to back. The judge ordered CAFCASS to investigate the allegations Mark had made of Emma's behaviour and treatment of Charlie and to look into the emotional abuse.

Mark held his breath, barely able to believe what he had wanted for so long was being acted on. But his happiness was short lived. Emma's barrister suddenly announced that they wanted an emergency hearing to have Mark evicted from the cottage. The judge also ordered a new contact order. Mark's barrister was concerned that Emma would provoke Mark to violence as her harassment continued. He took Mark aside

"Listen we are seeing a little light at the end of the tunnel, but I am warning you, that any violence will destroy your case at a stroke."

Mark nodded.

Mark's legal team were told that the emergency hearing would be in four days time. When Mark got home he packed his bags and went to stay with Tony and Tilly.

They welcomed him with open arms. Tony, despite Mark's tearful protestations, gave him £5,000 to start his legal fight. Mark knew that he really had no option.

Mark took the naïve view that as he was paying large amounts of money for the advice, it must be good. But Andreas Sims had never dealt with an opponent of Emma's ruthlessness. He often reassured Mark that Emma would not be able, in law and according to the edicts of the court to do various things. But Emma paid little heed to procedures, deadlines or edicts and simply refused to answer questions. Regularly Marks' legal team would be handed important documents as they arrived at court, instead of the customary days before, to allow time for study

Emma changed her solicitor many times. Mark liked to think the more ethical amongst them would not go along with her tactics. Mark knew that at least one of them had refused to act anymore until they got paid.

The emergency hearing was a disaster. Emma gave evidence first, then Mark, then Greg. The judge was a very pompous man. He upbraided anyone who pronounced words like harassment in the American way. To his credit he did not like waffle but Mark's heart sank as his barrister lost the plot twice while he was cross-examining Emma and Greg. Bizarrely for a barrister he was a very poor speaker and waffled a lot and he plainly irritated the judge.

Later the judge cracked a joke in poor taste, something about a baby bouncing down some concrete steps and there were muted sycophantic titters around the court. Mark's barrister proceeded to criticise the judge for his poor joke, and Mark cringed, as the man would not let it go, digging a bigger and bigger hole for himself.

Eventually the judge summed up. He started by saying that he had to make a decision, but he did not know which story to believe, Emma's or Mark's.

He eventually decided to believe Emma for a list of reasons, largely it seemed because Greg backed up many of her stories, as a witness. One example was that Greg said he had witnessed Mark deliberately run over Emma with the car. He said he was in the barn dealing with the goats over 200 yards away. Apparently he had seen Mark cutting electric fencing, leaving gates open and interfering with the milking parlour. On top of that he claimed that Mark had harassed the staff.

Exhausted from the fight, Mark discussed the future with Emma and they decided the best option was to sell everything and split the proceeds.

Emma's idea of a split was 90:10, while Mark's was 50:50. On that basis Mark said he would write to various farmers that he thought would be interested in buying some of the rare breed stock. Mark gave Emma a copy of the letters. These were produced in court as evidence of Mark trying to sell the stock behind her back.

The organic status of the farm and business was under the Organic Farmer's and Grower's Scheme. As Mark had started as a sole trader years previously, the license had remained in his name. Over the years his business as a sole trader had evolved into a partnership and then a company. When Mark raised the point with Emma that the farm had been in breach of many of the organic regulations since her coup, she told Mark she did not care.

Mark wrote to OF&G to say that he no longer had any control of the management of the farm or business and was therefore not responsible for it's current problems. He wanted the license put in the company name! Naturally they wrote to Emma to clarify this. Mark had strong environmental and "green issue" views and was determined to safeguard his reputation in the industry and distance himself from any liability for accusations of fraud. When the annual inspection came round many lapses in the regulations were found. All of this was presented as evidence that Mark wanted to destroy the business. The judge ruled that Mark had interfered with the business. As Mark had been arrested for assault and had admitted locking Emma out of the house, Mark was found to be guilty of harassing Emma. None of her behaviour was deemed relevant. The judge ordered Mark to sell his share of the company to Emma for £1, ordered an exclusion zone of 250 yards around the farm from late in June, and Mark was to vacate the farmhouse from midday on the same date. Mark had three days.

The next few days were very difficult in the house. Emma was delighted with her triumph and gloated constantly.

"Ah what a pity Charlie Daddy's is going to have to move out, boo hoo!" she balled her fists and rubbed her eyes.

Mark walked away.

Later as he brought the dogs in from their walk she accosted him.

"Oh and don't think that you are going to get way with running me over with the car!"

"Emma, for God's sake, we're not in court now, you can drop the act. You know very well that I did not and would not ever run you over."

"You liar!" she shouted.

"Look Emma you do what you want, in fact, I would welcome it. There are a couple of real witnesses, and Greg would be torn apart by a good barrister. Still want to pursue it?" Mark stared at her. "My barrister did not show up the common phrases in Greg and your own testimony although it was obvious that Greg was coached in his evidence, but reopening the subject will give him the chance to do that." Emma stared back at him her face venomous.

"So be my guest because I know he would welcome the chance to point that out. Who knows you might both be found guilty of perjury. After all with this particular case, you can't hide behind your so-called maternal status, this has nothing to do with Charlie. I wonder if the court will be so easy on you without him to hide behind?"

Emma stormed off and Mark felt a small thrill of triumph.

On the 22nd Mark took a carload of possessions up to Tony and Tilly's house. Emma was furious that Mark had taken the new fridge-freezer that he had paid for. On the last day Mark started loading up his belongings at 10.30am, but true to form Emma argued about most things and as fast as Mark loaded things, she unloaded them.

In her usual style Emma called the police.

When the police came, Emma found that her plan had backfired. Mark was able to load in peace. But then the officers had to respond to an emergency call. Emma promptly started unloading things again. She parked her van across the drive so that Mark could not leave by the midday deadline. Mark rang the police to say that he was unable to leave. After three phone calls they sent a car, and Mark eventually left the farm just after 1pm.

The following day Mark drove back down to the farm to have contact with Charlie. (The exclusion zone was lifted for contact). When Mark arrived there was no one at the farm. Mark waited an hour, before Emma turned up.

"Oh I wondered what the bad smell was, I thought you must be somewhere in the vicinity" she said holding Charlie back from Mark as the child excitedly held his arms out to his father.

"Cut it out Emma, I'm just here to see Charlie. I'm not interested in a slanging match, and nor should you be in front of the child."

"So where are you taking Charlie today? Going round to see your fancy piece are you?"

"I'm not going anywhere for the moment, I've got a puncture." Mark said and Emma threw back her head and laughed.

"Oh dear oh dear, it just looks like nothing is going your way, doesn't it?" Emma walked away Charlie on her hip, laughing as though she had heard the funniest joke she had ever heard.

Mark took Charlie back to Tony and Tilly's and had a lovely time as the little lad showed genuine delight at seeing his friends who always spoiled him rotten. Tilly was careful though, to make sure that she and Tony did not monopolise the boy, although both found it difficult, since he was so enchanting. Mark could see the difference in his son, away from the terrible atmosphere between his parents. He never whined and beamed happily all the time when he was with Mark away from the farm. Mark felt his heart break a bit more.

When Mark returned with Charlie, Emma was putting boxes of his belongings down the side of the drive. She said the boxes would stay there till Mark picked them up. It started to rain. Mark drove off to collect his puncture repair before the tyre company closed, and then drove back and parked on the ridge road that overlooked the farm. The boxes were still on the drive getting wet. Mark rang the police but, as he knew they would, they said it was not a matter for them to deal with.

As summer blazed, contact was much improved in July. It had been changed to Wednesdays and Saturdays. Mark speculated on why Emma had loosened her strangle hold. It was possibly because Emma felt she had won a great victory, in getting him out of the farm or simply because contact was now away from the farm. But it was still far from ideal. Whenever Mark returned with Charlie, he was pulled unceremoniously from the car before Mark could get out to hug him and say goodbye. Mark had to lock all doors and so that Charlie could climb through to the front to have a hug and a kiss before Mark gave him back to his mother.

He and Tilly and Tony sat up late into the night talking about the legal struggle that he was having. After one particular discussion Mark fired his legal team and spent a long time choosing a new one. Eventually Mark hired a well-known firm from Marlborough. Mark was very impressed with his new solicitor Christine Eaves. He was sorry to say goodbye to Andreas but thought that he saw a look of relief in the man's eyes. He knew he was out of his depth. The new firm was unusual in that it did not waste money on flashy premises.

With contact on Wednesdays and Saturdays Mark found it difficult to get a full time job and signed on for Job Seekers Allowance. Mark eventually ended up with two part-time jobs. No sooner had Mark moved out of the family home, than Emma applied to the CSA to chase him for money. The irony was that Mark should have been getting money from his company, the farm, but Emma refused to pay him anything; so she had it anyway!

Mark's new legal team were perplexed and disappointed at the advice and defence strategy Mark had been given by the initial legal team. The general advice was that although Mark had been knocked down by the injunction fiasco, he was not out. It was deemed a waste of time to appeal the judgement, as it would still boil down to Emma's word against Mark's. With regard to her erratic and confrontational behaviour the strategy thought most appropriate in the long run was to give her enough rope to hang herself.

And then in August Emma's mother died.

Mark could feel nothing but relief that the woman would be able to influence his son no more. She had done enough damage to her own daughter, and it had ripped his heart out every time he knew that she had care of Charlie.

The contact times with Charlie continued to be good in July, August and September. Father and son went on all kinds of outings, and spent time with Mark's sister Laurie as well as happy hours on a blanket in Tilly and Tony's back garden. They had bought a swing and slide set for Charlie and when it was hot, they would blow up a little paddling pool for the boy to splash around in. The main problem was picking Charlie up and giving him back. Emma was so vicious and difficult that it obviously upset Charlie. Often he would arrive to find no-one at home, so after waiting an hour Mark would drive home again. Emma always found fault with something. Usually it was the car seat, at other times it would be over some sandals Mark had bought Charlie to wear in the hot weather. Emma was unfailingly unpleasant, which upset Charlie. A few times Mark had to ring the police in front of her to get her to behave reasonably. Mark would then cancel the police car before it arrived.

Emma delayed divulging the contents of Gladys' will. It eventually transpired that the will was changed three days before she died in favour of Charlie, not Emma. The lack of information around the will made the preparation for the final financial hearing impossible so it was delayed till mid December and Emma was ordered to provide the outstanding information. Emma had by now formally changed her position and declared that she wanted the farm and business sold and the proceeds split 60:40. She had started from the position that she wanted almost everything. Now that Charlie was to inherit at least £250,000, she could hardly claim she needed everything to care for him.

They were also gearing up for a final hearing for chid matters and contact. Mark's solicitor said he had never seen or heard of a statement like that produced by Emma about cruelty to animals. Emma was also going for an interim hearing to reduce his contact time. She claimed that Charlie was showing disturbing behaviour. Charlie was allegedly masturbating and spreading excreta around the house. He would be in a manic state after contact. The court hearing was set for September.

In the run up to the hearing contact was denied because Charlie had a cold. One contact was halved but Mark saw no sign that Charlie had a cold. Mark saw very little of his son in September. At the court there were 8 other cases before the judge that day. They went before the judge last thing before lunch and then back after lunch for a little more than the half hour pencilled in for the case. The judge would not consider Mark having overnight contact with Charlie. Mark suggested that Emma and Charlie move into Charlie's inherited house, two miles from the farm. Mark would move back into the farmhouse to make contact easier. Emma vetoed this. The judge allowed Emma to swap the Saturday contact with Friday so she could have weekends with Charlie, unless or until Mark had a job that conflicted. He ordered psychological assessments of Emma and Mark, and CAFCASS to report on contact for a final hearing in December. A new CAFCASS officer, John Liddle, was assigned to Charlie's case. In early October he came to visit Mark at Tony and Tilly's house, to interview Mark and see where Charlie would be staying.

Mark received a summons from the local council for council tax arrears. Emma had not forwarded the bill. She had also not paid his National insurance as a company employee for over a year.

In preparation for the final hearing Mark talked to Dot, the farm's best and most experienced dairy worker who had worked in the processing room from before Charlie was born. She had witnessed Emma's unreasonable behaviour and how she treated Charlie in the yoghurt room, and Emma's efforts to keep Charlie away from Mark. She was prepared to be a witness for Mark and wrote a statement for the court. Mark also went to see Greg's previous employer. When Mark asked her if Mark could speak to her about Greg, her first exclamation was "what that bloody thief?". She said he was a good stockman, but when the work tailed off in the autumn he would leave the gates open so he would have to spend extra time rounding the sheep up. He was paid by the hour. After a while he kept threatening to leave. Also he had claimed to have been in jail for GBH. When she finally sacked him, she said lots of equipment from around the farm went missing. Dot also told of Greg bragging that he had been in prison for violence. He was to deny all these claims in court. Mark discovered that his hypnotherapist's suggestion that he was a fantasist had turned out to be true. Mark also went to see his MP, to discuss his problems with the legal system. But typically, perhaps, he was dismissive of any suggestion of bias in the courts or CAFCASS.

Towards the end of October Emma rang to tell Mark that Charlie had the flu and therefore would not be available for contact for at least a week. She said Charlie had not gone to nursery. Emma then changed her solicitors again making communications difficult and delayed.

The new solicitors claimed that until her public funding certificate was transferred to them they did not get paid, so they would not act for her.

Mark started work as a night porter at a local Health and Fitness Spa on Sunday and Monday nights. Mark also started work for a tree nursery as a part-time tractor driver. Mark told Emma that he would have to see Charlie on Saturdays and Wednesdays, because he now worked on Fridays. The contact order had allowed for this.

"Oh yes? How do I know you have a job? Don't think I was born yesterday Mark? I want to see some proof. This is so typical of you to try to get one over on me!"

She refused to allow Mark to see or talk to Charlie. Mark went round to Charlie's GP's surgery and asked for confirmation that Charlie had been seen and diagnosed with flu. The practise manager rang Mark later to say that she had contacted social services who had advised the surgery that they could not give out that information.

Mark was livid. This was the second time social services had advised against his legal rights as a parent. Mark had to get his solicitor to write to the surgery at his own expense to clarify his parental rights.

Mark saw Charlie in the middle of November for the first time in ages. A neighbour was collecting the dogs to take them on a walk when Mark arrived so Emma was, for once, civilised keeping up a façade for the neighbour. Mark was even allowed to play with Paddy and Saffy briefly as the animals threw themselves at him, clearly delighted to see him again. Normally they were locked away so Mark could not see them on contact days.

When Charlie appeared he let out an almighty yell of delight. "Daddy!" as he saw Mark and ran over to Mark as fast as his little legs could carry him to jump into his arms. Emma asked if Charlie could be returned early so he could rest before going to the Carnival in the evening. Mark agreed.

"I have only seen Charlie twice since October!" Mark said that evening as he and Tony sat in front of the fire in Tony's cottage. "I'm supposed to see him twice a week, not twice in two months!"

"Well, for a lot of that time Emma has said that Charlie was too ill to see you and he has not gone to the nursery. Don't get too paranoid mate!" Tony said.

Later that day a letter arrived from Mark's solicitor reporting that the GP's surgery had been very open and helpful. In the doctor's notes was a line saying that Charlie was not too ill to see his father.

Mark handed the letter wordlessly to Tony.

"Better get this to the court" Tony said.

Mark visited the nursery and the owner checked the attendance diary and wrote to confirm that Charlie had attended for all the period that Emma had claimed that Charlie had been too ill to go to nursery.

Mark produced his work contract letters for Emma, to prove he had a job on Fridays, but she refused to see them. She said Mark had to send them to her solicitors. Mark told her that it was ridiculous to waste £30 sending the letters via his solicitor. Emma slammed the back door in his face. Mark had to wait forty minutes before she produced Charlie for contact. Later that afternoon Mr Liddle came to observe Charlie and Mark at Tony and Tilly's. Emma had demanded that Mark return Charlie before it got dark because it was cold. Mark refused to shorten his contact time. It became very difficult in the winter months to find good warm places for contact other than Tony and Tilly's Many venues close for the winter. Often the weather was wet and windy, but they managed. Tony and Tilly loved having Charlie around.

After one contact, Emma rang to demand what Charlie had eaten that day. Emma claimed that Charlie had been violently ill all night. Mark's suspicion was that it was an invention, an attempt to prove that Mark could not be trusted to look after Charlie. This and other uncorroborated nights of sickness following contact were to form the basis of allegations of neglect brought by Emma in court.

On the next contact date Mark arrived very early and sat for a while looking down at the farm from the ridge road. There was smoke rising from the chimney in the house and the van was parked outside. Mark went into town to get a cup of tea. Mark turned up at the farm on time but there was no one around. Mark waited an hour and then, giving up, he was just driving out the entrance when Emma drove up in the van. Mark turned the car round and drove back up the drive behind her.

Leaping out of the van, Emma rushed over to the back door to unlock it and then ran back to Charlie's door of the van. Mark got out of his car and locked it as it had a lot of his legal papers inside. Mark went round to Charlie's side of the van. Emma had Charlie's door open. She backed up and turned to Mark.

"What are you doing here?" she asked hand's on hips.

"I've come for my court ordered contact", Mark said evenly.

"Well you can't see Charlie, nothing had been sorted!"

"There is nothing to sort! I've shown you my work contract letters showing that I work on Fridays. As prescribed by the court, I will now see Charlie on Saturdays!"

As he spoke, Mark got up close to Charlie's door and squeezed between Emma and Charlie.

"Get away from him!" Emma shrieked pulling on Mark's arm.

Mark was talking to Charlie and trying to unbuckle his seat belt. Emma started yelling and pounding her fists on his back. Charlie started to cry.

"Emma, for God's sake stop it, can't you see you are upsetting Charlie?" Emma kept pushing, pulling and hitting Mark. Mark pushed her backwards. Behind her was a pile of scalpings. She lost her footing and stumbled into the corner wall of the house, with her right hand out to balance herself and then fell over onto the wheely bin. Mark had undone the buckle on Charlie's seat belt and was trying to calm him, but Mark could not free him from all the seat belts.

Emma was back on her feet and now she was really angry. She pummelled Mark's back and then grabbed his arm and sleeve to pull him away from Charlie.

Mark felt dismayed as he and Emma tussled back and forth getting more heated, calling each other names.

"Emma I am going to call the police if you don't stop!" He managed to dial 999 as Emma tried to grab the phone out of his hand. When Mark got through Emma started to yell and scream for the police to come and save her son. It was difficult to hear anything with Emma yelling all the time. Mark told her to wait for the police to come. But Emma kept up her assault on Mark trying to pull him away.

"Emma, for God's sake stop this! I will hit you hard and it will hurt, so pull yourself together and calm down, for Charlie's sake!"

She ignored his threat. Mark closed Charlie's door. While Emma was pulling Mark hard, Mark turned and stepped towards her so she lost her balance. She stumbled over the pile of scalpings again. She put her right hand out to break her fall. She fell forward and her left hand skidded over the scalpings.

She got up and with a look of pure hatred she calmly said

"Mark, I am going to get an order to have you locked up and you are not going to be able to come near me and when this is over you are never going to see Charlie again".

She tried to get Charlie's door open but Mark blocked her. She then tried to open the van's sliding door to get to Charlie from the inside. Mark blocked her.

The dogs, Paddy and Saffy were in the back of the van were barking furiously. Emma said that they needed to be let out. Mark told her to open the rear doors.

Mark was breathing hard.

"You are completely mental Mark, you have completely lost the plot and you are going to be very sorry!"

"Emma you have to realise that you are sick and you need treatment, can't you see that you are just like your mother, who really was sick and evil. Don't you remember the misery she caused you? Please get help for Charlie's sake!"

"Lies, lies lies, that's all you can ever speak, isn't it Mark?" Emma responded.

"A liar am I? Well give me some examples!"

For a moment she was silent but in the event Emma did not come up with even one example.

"Look Mark you're not Charlie's father, so what is the big fuss about? Just leave us alone!"

"I am as much his father as you are his mother!" Mark said

"Oh is that so? Don't think that I don't know about the walker that you bored to death with your drivel and told that Charlie was not your son!"

Mark shook his head.

Charlie had quietened down and was sucking his thumb, looking at Mark. Eventually Emma and Mark faced off three feet apart leaning against the van.

The police arrived. Emma immediately started to cry and sob that they must save her son from Mark. A young policeman, took Emma inside the house. The sergeant spoke to Mark. Mark took Charlie out of the van and cuddled him giving the policeman a brief account of events. The sergeant suggested he and Mark went into the house. Mark stayed in the utility room with Charlie. He fetched the contact orders and two pay slips to prove what he was saying.

Over the police radio the officers got confirmation of the previous contact order. Mark was left with Charlie for a while and they hugged and laughed together; the little boy seeming to have got over the trauma. Then the police returned.

"Mr. Richards, we are duty bound to arrest you due to your wife's demonstrated injury to her hand.

For the second time, Mark found himself in a police cell.

Chapter 18

Despair

After being processed Mark was put in a cell at about midday. At 3.10pm the duty solicitor arrived. Mark was interviewed on tape with the solicitor present.

"Did you attack your wife?"

"No."

"How did she get her injury Mr. Richards?"

"She fell onto some scalpings, and grazed her hand."

"Did she fall or did you push her?"

"We scuffled."

"Scuffled? How tall are you Mr. Richards?"

"Six foot three"

"Your wife?"

"Five foot six."

"Would you say she was a big woman?"

"No."

"So in a scuffle you were obviously going to get the better of her."

"Yes, but, look I have never been violent toward my wife!"

And so the torture continued and Mark gave way to tears out of sheer frustration at the law. Mark then had his fingerprints taken, was charged with common assault and told to attend the Magistrate's court in Newbury. Mark drove to Tony and Tilly's house, emotionally exhausted. When he arrived there was no one in. He drove the car into the garage that he had been tidying up for Tony and Tilly and in which a lot of his things were stored. He had been going through them and sorting out what he wanted and what needed to be thrown away. His exit from the farm had allowed him no time to sort through things properly.

Mark sat staring at the dusty garage wall. He wondered why he had kept the old rusty watering can with the hole in it that stood on a shelf he had been meaning to fix. He smiled to himself. What did it matter? What did any of it matter? He looked at the unopened pack of cigarettes on the dashboard. He had given up many years ago but had thought that just once more he would like to savour that 'just opened pack smell', light one of the fragrant cigarettes and inhale the acrid fumes. But he knew that after so long the first drag would make him cough, and would probably taste rank. He hesitated, his hand half way towards the pack before he dropped it back into his lap again. Tears were coming now, streaming down his face and making his nose run. His brain was working overtime. Almost as though it knew what was coming. He thought about his childhood, happy innocent days. He thought of the photo he still had of his 5-year old self-standing with bruised knees in short trousers, his hand being held by someone out of the picture. His face was unlined, his gap toothed smile wide. The tears were coming faster now as he thought about another little boy whose hand he should have been holding, on his first day at school. The pain of his loss was like a heavy weight on his chest and he wondered if he was having a heart attack. He smiled through his tears. What did it matter? He got out of the car and checked the hosepipe he had connected to the exhaust. It was in place, passed through the passenger side window, wound up so that it held the pipe in place but was not squeezed tight enough to cut off the fumes. He looked at the pack of cigarettes again and opened them, breathing the fresh smell of tobacco in. But he did not light up. Instead he held a small tee shirt with Thomas the Tank Engine on the front it to his face smelling the familiar child smell and as he did so, he turned the key in the ignition.

It was some time later that he heard the banging on the door of the garage and then through half closed eyes saw Tilly's face, her hand over her mouth at his window.

Mark realised that he would have to lock the driver's door, to stop her getting it open but he could not raise his arm. Tilly opened it and he tumbled out of the car onto the garage floor. She reached in and turned off the ignition, dropping down beside him.

Tilly was pulling at him, trying to get him to stand up and he half crawled out of the garage with her, until they fell exhausted on the grass outside the garage.

For a time, Tilly said nothing; she just cradled his head on her lap in a soft rain that mingled with her tears falling on his face. He could taste the salt in them and he could see the sky and he realised that for the first time in a long time he was happy, happy to be alive. He wondered if it was the effect of the fumes, but he knew it was more than that. He had wanted to die, that was true but now he knew that he wanted to live more! The thought of never seeing Charlie again was too horrible to contemplate. In his hand he still had the Thomas the Tank Engine tee shirt and he held it to his face.

"I'm so sorry Tilly, I'm OK now!" Mark said struggling to his feet and holding out his hand to Tilly. Supporting each other they walked into the house.

"Oh God Mark, I can't believe that you would try to . . . ."

"I'm sorry, Tilly, I really am It was stupid and heartless and selfish and all the things that this has turned me into!" But it had taught Mark one thing, he very much wanted to be alive! Somehow in the depths of his despair he felt strength returning to the parts of his heart that he had thought damaged and shrivelled for ever, all he had to do was hold up his love for Charlie high, like an Olympic torch bearer, and let that lead him forward.

Tilly looked at him doubtfully but something in his eyes must have convinced her. She drew herself up and squared her shoulders.

"Right then, we won't say anything more about this. I won't even mention it to Tony."

"Where is he?"

"He went down to the police station, he was not sure if you had your car.

"I didn't but they gave me a lift back to the farm to collect it."

"Did you see Emma?"

Mark shook his head. "I just took the car and came back here."

Tilly opened her arms and Mark and she stood hugging each other. When they finally let go, Mark kissed Tilly on the cheek.

"I should never have let you go!" he said.

"Ancient history!" she laughed shakily and put the kettle on.

Mark appeared at the Magistrate's court. After giving his name, address and date of birth in the dock, Mark entered a plea of not guilty. Bail was to be kept. One of the policemen was to be a witness for Emma. They would have to wait hours for dates to be agreed with him for a trial. Before Mark left he asked the Magistrate to clarify contact. Mark felt himself go cold as the magistrate said in clipped tones that there would be none till the Family Court had addressed the matter.

The contact and child matters hearing had already been booked to be followed by the final finance hearing on in December. The trial in the Magistrates court was set for January.

Seizing what she saw as a golden opportunity, Emma tried to postpone the contact hearing until after the magistrate's court date. There was a pre-trial review hearing on the 10th December before a district judge who in an almost comic twist had a terrible stammer. He agreed that the contact issue needed d d d discussing and ordered the contact hearing to go ahead. Mr. Liddle, after Mark's arrest and without talking to Mark, had written to the court asking for the hearing to be postponed and added that his report was now out of date following the arrest. It seemed Mark was to be judged guilty of assault even before his trial. It was the first time Mark had seen Emma's new solicitor, Ms Alice Lyons who was extremely prickly and aggressive. Over the years ahead Mark's barrister and other solicitors would remark that she was an extension of Emma. She invariably refused to talk in a civilised way and often broke the rules and procedures for document presentation at court. Opposing solicitors often get together to try to find ways forward and to try to solve problems: not Ms Lyons!

Mark's legal team complained that she was always obstructive. Often Mark would laugh a wry laugh and say that Emma had finally found someone like her, who would do her bidding. In fact one of Mark's solicitors got so frustrated with her attitude that he investigated her legal background. With great indignation he claimed she was not even a fully qualified solicitor!

At the next hearing they were before Judge Steven Brown again. After heated argument contact was reinstated but Mark was not allowed to go to the farm for exchange. Apparently Emma was too frightened. It was agreed that they use the nursery school for exchange. John Liddle did not appear, but he was ordered to produce another report by April and organise the psychologist Lesley Norman to assess Mark, Emma and Charlie and also report by April.

Mark called round to see the farm mechanic, Ryan Morris, who over the years Mark had come to consider as a friend. One of Emma's statements had quoted him as saying something unpleasant about Charlie and Mark together. When Mark showed him the statement Ryan was angry and said it was not true, and that he had never discussed Mark and Charlie with Emma. The day before the final finance hearing Emma came up with a series of last minute offers for settlement. Mark ignored them; he wanted the judge to decide.

Mark's solicitor came to the final hearing with an ancillary relief barrister. He had always said there was no point in going with his child matters barrister as it was just duplicating costs unnecessarily. He actually did a lot of the drafting of the final agreement and gave lots of good advice on the day during the negotiations. Mark arrived at court and the negotiations started.

If a negotiated settlement can be made, then it goes before the judge to rubber stamp it. If no agreement is reached the judge imposes what he thinks is fair. Just previous to the hearing Emma had changed her position. She now demanded she be allowed to keep the farm and business to provide her with an income. Mark was sure she did not want to farm, and pointed out that the processing business could be operated from an industrial estate locally. The farm had been given a ridiculously low value in his opinion. A few years before the separation the new yoghurt building had been erected at a cost of £70,000. It had been carefully designed to allow for conversion into two holiday cottages at any time in the future that Mark and Emma decided to retire from the dairy business. The valuer had refused to put a value on it. Later Emma was able to rent this 'valueless building' out for £150 per week! Stupidly Mark had agreed to the initial valuation as the arguments over it had already accrued a bill with the solicitors for over a thousand pounds. As the sale of the farm had been agreed Mark thought the valuation was fairly academic. Now Emma had changed her demands and once again Mark had been outsmarted.

Mark's barrister spoke to the usher to tell him that no useful negotiation had been forthcoming; they were ready to go before the judge. Miraculously the opposition's offers improved from a start point of £80,000 for Mark and maintenance for Emma to £195,000 with a clean break settlement. A clean break settlement meant Mark was not liable to pay any maintenance for Emma afterwards. Mark's bottom line was 49% of the valued assets (less a range of costs) at £200,000. Eventually Mark was able to present this in a way that Emma agreed to. They moved on to possessions. Emma refused to relinquish many of the items on his list. Mark also refused to budge, to the point where his own barrister was pleading with Mark to give way as the whole agreement was in danger of coming adrift.

But Mark could not let go, not this time! Mark stuck to his guns, and when the usher informed them that the judge had dealt with the other cases before him and now wanted to hear their case, Emma agreed to sign.

It took some time to draft the agreement before the judge signed it off. Mark simply asked for all his possessions before the marriage to be returned and one painting by a relative that had been given to them as a wedding present. Mark made no claim on any of the other wedding presents or any of Emma's possessions left to her by her father. There were a few small items, things that they had bought together that Mark wanted to keep, along with all the birthday presents given to him by Emma during the marriage. Unfortunately Mark was never to see most of them.

Although he had bought them, Mark did not ask for the dogs, as he did not want them split up. Sadly when the order was transcribed by the court stenographer the first sentence was omitted. It now read that Mark was to receive the items to include . . . . . . then the list. Mark's team did not spot the error until they tried to enforce the order. Mark had no idea how difficult enforcing it would turn out to be. A lot of effort had been put into the wording of the settlement so that Emma could not wriggle out of it, especially the default arrangements for the financial settlement.

Mark had contact the following Tuesday. Mark picked Charlie up from the nursery and father and son went to

Farmland, a play farm for young children and one of the few venues still open in the winter. As they walked around the farm Mark led Charlie into one of the lambing sheds. The farmer came in and asked if any children wanted to help him feed the lambs with a bottle of milk. Far from shouting "me me!" as the other children were doing Charlie looked uneasy and worried and whispered.

"He's a man!"

"Yes, he is, what do you mean, what's wrong?" Mark asked.

"I don't like men!" Charlie whispered, his eyes wide.

"Well Daddy's a man, don't you like daddy?"

"Yes" Charlie nodded.

"Did mummy tell you that she did not like men?"

Charlie nodded.

"You know Charlie, one day you will grow up to be a man."

Charlie looked at him, naked fear in his eyes.

Mark's heart broke.

Over the Christmas holiday Emma took Charlie to stay with her cousin Jane Taylor. Mark had two contacts, both after Christmas. Mark picked up Charlie from the Taylor's' house and went back to his aunt and uncle's house where is mother joined them. This was really the first time since he had been a baby that Charlie had mixed with any of his family except Mark's sister Laurie. Charlie met his cousin Stevie and they played together happily.

Mark's mother wept for most of the visit, but Charlie let her cuddle him. The day was a great success and Charlie had a lot of fun, letting his guard down and laughing and playing with his cousin. Charlie slept all the way on the two hour drive back to the Taylor's house.

As the nursery was closed on Saturdays various ideas were put forward for contact exchange including paying a private child minder. After Emma had interviewed them, they all mysteriously changed their minds and withdrew their offers. One reported to Mark's solicitor that she felt like she had been threatened by Emma. The only option that Emma would agree to was to use a contact centre. Under the rules of the contact centres Mark was not allowed to leave with Charlie. The centre had been told by Emma's solicitor that Mark was a danger to Charlie.

It was all very cloak and dagger. Mark arrived and waited. Emma arrived by a different entrance and Charlie was brought through to him. Emma then remained on the property in her van. There were four volunteers of retirement age that supervised the centre. There were other dads with young children in the same room. Mark was not left in peace with Charlie. Mark became very irritated with the constant chivvying by the volunteers to use the toys and equipment provided. Mark took Charlie outside to kick a football around. Mark had to leave the door open so they could watch him playing with Charlie! They made Mark feel like a criminal. Charlie was very distracted and subdued with all the strangers around. He was not at ease and clung to Mark's legs. Then Charlie spotted Emma in the van outside and that proved a further distraction. Emma refused to leave, waving and blowing kisses to Charlie as she stood leaning up against the van.

"I'll be taking you home soon darling! Don't worry, mummy's here!"

Emma refused to leave saying that she needed to be there for Charlie's safety. At one point Mark went to get Charlie's bouncy ball from his car and was told that he would have to be escorted!. Mark got more and more frustrated and angry at what was happening to Charlie and his contact time with his son. Mark was also angry that he could not take Charlie to his father's 90th birthday party the next day. There was a gathering of many relatives, including Mark's eldest brother over from America.

The day after that, Mark appeared at Reading Magistrate's Court to answer the assault charge. He was introduced to a young friendly counsel, who disappeared to discuss the case with the Crown Prosecutor. He opined that the case should have been dealt with in the civil courts. He also suggested that rather than go to trial, Mark should be bound over to keep the peace. His counsel took Mark to one side to explain this. The prosecutor took a long time to persuade Emma not to go to trial. There was another trial being heard before their case. Eventually Emma agreed.

Mark was ushered into the dock and the panel of three magistrates came in. The chairman was his retired organic farming mentor. When he saw Mark he left the room immediately. There was much debate and it was explained to Mark that he could not sit in judgement in the case, as he knew Mark.

Mark was transferred to court number two and stood in the dock as the lady magistrate read out and explained what was entailed in being bound over to keep the peace. She then dismissed the case. Bail conditions were lifted and if Mark kept the peace there would be no conviction.

Mark went to say goodbye to his counsel. The Crown Prosecutor walked past them and came over to thank Mark for his honest statement and remarked that he was irritated that the matter had come to court, and that he considered it a waste of everyone's time. They shook hands and Mark left. Mark drove home in time for his night shift at the local spa hotel.

Mark saw Charlie the next Wednesday, picking him up at the nursery. When he saw Mark, he shouted to everyone "there's daddy". In Charlie's haste to get to Mark he knocked several children over. Mark could not hide his delight at his son's excitement to see him as he helped to get the children back on their feet.

"Well, that's a happy young fellow if ever I saw one!" the nursery owner said. "He's been telling us all morning since he was dropped off by his mummy that he was going to see his daddy! It is a joy to see Charlie so happy!"

Mark blinked away the tears in his eyes. When Mark returned Charlie to the nursery later that afternoon, he left with tears in his eyes. He had forgotten what it was like to be carefree. He was exhausted from living on his emotions, but a day like this with Charlie so obviously delighted to see him made it all worth while. Mark could only see Charlie on Wednesdays as he refused to use the contact centre. This was partly because Emma insisted on remaining there during contact; partly because it gave entirely the wrong message to Charlie; that daddy was not to be trusted or was dangerous and could not be left with Charlie on his own; and because his barrister was worried it would give a subliminal message to the judge that Mark was a danger to Charlie.

In February Emma started sending Charlie off for his contact with a packed lunch. It was another subtle antagonism, she was not present at handovers so was unable to say unpleasant things or attempt to wind Mark up. Father and son started to go to London on the train more in the winter and went to London zoo several times.

Mark drove down to Devon for his appointment for the court ordered psychological assessment. Mark filled in a long questionnaire and some multiple-choice questions. The assessment was three hours long. It seemed to dwell on his parenting skills and issues about anger. In her report, the psychologist, Lesley Norman wrote that his old fashioned attitudes to parenting did not sit well with modern parenting methods. Although, she wrote, she thought that Mark did not have a problem with anger per se, she thought that he was angry. Her assessment of Emma was that she suffered from high a level of anxiety over Mark's involvement with Charlie and would benefit from some counselling. At the time Mark thought that the assessments gave such little insight that they were almost a waste of time. These assessments cost several thousands of pounds, a complete waste of money. Later assessments were far more in depth. A week later at Tilly and Tony's place the psychologist came to observe contact between Charlie and Mark. She declined to have lunch with us, but observed Charlie. She commented that Charlie was obviously enjoying himself. She said she had seen enough and left.

A few days later Mr Liddle came to see Mark, for an hour. Mark had finished a night shift a couple of hours earlier. He asked Mark about the Magistrate's decision. Emma had told him Mark had been found guilty!

Mark explained what had happened at the incident in November and the outcome of the court. Mark had the distinct impression that he had already made up his mind. A fortnight later Mr Liddle came to see him at Tony's house for about an hour to observe contact between Charlie and Mark. He then went to Emma's house immediately afterwards to observe Charlie's behaviour after contact with Mark. Presumably this was in response to Emma's claims that Charlie was so distressed by contact that his behaviour was extremely worrying. He later explained that children often learn to compartmentalise their experiences with each parent. If one parent questions the child about the other parent it is normal for them to clam up and refuse to talk. He observed this with Charlie, but did not find his behaviour unusual or a cause for concern.

When Mark picked up Charlie from the nursery on a warm spring day in April for their contact, the apple cheeked owner that Mark had come to like, told him that Charlie was being removed from the nursery. That meant that contact exchange could not continue at the nursery.

With the final two day hearing about Charlie in a fortnight, Mark had no choice but to accept the situation. He knew that this was Emma's reaction to seeing the evidence from the surgery and the nursery that would prove that she had lied. She was also threatening to change doctor's surgery.

The case went before the District Judge. Evidence from the experts in behaviour was heard and the judge decided that the thrust of Emma's argument, that Mark was a danger to Charlie because Mark was allegedly cruel to animals, was not admissible as neither expert would agree with Emma that there was any link between cruelty to animals and cruelty to children. Emma's whole argument was based on the premise that if a person was cruel to animals it was automatic that they would be cruel to children; information gleaned from some obscure American web site.

The judge ordered a recess for Emma's team to discuss whether they wanted to pursue the cruelty angle. When recalled they declined to pursue it.

Mark was questioned. The judge ended the session for the day. Emma's barrister, a woman, tried hard to get him angry. Bombarding Mark with questions so fast that he could not answer one before another was barked at him. Mark got flustered. He could not remember how to properly address Emma's barrister. Now the woman was almost shouting at him. Finally Mark raised his voice and said "listen lady, slow down".

The judge rebuked Mark for talking improperly to counsel although Mark's barrister thought it was hilarious and said Mark reminded him of a taxi driver getting on his high horse. But the interruption had allowed Mark breathing space and he apologised to the court. In fact the proceedings were not being held in the formal court, but rather in what appeared to be a large office. All parties sat along a line of tables facing the judge and the clerk.

A few times, when Mark got to the Circuit Court hearings were held in the old courtrooms. Only twice, over more than 50 hearings, were the barristers and judges wigged and gowned.

Emma gave evidence. Her barrister asked her only one question. Mark's barrister had a very laid back style. Because Emma rarely answered a question in a straightforward manner, he often asked the same question in anything up to five different ways. Sometimes he would have to ask the judge to order her to answer a question if she stonewalled him completely. At one point he asked Emma how important it was that Charlie saw her father.

Emma replied that seeing Mark was about as important as Charlie being able to play with his peer group at nursery. The judge was so shocked by this attitude that he referred at length to it in his summation. The judge gave his summation and judgement after lunch. During lunch both sides had to put forward proposals for contact. The judge took from both sets of proposals. He wanted exchange to take place at a contact centre, but no one was able to give details of any local opening times and availability.

This hearing was very important as previously none of the facts and problems had been properly investigated or discussed. The Judge ruled that there was absolutely no reason why there should be any restriction on contact and said that contact should be introduced slowly and expanded till in September Mark could have Charlie every other weekend from Friday 4.30pm till Sunday 4.30pm. There was not enough time to deal with the exchange arrangements, so he ordered the solicitors to sort something out within a week. He also said he would deal with the problems Mark was having getting hold of his possessions, by correspondence. Emma was refusing to allow Mark to go to the house to pick them up. The judge agreed with the expert psychologist in saying he thought Mark got angry at specific events, but did not have an anger problem. Likewise he thought Emma was over anxious and would benefit from some treatment. He disagreed with Emma's assertion that Mark was a danger to Charlie. He spoke at length about his decision to make a "no residency order". He explained that as Charlie was not living with Mark for any of the time he could not grant a shared residency order. Then as Mark tried to keep the smile from his face the Judge specifically refused to grant Emma residency criticising her refusal to observe Mark's parental right to be involved in the big decisions in Charlie's life, such as the choice of nursery. He said that he had the feeling that Emma may be encouraged in her incorrect attitude if he were to grant her residency.

The judge had ruled on the first day that there would be no time for witnesses to speak; so they were all sent home.

There was no contact for nearly a month after the hearing. Emma vetoed all the child minder options. None of the contact centres were reliably open.

A first instalment of £100,000 was forwarded from Emma's solicitors. Emma sold all the stock, both live and dead and all the farm buildings with some of the land. (Deadstock was farm machinery and equipment, not piles of dead goats!) This was surprising, as only a few months before in court she had maintained she needed the farm and business to provide her with an income!

Mark had already bent over backwards to extend Emma's payment deadline, to avoid penalty interest payments being incurred. The final payment was many months after the deadline and she still refused to comply with the whole financial agreement. Eventually Mark said the penalty clauses would have to be enacted. It was to take another two years to get them enforced!

As an interim measure Mark agreed to meet Greg at the farm gate with Charlie for the contact exchange. Mark was angry at the stockman's perjury in court and he was the last person Mark would have wanted involved with Charlie at the handover. But Mark wanted to see Charlie, so he agreed to the arrangement. Charlie first asked if they could go to the zoo.

As we drove to the railway station at Newbury to catch the train Charlie said he had not seen me in the last week. Mark told him that he had not seen him for several weeks. Charlie then repeated that he had not seen me for several weeks and that he was very upset!

Mark was amazed at his son's vocabulary and indignant tone: he was not quite three years old! On their return Emma was in her van parked five yards from the gate. Mark smiled as Emma got out to receive Charlie.

Could this be the beginning of a new phase? For a moment he remembered that dark day in the garage, as his son kissed him on the cheek and he stroked the perfect soft skin of the child's face. He said a silent prayer of thanks. He was still here.

Chapter 19

The legal Machine

Mark's solicitor got another contact hearing arranged for June. Contacts were denied until that hearing. Mark had only seen Charlie once since the big hearing in April

Mark felt his heart break a bit more as Charlie's birthday came and went

In early June there was a bizarre incident at Tony and Tilly's house. An envelope arrived addressed to Mr and Mrs Charles Richards (Mark's father's name). The address was complete with postcode to the cottage. Inside was a plain A4 sheet with a note written in felt tip in capital letters. It said

YOUR SON IS A PERVERT. P.S. CHARLIE IS NOT HIS CHILD. YOU ARE SPENDING ALL THIS MONEY ON ANOTHER MAN'S CHILD.

It was like a blackmailer's note in a T.V. thriller. The more Mark thought about it , the more he reasoned it had to be from Emma. Apart from Greg no-one else was aware that Charlie was not genetically linked to either Emma or Mark. Greg was barely literate. The writing on the envelope was completely different from the note. The only person who knew his father's name was Emma, similarly Tony and Tilly's address. Mark's father lived in Cornwall! At the time Mark found the note unnerving. As he lay awake at night he wondered what this new form of torture was designed to achieve.

Later that month, Mark supported the Fathers 4 justice campaign for a better deal for fathers by joining a march through the centre of London. Mark also joined a Families Need Fathers support group in Farnham. The group met once a month on Wednesday evenings. They had a simple discussion forum. It was good to talk to and to hear from other fathers with contact problems. There was a strong body of opinion that father's like Mark should not waste money on expensive legal teams, but instead should represent themselves. Mark reflected that although this was undoubtedly good advice he had lacked the confidence to represent himself early on and had never imagined that the process would go on so long, chiefly the result of the judges apparently being so ineffectual. Later when Mark did represent himself, he did wish he had done so earlier. The Families Need Fathers charity produced a useful newsletter/ magazine. Mark also went to a few Fathers4justice meetings in Portsmouth but came away feeling that there were a few too many fathers who seemed more focused on the publicity of doing whacky stunts and who had, to Mark's way of looking at things, extreme views. Many simply seemed to be misogynistic.

The next court hearing was disappointing. The judge did not get to grips with any of the outstanding matters. He seemed to Mark to be in cop out mode. Both parties eventually agreed to a new exchange venue—a nursery in Kingsclere.

Charlie and Mark had an emotional first meeting at the new venue. Mark gave Charile his late birthday presents. By now Mark should have been having alternate Friday to Sunday staying over contacts. But Emma, true to form had managed to frustrate the plans ordered by the Judge. A fortnight later Mark had Charlie for the first staying over contact. Mark thought it unfair that he had to carry the burden of paying for the nursery owner's time at the exchanges. Because the nursery was not open on Sundays, it was agreed Mark drop Charlie back at Emma's neighbours. Charlie asked him

"Why don't you pick me up from mummy's house? "

"I would like to but mummy won't let me."

"Yes, because you hit mummy when you were angry!" Charlie said and Mark felt his blood run cold.

"Charlie, that is not true, I have never been so angry I hit mummy!"

"Well mummy doesn't like you!" Charlie said.

"Mummy hits me and Paddy and Maggie, the doggies when she is cross."

Mark gritted his teeth.

"What about the cat, does she hit her too?"

"No not now, pussy cat has gone because mummy got cross when it got into the van."

Many times over the next year Charlie would get in the car at pick-up and within minutes he would be saying,

"Why are you a nasty man, mummy says you are a nasty man?"

Mark would ask Charlie what he thought, and after a pause he would say

"I don't think you are a nasty man!" then after some thought, "Mummy hates you, but you don't hate mummy!" Sometimes he would unbuckle his seat belt and reach over to hug Mark round his neck over the back of the car seat." Mark would feel his throat ache as he held back the tears. It was only when Mark said he would get into trouble if a policeman saw them driving with Charlie not in his car seat that he would agree to get back in and do the seat belt up again.

Mark's solicitor left the firm. There was a period when Mark was without a solicitor until a locum settled in. In the middle of August, Mark had a court order to go and pick up his possessions from the farm. Emma and Greg were ordered specifically not to be there. Steve Jackson, a neighbour, had agreed to monitor the process. Mark drove down with Tony to help load the furniture into a van.

When Mark arrived Emma and Greg were waiting. Emma was very aggressive, and showing no sign of being afraid of Mark! Obviously that was only when it suited her. Mark was not going to be bullied so he rang the police. They arrived 30 minutes later and after reading the court order persuaded Emma and Greg to go inside the house. All the possessions for collection were in an outbuilding away from the house. As Mark loaded up it became apparent that many items on the list were missing, some had been exchanged for something similar (like a radio that did not work) and many items had been vandalised. Mark expressed his anger and disappointment toSteve. Mark was particularly annoyed that his father's dining table had been scratched badly all over its surface. Mark had to have it professionally repaired by a French polisher. The chainsaw had its controls broken off and the tools and safety equipment were no where to be seen. The strimmer was similarly vandalised and none of the attachments provided, so it was useless. Mark took all the possessions to Tony's house where he stored them in a barn. The next two contacts were cancelled at the last minute and the neighbour now said he was only prepared to facilitate the Sunday exchange once a month. So Mark arranged to see Charlie for the day on Saturdays instead. At the end of September Mark went to pick Charlie up for the weekend and the nursery school owner rang to tell him it was cancelled. As Mark was already in the village the nursery owner invited him to have a coffee.

They had an interesting chat and then Mark drove home again.

It was not until the 10th of October that Mark saw Charlie again when he came to stay for the weekend. They had a lovely weekend. On the Sunday at the end of lunch Charlie wandered out on to the terrace, within view through the glass panel door. He tripped over one of the swimming pool cover ties and fell onto the cover. We all had a good laugh and thought nothing of it. When Mark took Charlie back to the farm, Greg had his car across the entrance to the drive. Mark let Charlie out to walk to him. A few days later a letter arrived from Emma. She was refusing all contact in future because she insisted that Charlie had told her that he had fallen in the swimming pool. Emma applied to court to vary the order. We had to wait for a hearing till November. Emma changed her approach and now laid allegations of mental and physical abuse of both her and Charlie. She also produced a medical report from the local hospital with an evaluation of possible sexual abuse of Charlie.

The report specifically said there was no evidence to suspect sexual abuse. The only reason to produce the report was to smear Mark by bringing up the topic of sexual abuse and by so doing, introduce further doubt in the judge's mind. Mark was livid that Emma had put Charlie through such an ordeal and the inevitable questions about daddy. He knew very well that mud usually sticks!

Mark's barrister was angry that the judge did not reprimand Emma and her legal team for such reprehensible behaviour. Emma then produced a schedule of Charlie's supposed problems sleeping and difficult behaviour after each contact. This formed the basis of her demand to stop staying contact and reduce other contact to a couple of hours at a time.

Mark felt a cold feeling in his stomach as he began to realise the depths that Emma would stoop to in her fight to stop him seeing Charlie.

The barristers tried to do a deal before going before the judge, but Mark refused to reduce his contact time or to give up staying contact. The judge refused to substantially change contact. He wanted the first two consecutive Saturdays to be day contact to reintroduce Charlie to Mark. He was taken aback by Emma's furious fight to get out of sharing the travelling by picking up Charlie from Tony and Tilly's house. The judge also gave dates for Mark to have Charlie over Christmas from the 28th to 1st. Both barristers requested that a Circuit or High Court judge should in future hear the case. The judge granted the request that Greg be ordered not to be present at future exchanges. As the nursery owner in Kingsclere had written to the court to say that Charlie had no behavioural problems when handed back to her after contact, Emma refused to allow exchanges to carry on there.

Mark drove down for the first scheduled contact only to find there was no one at home. This was becoming a habit that Mark had come to expect after any hearing that did not go Emma's way. The next Saturday Mark arrived to find Emma and Greg waiting in the driveway. They let Charlie run over to Mark.

"Here is the loser again!" Greg said.

"Sad, sad man, what a waste of space!" Emma goaded.

"What do you expect from a wanker like him? Greg said.

Greg had his vehicle blocking the drive. Charlie was caught in the middle and was increasingly badly affected by the tension and hostility emanating from his mother. On the way to Tony's house he suddenly announced that he would chop me in two and eat me, then he would get a nice daddy. Charlie was obviously very troubled. Mark suspected, and it was later admitted, that Emma had told Charlie all about the court actions and kept telling Charlie that Mark wanted to take Charlie away permanently so Charlie could never see his mother again.

There seemed to be no depths that Emma would not plumb. On the way back from Tony's house to the farm, Mark drove to the local supermarket car park, about a mile from the farm. Mark told Emma to pick up Charlie from there. Mark feared at some point Greg would provoke him to respond to his verbal abuse. Mark thought a public place would be a wiser option. Eventually Emma turned up with Greg. Emma got out of her van and waited. She told Greg to get out too. Mark got back in his car and as Greg came over Mark centrally locked the doors. Greg circled the car calling to Charlie. He came round to his window and in a low voice said.

"Don't worry Charlie, we are going to get you away from this horrible man. He is evil and he is bad and we are going to save you!"

"Look Greg, back off, I don't want anything to do with you, you know as well as I do that you have been ordered by the court not to be involved with this, it's nothing to do with you!"

342

"Fuck off, you miserable low life!" Greg answered, oblivious to Charlie's distress.

Mark called the police.

As Mark ended the call Emma appeared in front of the car.

As Mark gave a running commentary to the police controller he let Charlie out of the car. Mark apologised to the police lady, but said that the phone call had probably prevented an incident. Mark drove off without a word to Emma. The next contact exchange took place in the supermarket car park. Emma had a neighbour with her. Greg was parked in a car two rows back. Mark took Charlie down to stay with his father in Cornwall for the weekend. Charlie seemed very relaxed with being there and enjoyed the playing with some older children whom lived next door. When Mark and Emma met to hand Charlie over, Emma brought Greg along again.

The afternoon before his next contact Mark's solicitor rang to say that Emma had refused all further contact till at least the middle of the next year. This was to allow Charlie to have some counselling in peace to overcome the trauma of contact with Mark!

My new solicitor, Ian Hamilton made an "ex-parte" application to attach a penal notice to the last order for Christmas contact. He managed to get an emergency hearing, the last slot on December 23rd before the court closed for the holiday. Mark's barrister could not attend, so Ian Hamilton made the application before the circuit judge. Emma's barrister, who had a very bombastic and aggressive style, was reprimanded by the judge for trying to delay the proceedings on a technicality. The judge told us to sort out the Christmas dates between us. Emma still refused contact so we went back before the judge. The judge explained that he expected an order to be obeyed, otherwise some sanction would be applied, even to the extent of removing Charlie to live with me. There followed one of the funniest and most surreal moments in court. The judge then asked Emma's barrister to ask Emma if she had understood and would obey the court order. The barrister stood wringing his hands looking very uncomfortable and replied that his client understood but had instructed him to say she would not obey. The judge was completely taken aback. He repeated the question, adding that he thought she did not understand the gravity of the situation. Her barrister asked Emma again; she again responded negatively. Her barrister, looking even more uncomfortable, in a very quiet voice relayed the negative response to the judge. So the judge told Emma to stand up, and addressed her directly. He explained again and at length the consequences of disobeying a court order, of being in contempt of court. Emma replied in a level and calm voice that she would not obey the order. The judge was visibly shaken. Ian and Mark had trouble restraining their mirth. At last someone else was getting a taste of Emma's totally unreasonable and confrontational behaviour!

After a minute or two of silence the judge closed his file, and declared that he would not at this stage attach a penal notice to the order as he expected the order to be obeyed. He ordered all parties to appear before him on the 10th of January to review the situation. Ian insisted that when Mark drove down to the farm to collect Charlie he go with a witness to corroborate whether Charlie was made available for contact. Mark was not impressed with Ian's performance in court. He was a poor speaker and seemed unable to recall facts when required. But the hearing had been entertaining.

In January they all assembled in court again. The District judge made no comment on the lack of contact or contempt of court other than to acknowledge that both had happened. Emma again indicated she would not obey the order. The judge adjourned the case to be heard by a circuit judge. He announced that there was a convention at the Reading courts that only a circuit or more senior judge should attach a penalty notice. The order for contact was to stand. Later the judge discovered that the earliest opportunity for a suitably senior judge to hear the case would not come up till the end of May. He sent a note to all parties that the period without contact would be damaging so made a hearing date to bring the matter back to court in February.

At that hearing Emma still refused to obey the order. She wanted contact to go back to being restricted to a contact centre. (Back to square one and an option intended for father's proven to be a danger to their child.) After much discussion the judge ruled that the order was to stand with some minor adjustments. As Emma had indicated that she would not obey, a penal notice was attached to the order including a clause that prohibited Greg's presence at the handovers.

Contact was delayed as Mark had a holiday booked for three weeks in Botswana in March. But he felt a small sense of triumph, it seemed that a district judge could break convention!

Pressure had been applied in the pre-Christmas hearing for Mark and Emma to try mediation again. In early February they met with a mediator in Reading. Emma spoke first and refused to talk about her family background. Most of the time she revisited the history between her and Mark and wanted to get off her chest all the things that upset her. The mediator proved totally unable to control or direct the topics talked about.

When Mark's turn came to speak, Emma picked up her bag and left. The mediator was a bit non-plussed and said she would report that mediation was not appropriate.

Finally at the end of February Mark moved out of Tony and Tilly's house and into a rented two bedroom house two doors away. Although he was not going far their parting was tearful, Mark knew he could never thank his friends enough for their support, always encouraging and ready with advice when appropriate but somehow knowing when to leave him alone with his frustration. Mark thought back to that awful day when Tilly had found him in the garage. He did not think she had told Tony. She had said she would not, but he knew he owed her his life.

His friends had provided a relaxed atmosphere for Mark to try and deal with the emotional roller coaster he was on. Because they were also very sociable people and had soon become stalwarts at the heart of their community Mark had been unable to hide away or get into a cycle of depression and bitterness.

Most days there were guests for meals or people staying in the house. Mark was not allowed to mope. Mark was also thankful for the opportunity to get to know them better. Mark's frustration and deep anger at what Emma was doing to Charlie and their father son relationship affected Mark's health considerably. He was constantly down and had trouble sleeping, that caused him problems at work. Half the time he felt as though he was on automatic pilot, somehow not connected to his body. In order to stand on his own two feet Mark needed to earn enough to live on.

Housing costs in the area being, as it was, close enough to London to commute, were impossible to meet on minimum wage. The manager at the tree nursery wanted Mark to work full time, so they matched his pay rate for the night porter job at the local Spa Hotel. Mark stopped working there at the end of October 2004. This meant that Mark no longer had to do a night shift followed immediately with a day's work at the nursery. After doing that for a year the shift pattern had had a lot to do with exacerbating Mark's poor sleep pattern.

And then in 2005 Mark did not see Charlie at all. It was an all time low.

At the end of May Mark left the nursery. They had been a very understanding employer. Mark had enjoyed working there but simply could not earn enough to live on. Mark joined a driving agency, doing ad hoc work driving lorries, private buses or vans with the occasional chauffeur job. Mark's mother was also causing him concern. She had early dementia and was not coping with living on her own very well. She ended up in hospital several times because she neglected herself. Mark was the nearest to her so accompanied her to doctor's appointments etc.

As an agency worker Mark could refuse work if he needed to do something with or for his mother. His own health was suffering, but there was nothing he could do about it.

Misery seemed to be Mark's constant companion. He went down to pick up Charlie several times after the February hearing, only to find no one at the farm. After a pattern emerged Mark's solicitor wrote to the judge to ask if Mark had to continue to waste his time going down to the farm for contact, only to find Charlie unavailable. The judge agreed that Mark did not have to waste his time with further fruitless journeys for contact.

In June Emma appealed against the February order for contact on the grounds that the judge had not understood the danger that Charlie had been in from having contact with Mark and had not taken into sufficient account the distress the contact had on Emma herself especially in not permitting her to have the support of Greg at handovers; nor the effect her emotional breakdown was having on Charlie. The judge heard the case and Emma lost the appeal, and was found in contempt of court for not obeying the contact order.

Mark's solicitor made an application for committal proceedings, to send Emma to prison. This was heard by a circuit judge. In his order he upgraded the CAFCASS officer to the position of Charlie's court appointed Guardian and authorised legal representation for Charlie on legal aid. To save me making wasted journeys he ordered Emma to notify me more than 72 hours in advance of contact if Charlie was to be made available. The February contact order would remain. Crucially the judge adjourned without any consideration of penalty for the contempt of court. Unbelievably Emma was not even reprimanded.

Emma made sure that Mark did not see Charlie so they went back in front of the judge in October. On this second occasion before him the judge looked Mark in the eye and declared that he would deal robustly with the case and he assured him that he would not just duplicate the excellent work of the District judge. Sadly he went on to waste everyone's time and money by passing the buck or sitting on the fence till he eventually sent the case up to the High Court. He continually adjourned the decision about a penalty for the contempt of court. Similarly he continuously adjourned any decisions on costs being awarded against Emma. Mark was frustrated and furious as at hearing after hearing, costing £3,000 a time where the judge could have either forced Emma to comply or moved the residency to Mark, he did nothing. At the same time the CAFCASS Guardian was equally unwilling to meet his responsibilities. He started from the position of fairly blatant support for Emma over the false assault charge. After a few hearings Mark became quite wary of him as he would say things privately when visiting Mark to discuss the case, and then in court would take an opposite view. All the advisors and professionals connected to the father's support groups like Families Need Fathers had advised Mark not to cross or unduly upset the CAFCASS case officer: he has the power and position to decide your child's future as his job was to advise the judge about what was best for your child. There are many horror stories of the consequences of personality clashes between fathers and CAFCASS officers. As a man he was easy to get on with, and easy to talk to. But over the years Mark realised he had little backbone and avoided making any decisions if he could. Indeed at one hearing he leant over to tell Mark that the judge wanted him to make the decision for him. Over the years in his reports he put forward the ideal result for Charlie being that he should have regular contact with Mark. We all agreed, but given Emma's attitude to contact this became an increasingly impractical option. He trundled on right up to the end advocating contact as the answer even when contact was impossible to maintain! Towards the end of his participation in the case, as he left the court hearings, he would comment that the contact arrangements ordered by the judge would not work. Yet he had pushed for those arrangements, against everyone else! As things got more difficult he admitted to being intimidated by Emma. He had admitted to Mark early on that in his opinion he would only recommend moving a young child if the mother had been found guilty of physical abuse. In his view it was not possible to prove emotional abuse, so he could or would do nothing about that.

But then in early 2005 to Mark's great surprise, he suggested that Mark apply for residency of Charlie. He said Mark had good grounds. Not for the first time, Mark felt hope light a small fire in his heart. But when they got to court, the CAFCASS guardian said there was no reason to consider changing residency, as he was confident that contact would work! It was another bitter blow.

In order to get contact restarted the Guardian arranged for some meetings at his office in Reading. Emma took Charlie along to two initial meetings for Charlie to get to know him. Then Mark was to meet Charlie under the Guardian's supervision in his office the following week. When it came to Mark's meeting, Emma brought Charlie to the office lift, but then promptly turned around and took him home! No contact.

The judge had also ordered an expert psychologist assess and report on Emma's ability to support Charlie's relationship with Mark. There would be a three-day hearing at the end of February.

Despite the seemingly never ending misery of his life, in the autumn of 2005 Mark met a lovely lady, Karen Brown, and the two of them became close friends. Mark started to spend some time at her house in London; partly because the driving agency gave him a lot of work driving lorries in London. The stress of the endless court hearings and not seeing Charlie had taken their toll. Karen was very supportive of Mark's fight to see Charlie and would come down and wait outside during the hearings. She endured Mark's highs and lows, and helped him to enjoy brief periods of relaxation. When contact was finally restarted her experience as a nanny and experience with children in general was very useful and helped Mark enormously. In mid-march Mark moved in to her London house. It felt good to be sharing his life with a woman again and Karen's calm and kind manner soothed him when he was at his most frantic. Her gentle support helped him to go on with his fight and her gentle care for him almost broke his heart, he was so unused to it.

At the February hearing the Guardian produced a plan designed to increase Mark's contact with Charlie. The first stage was to set up a "chance" meeting with Charlie for about 15 minutes at the duck pond in the centre of Newbury Park. Charlie was with a new friend of Emma's called Alex Finn. Mark walked past the man and said hello Charlie. The Guardian, with more than a hint of Inspector Clouseau, was watching from behind a newspaper, from a park bench nearby. After feeding the ducks together Alex took Charlie away with the boy looking back and waving at Mark till he was out of sight. A fortnight later Mark had Charlie for 90 minutes again with the Guardian observing from a distance in the Park. Mark then had Charlie for three consecutive Saturdays from 10 till 4pm. The exchanges were in a local pub car park with Alex always accompanying Emma. Most times Karen came with Mark. The contact schedule had three phases. Phase one was the two introductory visits. Phase two was the consecutive Saturdays. Phase three was overnight staying on alternate weekends. This involved Mark picking up Charlie at the pub car park, but also required Emma to collect Charlie from a place near Tony and Tilly's house. During the hearing an expert psychologist, had given evidence in addition to her report. There was a lot of detail, but the main thrust of the report was that in her professional opinion Emma was deliberately obstructive about contact, believing that Mark had nothing to do with Charlie's birth, so Mark was not her father and as such Mark should be dispensed with as soon as possible. Her opinion suggested that Emma's dysfunctional attitudes to men and her relationship with Mark could be traced back to her mother's influence during her upbringing. She described Emma as very narcissistic. She explained that Emma feared that Charlie's relationship with his father would dilute her own relationship with the boy. The report was 65 pages long and very detailed. In her oral evidence the expert said that she believed that Emma was very unlikely to change her behaviour without a lot of therapy. One of the surprising things to be revealed at the hearing was that at home Emma never referred to Mark as daddy. Mark was referred to by his initials, M.R. and that had become Mister. The judge thought that this in itself would be enormously undermining of Charlie's relationship with his father. Apparently Charlie referred to Mark as Mister in front of his mother, only Alex called Mark daddy.

The Guardian expressed doubts about whether Emma could or would benefit from therapy. He had further doubts as to the impact on Emma if residence was changed and whether, if this came to pass, she would be able to have beneficial contact with Charlie. He wanted contact restarted, and he wanted Emma to undergo appropriate therapy; but added that if this did not work then changing residence should be considered.

Mark dared to hope. There had been many false dawns, that was true and he tried not to give way to optimism, but something in him would not allow him to give up.

Chapter 20

Charlie's voice.

When they all arrived in court again, Emma, her face composed into a picture of contrition, assured the judge that she had seen the light, and was now converted to the benefits to Charlie and herself of re-establishing a meaningful relationship with Mark.

It was just what the judge and the guardian wanted to hear. Mark did not believe a word of it. Emma agreed to start therapy with someone approved by the expert, and to implement the contact plan. The judge ordered them back for a review in July. Mark had not seen Charlie for 15 months. Emma had delayed and controlled everything by pure brinkmanship with the judges. When the mood of the court changed to seriously consider the issue of a change of residence, Emma confirmed that she had had a miraculous U turn! The judge grasped at that particular straw and adjourned all outstanding issues of costs and the penalty for the earlier contempt of court. Mark got the distinct impression that he was glad to back away from a situation he had probably never encountered before.

The hearings scheduled for July were arranged to allow a detailed discussion of the report on the therapy Emma was to undergo and how progress with Mark and Charlie's contact was going. Emma delayed the start of therapy to such an extent that that they had to get an emergency hearing at the beginning of July to high-light the problem. But at least contact was continuing as prescribed and was going well.

Charlie had been to London for a few weekends. He was not so keen on the long journeys, which was not surprising. Mark thought back to the hours that the boy had sat in the van with Emma on her deliveries, it was no wonder he did not relish the lengthy time he had to be strapped into his car seat.

"Are we nearly there yet Mister?" Charlie's plaintive voice would call out from the back seat. Mark had to use all his will power to stop himself breaking the motorway speed limit! Seizing on this fly in the ointment, Emma began to make an issue of it. Emma delayed seeing her therapist until the middle of July. This left no time for any meaningful report on progress at the hearing that was scheduled for later in the month.

Mark's was told that his replacement solicitor, Ian Hamilton, was to continue with Mark as the maternity leave he had been covering had become a permanent departure. This was quite a blow as Ian was nowhere near as competent or talented as Mrs. Eaves. Ian was an extremely affable man, always good company with plenty of amusing anecdotes. But his work was not nearly as thorough and he could not grasp the situation as quickly nor think on his feet as Mrs.

Eaves had been able to do. In short he lacked a nimble brain. Mark was always aware of the cost of his legal advice. Letters and calls were costed at set rates, so Mark only dealt with his solicitor if it was something important. Mrs. Eaves had been keen to keep Mark's costs down and Mark rarely saw her in her office. She had only come to court for the final hearing in the Ancillary Relief (finances). Ian Hamilton was the opposite. Mark had to order him not to attend hearings. He insisted that he attend the final hearings. As it happened there were several final hearings in the child matters. He turned out to be more expensive than Mark's barrister despite having virtually no input at the hearings!

Before her maternity leave, Mark had given Mrs. Eaves written instructions that the firm should not allow Mark's costs to exceed £10,000 at any one time, without him being warned. Mrs. Eaves had presented Mark with invoices regularly, so Mark could manage his accounts efficiently. Ian, again, was the exact opposite. In April 2006 Mark had asked for a statement of account and got an invoice for around £10,000, which he paid. A couple of weeks later Mark received another invoice for £13,000. Mark had bought some land just outside Thatcham with a view to starting an organic market garden business and most of his money was tied up with that. Mark had no idea that his legal bill had been allowed to mushroom so fast. Mark was embarrassed that he could not pay the bill, but he was also angry at Ian for not dealing with the invoicing efficiently.

Mark arranged a meeting with the senior partner. But the sour faced man would have no truck with what Mark had to say and threatened legal action if Mark did not pay.

He agreed eventually to allow several months to sort the situation out.

"I'm going to have to sell the land I have just bought to pay this bill!" Mark said with resentment. "That is going to take a few months."

"Very well, we will allow a few months, Mr. Richards." The ancient solicitor looked at Mark though pinz—nez perched on a narrow nose.

That evening over a meal with Tony and Tilly he told them the story

"But if you gave the bloody people instructions about your billing, it's their fault if they got it wrong, surely?" Tony said indignantly. "If I were you I wouldn't give them a penny!" And then, out of the blue, some weeks later Mark took a call from Laurie's ex-husband Jack.

"Hi Mark, how's things?"

"Don't ask" Mark laughed "You really don't want to know.

"Yeah," Jack said," listen, I want to pay the solicitors bill for you."

Completely taken aback Mark stood gob-smacked, the phone to his ear.

"Mark are you there?"

"Yes, but, Jack, I never , I mean I didn't, ..."

Jack laughed.

"Listen Mark, you know what I say, don't let the bastards grind you down!"

The next weekend Mark met Jack to discuss his offer. As they sat in the sunshine outside a bar in Marylebone Jack said to him.

"Look Mark you've had a pretty rough ride, it's incomprehensible to me how any woman could be as bloody evil as Emma and I feel for you. As well as the £13,000 I want to pay for future hearings."

Mark was completely stunned, but before he could speak Jack went on.

"Look mate I think your case is reaching a conclusion with that "final, final hearing" due. You know that I'm a private financier, I'm not short of a shilling or two, and I want to help, you're a decent bloke Mark, I'm in a position to help and I want to."

Mark blinked tears away. It was true, Jack was very successful in the city. But this was more than generous considering Mark's sister had divorced him! The family had remained in contact with him and at times this had caused a bit of friction. But now as Mark sat opposite Jack he could not summon words enough to thank him.

Mark was able to resolve the conflict with his solicitor although it left him very wary. He did consider finding another firm but he did not want to delay the court process.

Mark was also wary of the cost of moving solicitors. When Mark left the Newbury solicitors they had charged him £750 for photocopying the files! At this stage Mark calculated that he had about four times more paperwork to copy!

As the summer months wore on Mark's mother was a constant source of worry as she became more resistant to any extra help the Social Services tried to provide. She refused meals on wheels but did, at least allow nurses to visit morning and evening to ensure she was taking her medication. The family were trying to arrange for her to be supported so that she could remain in her own home for as long as possible. Because of her dementia she often forgot or became confused about what was arranged.

Marks relationship with Karen had developed to the point where they were talking about getting married. She had inherited part of her father's estate, and wanted to buy a house out of London for them to live in. As they dashed about looking at houses, Mark began to allow himself to believe he might be able to be happy again. They told the guardian about their burgeoning relationship.

The so-called second final hearing was reduced to two days at the end of July. Because of the delay in starting therapy, no assessment of Emma's progress in this respect could be made. This was crucial to discussing the future of any contact or the possibility of a change of residence. The judge ordered another final hearing in January 2007. All parties were to report on contact progress and proposals for a change in residence. The various experts were to report too—the therapist, and the Guardian. He also ordered that the weekend contacts start on Friday afternoons, and that in the summer holiday Charlie would have 5 days at the end of August and a similar 5 days at half-term in October with his father. For Christmas Charlie was to spend 7 nights with Mark including Christmas eve and night.

Once Mark and Karen moved to the house in Westbury, the judge ordered that Charlie be picked up from the garden centre next door.

For the first time in years, things seemed to be going Mark's way. The contact over the summer and autumn was fantastic. Charlie had a real chance to settle with the two night visits and the longer stays. Mark and Karen started to introduce him to more of Mark's relatives and some of Karen's friends that had children. Emma often tried to make a fuss over Charlie's clothes, so Mark bought him another wardrobe that stayed in London. On the odd occasion that new things went back with Charlie, they were never returned!

The exchange for contact remained the difficulty. Emma just could not help being awkward and unpleasant. Amusingly a couple of times Alex who was present at some of the handovers, told her to shut up. Very often Karen would get more wound up than Mark and it affected Charlie badly. When Mark was first introduced to Alex he was told he was just a friend. Mark learnt that Alex and his wife Claire rented Charlie's smallholding that he had inherited from his maternal grandmother. When Mark declared his relationship with Karen, Alex very swiftly began to be referred to as Emma's partner. In the first few contacts in April Charlie would talk a lot about Alex. The child seemed very confused about his role, even referring to him sometimes as daddy. By the July hearing Alex professed that he wanted to marry Emma. Apart from the fact that he was already married something did not feel quite right. Not least as there appeared to be no intimacy between them, no body language to suggest that they were in any way connected romantically. Mark was very sceptical. On the one hand he was pleased for Charlie as he sorely needed a good role model and someone to balance Emma's extreme views. (Putting aside the fact that he was two timing his wife!) On the other hand Mark suspected it was a sham to counter-balance what Mark thought Emma perceived as a real threat that the court may look upon a settled couple as a better environment for Charlie to be raised in and therefore increase the likelihood of changing the residence order to Mark with Karen. Emma even wrote in her sworn statement to the court that she had a happy and fulfilling regular sexual relationship with Alex. Her therapist, also referred to this in his letter to the court!

Mark expressed his doubts to the Guardian and was surprised to find that he shared Mark's misgivings. He, like Mark, had noticed a complete lack of intimacy when they were together. He commented that when he saw them together Alex left at the same time as he did. He said he would have thought Alex would have stayed on to discuss their meetings with Emma, as a normal couple would do. Later on when his relationship with Karen came apart, and Mark indicated that it would not be rekindled, Alex faded away! Emma's neighbours became involved with contact handovers. Charlie's solicitor on one hilarious occasion in court had to explain the intricacies of a "ménage a trios" to the judge. The judge took several minutes to fully understand the impact that mother's lover was also Charlie's prospective father figure and also Charlie's tenant, who also still happened to live with his wife in Charlie's house. As Mark's barrister put it, you couldn't make it up!

But time had gone on and shockingly, Mark realised, he had been fighting for nearly 5 years to have a normal father-son relationship with Charlie. For a long time Mark held on to the hope that Emma would emerge from this spiteful, bitter period. Mark went out of his way not to paint her character as black as it was. Mark even urged the judge to find an alternative to prison for the contempt of court. Mark had been married for 18 years to a woman he had loved. That meant something to him, even though their relationship had been all but impossible at times. He realised at last that this was not a phase that Emma was going through. If she could get rid of Mark permanently without repercussion, she would have done so in a heartbeat. She was not going to change. She was becoming as evil as her mother. What she was doing she planned carefully, being completely aware of the consequences to Mark and to Charlie. It was premeditated and evil. She was determined to force Mark out of Charlie's life.

Desperate to find any way to move forward, Mark had agreed in court to having two joint sessions with Emma's new therapist. In both sessions it appeared to Mark that nothing had changed. Emma wanted to use the sessions to expunge all her previous bad behaviour, rewrite history and blame Mark for it. In the first session Mark was completely taken aback by the barrage of accusations that issued from her. Half way through Mark asked to leave as there was no point in engaging in fruitless argument. The therapist persuaded Mark to stay but proved unable to control the session. Mark said he was not keen on a second session if it was just going to be used to rewrite history according to Emma's whims. Mark also said that just because she had been telling the same lies for years did not make them true. She may have convinced herself that they were true by repeating them so often to anyone that would listen but Mark had written a diary from the beginning containing many facts that could not be challenged or changed. Mark also pointed out that her aggressive attitude indicated little or no progress in her therapy. Mark repeated what the Guardian had said in court—you can lead a horse to water (therapy) but you cannot make it drink!

Emma had proved time and time again that she was sufficiently clever and cunning to fool people, Mark included! As quixotic as a chameleon Emma changed her tactics again and throughout the summer alleged that Karen and Mark had been saying inappropriate things to Charlie while he was with them. She insisted that this was undermining her relationship with Charlie. She claimed Charlie was having psychological problems and that his behaviour at school and at home was deteriorating and that he was having trouble sleeping.

Mark found this very difficult to deal with, largely because what she was describing was precisely what she, his mother, did to Charlie. In spite of repeated orders from the court and the experts and other professionals that Charlie should not be party to the proceedings of the court, Emma constantly briefed the boy about the legal proceedings against his father. There was nothing Mark could do. It really angered Mark that she would then accuse *Mark* of what she in fact had done! Karen and Mark had made a real effort not to question Charlie about his mother, except if he asked them a direct question. They evaded any discussion about the court process, except to refute what his mummy kept saying; that Mark wanted to take Charlie away and to not allow Charlie ever to see his mother again. Eventually the judge made a "finding of fact" that they had not been guilty of any inappropriate behaviour to Charlie.

But with a tenacity that would have eluded even the most energetic terrier, Emma never gave up finding new areas in which to create conflict, real or imagined.

Mark saw Charlie for the bonfire night weekend in November,2006. After that Emma inexplicably stopped contact again. As part of the arrangements for the weekend contacts Charlie had to ring his mother at set times. Although this felt like an intrusion at the time, it did get Charlie used to using the phone.

In mid December there was a hearing for Emma to challenge Charlie's Cafcass Guardian's status. She accused the guardian of not protecting Charlie from Mark, nor considering what was in Charlie's best interests as well as failing to research matters fully.

On the face of it, it was an extraordinary tactical error: in court, the guardian, John Liddle, had consistently supported her position as primary carer and acquiesced to many of her demands over contact. He had bent over backwards time and again to give her the benefit of the doubt and chance after chance, much to Mark and his legal team's disgust. But she had now declared her position and in doing so openly distanced herself from the guardian by undermining his work with Charlie. She had decided that John Liddle was a weak man whom she could be prevent from doing his job properly. She ruthlessly set about intimidating him.

She prevented the guardian from seeing Charlie for the last two years of his involvement in the case and successfully prevented him from visiting Charlie's schools and talking to his teachers. But the judge dismissed the application to replace the guardian, saying that Mr Liddle was a Cafcass officer of enormous experience, one of the most senior officers in Berkshire; adding that he had enormous respect for his work. For his part Mark entirely agreed with Emma that the guardian was pretty useless, but Mark remained silent. It was also obvious that had she been successful in having the guardian replaced, the whole court process would have been delayed for months. Any replacement would have had to spend time meeting all the parties, especially Charlie and getting up to speed with the reams of paper work generated by the case.

Although contact had increased and improved since March, Emma became more and more difficult. She was particularly angry at the two 5 day contacts Mark had been awarded. There were a barrage of accusations levelled at both Karen and Mark claiming they were undermining Emma's relationship with Charlie. There were the constant allegations of inappropriate things being said to Charlie, such as Emma not being Charlie's mother. It was also claimed that Charlie did not want to go on contact. By November this became an issue. Charlie became reluctant to get out of his mother's car at the exchange. Confusingly, once we had driven off with Charlie he was happy and chatty. Once in November he refused to get out of his mother's car. Mark accepted his decision and left very disappointed. The same happened the next time. As a consequence Emma stopped further contact. Mark had expected trouble at Christmas as Emma refused to accept any dates put forward within the contact order. In the third final hearing in January, 2007, as the plan for increasing contact was implemented Emma became more and more angry at the rebuilding of the relationship between father and son. The further prospect of longer contact periods, up to 7 nights at Christmas, made Emma more and more anxious. As Charlie was a single child with to all intents and purposes a single parent he was very responsive to his mother's moods and especially her anxiety. Charlie, within the context of the two parental relationships, was desperate to please both. But his bond with his mother was considerably stronger. As Emma's anxiety levels rose Charlie would try to placate her by saying and doing what she wanted. This was not, as far as Mark could see, on a conscious level but it did explain some of Charlie's claims that inappropriate things were said to him and why he refused to go on contact. Charlie felt he was doing what his mother wanted. As he lived with Emma he was reacting to his mother's extreme anxiety levels at a subconscious level to reduce the tension at home. This was exactly why Emma needed the therapy—to deal with the issues around anxiety and to enable her to promote contact, not undermine it.

Mark had his second joint meeting with Emma's therapist and he made it clear from the outset that he would respond vigorously to any accusations or airbrushing of events.. At times the therapist had to call a halt to restore calm. Emma's basic position was that Charlie should not see his father because Mark was dangerous. After all she said, Mark was not Charlie's biological father and Alex, she thought, would be a better father figure. Mark felt depression threaten to overwhelm him. It was obvious that precious little progress had been made.

There was no more contact before the hearing in early January. Then one day in early January the phone went, Mark answered it.

"Mister? It's me, Charlie!"

"Charlie, are you OK?" Mark said

"Yes, but mummy's out!"

"Why are you whispering?"

"In case mummy hears"

Mark laughed.

"But you said she was out?"

"Yes, she is!" Charlie said, still whispering. It was obvious that he was very worried that his mother would find out.

The second time he rang Mark asked where he was.

"I'm hiding under the bed!" Charlie whispered.

In court Emma had said she had put Mark's 'phone number on the calendar in the kitchen, and she had encouraged Charlie to ring. Whatever the truth was, it was apparent that

Charlie wanted to speak to Mark but without his mother's knowledge. The child was obviously in turmoil.

Emma's therapist had been instructed to produce a report for the court to assess the impact of the therapy. Lesley Norman's report was a scant one page long in the form of a short letter in which Emma's therapy sessions were described as demonstrating good progress. There was no detail in the report.

At the hearing the judge commented that Emma's statement before the court, written at the end of November, continued to show that she believed that her "attitudes, beliefs and behaviours" were appropriate and that she was merely protecting her son from harmful emotional stress by refusing contact.

Emma, it was concluded, did not appear to be fully open towards the idea that there could be benefits to Charlie through being in a harmonious relationship with both his parents. Emma's therapist was later criticised by the judge for exceeding her remit. Lesley Norman had taken it upon herself to interview Charlie on his own. In her assessment in December she wrote that "Charlie should not be forced to go away for Christmas to Mark as she feared emotional damage to her child." The judge and guardian were made aware of this in a letter from Emma's solicitor. At the December application to remove the guardian some effort was made to sort the Christmas contact between Mark and Emma. In his summation at the January hearing, the judge said that this comment had influenced the guardian's recommendation to cancel the Christmas contact. He went on to explain that he had declined to address the matter in court as there was not enough time. He was critical of Lesley Norman exceeding her remit and attempting to advise the court on such a manner. This was a prime example of what Mark called the underhand and disreputable tactics employed by Emma's solicitors. They introduced matters that shouldn't have been introduced, knowing that it would influence the proceedings. They would drop their bomb then make a simple apology to the court, but by then the damage was done. On one occasion the judge was so angered by their disregard for procedures that he applied a financial penalty on Emma's solicitors.

A "tame" psychologist assessed Emma. A report was written and they tried to have it introduced instead of the courts independently solicited report. At the time the judge was so angry that he had to leave the court for several minutes to compose himself! At the three-day hearing the judge realised there was not going to be enough time to cover everything. He adjourned the proceedings and ordered all parties back to court in February. The judge made a detailed, lengthy judgement that amounted to 25 pages of transcript.

He ordered that no further sanctions should be imposed for the contempt of court that was still outstanding and no cost orders except for the fact that Emma had to pay the costs of the failed appeal hearing. Full residence was granted to Emma. Emma was to make Charlie available for such contact as was arranged by the guardian. The parents and the guardian were to identify a family therapist for joint therapy to assist in longer-term support for all parties over the issue of contact.

One of Emma's main arguments at the hearing was that her anxiety was incredibly heightened by not having legal residence of Charlie despite the fact that she had it de facto. The constant threat that Charlie could be moved, she insisted, made the situation intolerable for her and for Charlie.

It was Mark's argument that this threat had proved the only effective method of getting Emma to comply with contact and other issues. The judge said that he now accepted that Emma had completely reversed her views on contact and believed that she was going to support contact and foster the relationship between Charlie and Mark. It was in order to facilitate this and to remove the extra uncertainty that he granted her residency of Charlie. She assured the court that she would restart contact quickly. The guardian was ordered to explain the judgement to Charlie in simple terms, at school, to organise the resumption of contact, and organise the selection of the therapist.

Mark felt gloom descend. Given the history of the case and Emma's consistent implacable hostility, it was hard to believe the judge was so naïve as to believe that Emma had, for the second time, apparently 'seen the light' and accepted all the benefits of allowing Charlie to see his father regularly.

Prior to the hearing in January Mark had explained to the guardian that his relationship with Karen was breaking down. The stress Mark was experiencing was never going to be conducive to maintaining his new relationship. Since moving into their new house Mark had experienced a level of control from Karen that severely tested his concept of trust. Mark experienced echoes of the problems he had had with Emma and alarm bells began to ring, loudly! Mark decided to leave. But Karen remained very supportive and became one of his closest friends.

She encouraged Mark to stay till after the January hearing to lessen the stress that moving out before that would bring. The guardian informed the court of Mark's change in circumstances. Eventually, his heart heavy and his soul weary, Mark moved out and found a flat to rent in Thatcham.

Mark saw Charlie for a short day contact in January after the hearing. The handovers took place in a local park. Laurie had come up with presents for Charlie and Mark gave him all his Christmas presents too. It was a joyous day and Mark had to swallow a lump in his throat as he saw the happiness on his son's face.

At the January hearing the guardian commented on some behavioural problems Charlie was reported to be having at school. Mark applied to Charlie's school for all the reports they had sent to the guardian. As Mark read through the reports, he was surprised to find reports of bad behaviour dating back to 2005, especially after the visits to see the guardian at his office in Newbury. Mark had had no contact with Charlie for the whole of 2005 and early 2006.

Charlie was reported to be talking about "that bad man" meaning the guardian. He was also telling teachers about a bad Mister trying to take him away from his mummy. The source for all of this information could only have been Emma. Mark was completely unaware of these reports as Emma always refused to tell Mark anything about Charlie.

By January 2007 Charlie's behaviour was of such concern that the school counsellor was brought in to have discussions with Charlie. Mark saw Charlie on 20th of January. On the 22nd Charlie was reported as being distressed as his mother left him at the school gate. He was distracted and apparently unable to concentrate in class. He had run out of the class at one point and was found hiding in the outdoor playhouse. He said he was upset that 'Mister' had told him that his mummy had told lies in court. A few days later he upset some of the nursery children at playtime by saying he would lock them all up and put them in prison. When questioned by staff he said that 'Mister' was a policeman and locked people up. He had difficulty staying in class at times and was clearly confused and distressed. During counselling he expressed his worry that a judge might not let him live with his mother anymore. Charlie demonstrated considerable knowledge of the court process and found his parents arguing over him very distressing. Surprisingly, there was nothing in his school academic reports to suggest he was having any problems. Initially despite all the evidence to the contrary, Emma denied Charlie was having any problems. When the behaviour continued after contact was re-established, she turned it around and in her court statements blamed Mark for Charlie's behaviour.

Mark felt despair threaten to overwhelm him again.

Chapter 21

Hope Fading

Mark finally became fully aware of Emma's game plan in January 2007 and more particularly at the hearing in February. A school counsellor had seen Charlie up until May, when the contracted sessions with the school came to an end. She advised that Charlie needed and wanted to continue the sessions. Mark agreed to pay for them, but Emma refused to transport Charlie to and from the sessions.

"Don't be so stupid Mark, I'm with him every day. I can see he has improved. He doesn't need it!"

Emma also refused to warn Charlie that the sessions that the child was finding comfort in, were coming to an end. It therefore came as a shock to Charlie when the sessions abruptly came to an end. The School counsellor did write a report for the court later in the year expressing her concern that Emma invariably overrode Charlie's wishes when they did not coincide with hers. Charlie had shown that he could not express his views to his mother and had to keep anything good he had to say about his father secret from his mother. Now with the abrupt ending of the sessions Charlie's frustration had no outlet. According to the school professionals Charlie's behaviour did not improve. But Emma refused to allow any further counselling sessions privately with the school counsellor as she claimed that the counsellor was no longer impartial. In turn in her report the counsellor observed that Emma reacted very aggressively to any professional who tried to establish an independent working relationship with Charlie when it was in relation to Mark's request for contact and a relationship with the boy. In the end Emma took Charlie away from the school and enrolled him in St Bartholomew's junior school. She claimed the reason was because Charlie was being bullied at his other school—a claim that was strenuously denied by the school. It was a pattern Mark had seen often with Emma. She had often made similar accusation against any professionals that she perceived as being 'against her' or critical of her.

After a total of four days plus a day of final submissions and the judgement, Mark felt his relationship with Charlie becoming collateral damage and felt his closeness with his son slipping away. Mark felt the cold fist of fear in his stomach again, the future was uncertain. All the judges, had, over the years emphasised how important the court sees it that father and son have a good relationship, and maintained that the court was committed to doing everything in its power to promote this. Where there was continual obstruction the court could and would consider moving the child to the non-resident parent. Yet, Mark reflected, after 5 years of continuous obstruction no sanction had been brought to bear on Emma. The best period of contact had only been achieved after the threat of a penal notice and the threat that non-compliance could result in Charlie moving to live with Mark. Twice Emma had promised in court that she had had seen the light and would promote and support Charlie in a proper relationship with his father. Mark's legal team were frankly disgusted at the outcome and foresaw continued problems over contact. In fact Mark's barrister said that for the first time in his career he was ashamed of the profession he worked in.

Earlier in 2006 Mark's barrister had asked permission to send the case up to the High Court. The Judge Grey had said he was perfectly capable of dealing with the matter and refused permission. For judge Grey to refuse to punish Emma for the outstanding contempt of court or award any costs against her for the endless hearings to deal with her bad behaviour was extraordinary. Giving Emma all that she demanded from the court was tantamount to giving her the green light to carry on as before. She was being rewarded for her appalling behaviour! Mark did not know if the judge's actions were incompetence, prejudice or just bias. Mark discussed appealing to the High Court with his legal team, Mark's barrister was prepared to appeal but thought the chance of success would be low as the appeal judge would most likely rule that the judge was entitled to view the matter as he did. A more senior judge would be loath to overturn a judgement without strong cause.

Mark was emotionally and financially drained. After some thought he decided that there was just no way he could continue his fight to see Charlie with full legal representation in court. In the autumn of 2006 Mark had approached the senior partner to ask if one of the firm's other solicitors could handle his case. Mark did not think Ian Hamilton was up to the case. But looking down his nose over his pinz nez the legal fossil was dismissive of Mark's criticisms and assured Mark that Ian was an excellent solicitor. Mark thanked God that he had every confidence in his barrister. He was the lynch pin and main advisor in the process. Whenever Mark asked Ian for advice he always had to refer to the barrister or a senior colleague. But, Mark knew, you could only get your barrister through your solicitor, so if Mark changed firms he may have lost his barrister.

After the hearings Mark told Ian Hamilton that he could not afford to carry on. Mark intended to represent myself as a Litigant In Person (LIP). Ian was keen to pursue the adjourned costs matters. Mark said he had no confidence that they would be recovered, as Emma always seemed to wriggle out of everything. She always got off Scot-free. Ian was adamant that he could eventually recover the costs awarded. It was simply a matter of perseverance.

"Look Ian, I am finished scraping the bottom of the barrel now, I'm through to the earth beneath it! I simply don't have anything more, financially or emotionally."

"Come on Mark, surely you're not going to give up now? I'm telling you with more time I can win this one!"

"Well, if you're sure?"

"I am!" Ian smiled at him.

"Ok then," Mark sighed wearily, " I can get the money, but why don't you put your money where your mouth is and recoup the money with no further expense to me?"

"Yes, of course! I will just add my costs to the costs awarded to you!"

"Well, OK then," Mark extended his hand and Ian took it.

"Good man!" he clapped Mark on the back.

So Mark had, despite his better judgement, empowered Ian to continue fighting to recover the costs due whilst Mark would be LIP for everything else. Mark signed a form to inform the court that he would now be LIP in May.

Following the outcome of the five days of final hearings in January and February, the Guardian was supposed to organise contact and joint therapy for Emma and Mark with a psychologist. The judge had ordered a review hearing for May. Judge Grey also approved a Family Assistance Order, which, in effect allowed the guardian to access more funds to deal with the case. He wrote a letter to the court outlining the problems and lack of progress leading up to the new hearing. His letter stated that Mark was cooperative but that Emma was unwilling to engage in constructive dialogue over restarting contact and refused to pay for any part of the joint therapy. At one juncture it was pointed out that the court could order Emma to use Charlie's trust fund money to pay for this. The guardian had not envisaged that no contact would take place between the hearings as he had expected the new level of cooperation that Emma had promised in court. He wrote that Emma had indicated before the last court judgement that the outstanding matters of residence and penal notices hanging over her were extremely stressful and resulted in her being unable to comply with the previous contact arrangements. She just *knew* that she would be better able to deal with contact and joint therapy once these were removed. Judge Grey also commented on this in his judgement. The guardian went on to say

" I have to say I have seen no sign of this situation easing and no sign of any real intention on behalf of Emma Richards to solve the problem of Charlie's contact with his father by cooperation as outlined in the schedule of the court's last order".

As it turned out Emma appeared in court as LIP too. The judge ordered that Charlie's solicitor would handle the court procedures from now on. It is normally the applicant's (Mark's) legal representative that organises the case. Not much happened in the hearing as no substantive progress had been made since February. The judge acknowledged that Mark had agreed to pay for the joint sessions of therapy with a Mrs Michelle Lovelock. Mark and Emma were to pay for their own individual sessions initially. The court ordered a review hearing for July.

But far from being cooperative Emma delayed her solo sessions with the therapist so that the first joint session was not until July, just before the next court hearing. The hearing had to be cancelled and rescheduled for October. The second joint therapy session took place at the end of August. Emma claimed she was away on holiday with Charlie. They had a third session in the middle of September. The therapist had been ordered to file her report 3 days later when it had been envisaged that there would have been a minimum of 5 sessions to report on.

The guardian had only managed to have one meeting with Emma. That meeting was apparently dominated by heated discussion about a letter Mark had sent to Alex, Emma's so called partner. He was usually present when the guardian saw Emma, and indeed was often at the court hearings to support Emma. Further efforts to have meetings were frustrated by Emma. The guardian was adamant that contact could not take place unless progress was apparent in the joint therapy, or that if there was contact it would have to be supervised to prevent Emma further alleging inappropriate things being said to Charlie by Mark. He had envisaged supervising some contacts himslef but was unable to organise even his own appointments with Emma. At this time everyone was trying to persuade Emma to continue the counselling that Charlie was having at school. The guardian asked Mark to write some letters to Charlie but send them to him so he could deliver them to Charlie. Mark did as he had been asked, desperate for any presence in his son's life. The guardian never delivered or sent the letters to Charlie. Nor did he go to the school, as he had said he would, to explain the judgement to Charlie.

He did not see Charlie at all.

The Family Assistance Order had a time limit of six months. The guardian failed to make use of the extra resources within the time limit.

In July the guardian held a professionals' meeting at Charlie's solicitor's office. This was in response to concerns reported by Charlie's school to Social Services. Only Charlie's previous counsellor and solicitor attended. The joint therapist and school supplied written information. Social Services withdrew at the last minute. The meeting concluded that it was appropriate to await the outcome of the joint therapy before considering whether any further action was necessary.

Mark was getting more and more angry and frustrated at the lack of progress towards having contact with Charlie. It was blatantly obvious to Mark that yet again Emma had lied in court about her apparent 'conversion'. Mark also felt that judge Grey had, as usual, grasped at the easy option and acquiesced to all Emma's demands. Judge Grey then put the control of re-establishing contact in the guardian's hands, whom Mark knew would be no match for Emma.

The guardian came to see Mark at his flat in Thatcham. He surprised Mark again by actively encouraging Mark to seek a change of residence. As Mark had believed that this was not a realistic option for the foreseeable future he had taken a flat where the landlord expressly forbade children to live there. It was all right for weekend visits but not full time occupancy. So, Mark explained, if this was a real option, he would have to move. Luckily there was a six-month clause in the tenancy agreement. At the end of July Mark moved to a three-bedroom house with a garden and garage in the village of Headly. Mark also had to consider what kind of job he could do if Charlie came to live with him. Mark's agency driving work fluctuated a lot. Renting a house also meant Mark had to live off his savings as well. Rent and council tax was around £1000 a month, whilst Mark's agency work earned Mark about £800 a month after deductions and Charlie's maintenance. Sometimes there were weeks with no work. Mark tried to get weekend work and night shifts as the rates were much better. He decided to train as a driving instructor to give him flexibility if Charlie came to live with him.

By this time Mark was writing letters direct to Charlie, but Mark had no idea whether his son was receiving them. Mark was not allowed to ring Charlie and Charlie no longer rang Mark. It later came out in court that Mark's phone number had been put on the December calendar for 2006. When that was replaced by the January calendar, Mark's phone number was not made available to Charlie. Just before Mark moved to Headley he ended up in Basingstoke hospital. The stress and frustration of not seeing Charlie continued to take its toll on Mark's health. As he lay in his hospital bed tears running down his face, he wondered, not for the first time, just how much more he could take.

At the end of 2006 Emma demanded that Mark comply with the financial settlement order and send her the transfer of ownership of the deeds of the property. Mark refused, as she still owed the outstanding interest on the late payments for the financial settlement. Mark's solicitor had always advised him not to send it until full payment was received, as it was the only leverage Mark had left. Without the document to enable her to transfer the deeds into her sole name, she was unable to borrow money against the property without Mark's joint signature. Mark had discovered that one of her previous firms of solicitors was suing Emma for non-payment of her legal bill. She needed a loan to pay it.

Along with the non-payment of the overdue interest money that she owed, she had to provide proof that the original loan and mortgage had been transferred to her sole liability with the bank.

She had not complied with this order from the court.

At the February hearing the matter was negotiated between the barristers in the waiting rooms. Mark actually signed the form with Ian Hamilton beside him and Emma's barrister to witness this. Mark's solicitor said he would send the document on receipt of a cheque. Emma promised to send the cheque along with proof from the bank that liability had been transferred to her sole charge.

Unsurprisingly Emma never sent the cheque. She later claimed that a friend had lent her the money to pay the bill. But at every hearing from then on when she was still LIP, she asked the judge Grey to deal with the transfer of deeds issue. It rumbled on and on.

At the February hearing Judge Grey had again adjourned the outstanding costs issue from previous hearings but ordered that we were at liberty to apply to have it dealt with at another hearing. Mark's solicitor, engaged only for the costs issue, applied to the court to have it sorted out. As we had come to expect, Emma, now LIP, refused to supply any information to enable a hearing to be of any use. Finally they had a hearing back before the district judge to have an oral examination of Emma's finances. She had claimed that she could not pay as she was bankrupt. As she was LIP the judge was very patient and explained everything at length and even gave her advice on what to do if she wanted to contest the costs order. She did her tearful "I can't cope with all the extra stress" act, but, to Mark's huge relief, the judge would not change the substance of the matter. When they came before judge Grey the following month for contact matters Emma tried to win him around again with a tearful entreaty over the costs. Incredibly judge Grey criticised Mark for pursuing the matter and said it was another reason that things were so difficult between Emma and him and that this was impacting on Charlie. Of course Mark was not allowed to speak on the subject. His frustration in danger of overwhelming him, Mark wanted to shout that it wouldn't have been a problem if he had dealt with the matter properly two years previously! Judge Grey ordered a stay on the costs matter, until further notice. In effect he froze the proceedings, letting Emma off the hook yet again!

In July Emma was infuriated that the guardian had spoken to Karen Brown. He had needed to contact Mark and had left a message with Karen. He was aware that Karen and Mark remained close friends, even though they no longer lived together. Karen was privy to all the information that Mark had about Charlie and had been involved in Mark's discussions and interviews with the guardian. She discussed the situation with him. He said that Charlie was not doing well at school again. Charlie's counselling at school had come to an end at Easter and Emma was refusing to allow any further sessions. At the time Mark was left in the dark. The guardian said he was trying to get a statement for the court about the assessment of Charlie and his needs. Mark was told that the counsellor earmarked to make this assessment had had a difficult experience with a parent on a completely different case. That parent had physically threatened her over a report she was preparing on that case. Because of that experience she did not want to get involved with the court and she flatly refused to get into any communication with Mark. The guardian reported that the woman had found Emma's manner threatening at times. The guardian and Charlie's solicitors did eventually get a long statement from her in September. The counsellor was very critical of Emma and how she dealt with Charlie's emotional needs. For reasons Mark never understood, the guardian and Charlie's solicitor did not produce this statement for the October hearing. It did not appear until May 2008.

In September the guardian wrote an updating letter for the hearing that had been moved from July to October before judge Grey. In it he put forward three choices for the court to consider for Charlie:

No future contact till Charlie had grown up

Change of residence to father

Further attempts to arrange contact

The hearing in October turned out to be significant. When the judge was informed that the joint therapy had not got past three sessions he was very irritated. He threw his hands up in the air and exclaimed that he could not deal with the case anymore. He sent the case up to the High Court and ordered a directions hearing for November before judge Travers. At last, a year after Mark's team requesting that the case be moved to the High Court, he had admitted defeat and let a more senior judge deal with the case. In the two years that he had controlled the case they had not moved on with contact, nor from the judgement of the district judge!

A more detailed assessment had been made of Emma, that much was true, but overall all parties had spent an enormous amount of money with nothing to show for it, except an increase in stress levels! Judge Grey further ordered that Charlie be psychologically assessed and all parties were called on to agree on an expert to assess the likely impact on Charlie of:

An order for no contact,

An order transferring residence to Mark

Contact orders being made within continuing proceedings.

Mark felt his heart break a bit more. Another year lost, not seeing Charlie.

In the month before the October hearing Mark engaged the advice of Adrian Parker. Adrian was often a member of the advisory panel at the Families Need Fathers support group monthly meetings. After one of the summer meetings Mark and the tall fair haired man retired to a local pub to continue discussions. Adrian explained that he was about to start a business giving advice on contact and residence matters. He was not a solicitor nor a lawyer but he had successfully acted for himself in his own divorce. He had been on lots of legal courses alongside lawyers. He had been acting as a Mackenzie Friend for a couple of years. A Mackenzie Friend is a term given to a layperson that comes to court to support a Litigant in Person. The layperson cannot speak or engage in the court process, but may give advice or support like taking notes of the proceedings. An LIP has to ask permission for the Mackenzie Friend to be present. Until quite recently Mackenzie Friends were voluntary. Adrian outlined what he could do and his hourly rate. His hourly rate was about half that of Mark's solicitor's. Mark decided a few sessions might be worth a try.

Mark found Adrian's style quite difficult to cope with. At a solicitor's office there is an appropriate time period allocated for any meeting, and in most cases the appointment is uninterrupted. With Adrian working from home there were constant phone calls or people calling at the house. Conversations were often disjointed. With a solicitor and his back up team of secretaries some form of record and aknowledgement of the discussions takes place, usually in the form of a follow up letter. Adrian had no secretarial skills and Mark had to make notes, sometimes at an incredible rate as Adrian tended to get very passionate about his advice. He also had what Mark realised was a very aggressive approach to tackling problems. Everything was rather extreme. As an example he thought Mark should get Social Services involved to get Charlie taken into care. This would make the process of transfer to Mark easier to argue. Mark vetoed the idea because of the double stress Charlie would go through. First the stress of going to live with a stranger, then another upheaval of moving to live with his father and all with no idea of the time scales involved. Adrian commented early on in their association that Mark had obviously been the recipient of serious domestic violence as he was not assertive or demanding enough. By nature Mark was a conciliatory soul and liked consensus before doing things that involved other people. Adrian was very much an Alpha male. He also loved to trumpet his successes. It became such a problem and such a complicated protracted way of doing things that Adrian became more expensive than Mark's solicitors!

Even though Mark held his breath wondering if he was being rude, or if Adrian would take offence as he explained his concerns to him, Marks' complaints did not even seem to register with him!

Adrian accompanied Mark to the first hearing before judge Travers. He helped Mark draw up a position statement prior to the hearing. The position statement was drawn up in language that, compared to Mark's barrister's style, was very combative. It was a lot more technical, legal and demanding of the court, far from the cooperative style Mark thought worked best. They had to agree an expert child psychologist. Adrian was adamant that Mark had to put forward someone who had experience of dealing with residency change. In his opinion Cafcass would opt for a pliable psychologist who would deliver the recommendations they wanted. Emma put forward a name that had already been associated with the case, but the judge ruled there was a conflict of interest. When Mark's contender was named, the judge's demeanour changed completely. He became agitated and appeared to be irritated. He looked at Adrian and said he would not allow our choice as he foresaw endless appeals if that expert was commissioned. Mark was quite taken aback by the adverse reaction of the judge and it made him a bit wary of Adrian's advice.

In the judge's opening remarks Mark had been immediately impressed when he addressed Emma directly and said that the courts took a very dim view of any parent that prevented the other parent from having a good relationship with their children. He went on to say that the courts took the view that a child benefited enormously from having a loving relationship with both parents. He added that in cases of prolonged obstruction to contact he would have no hesitation in changing residency. Naively, Mark thought it sounded like judge Travers might actually get to grips with the case and for the first time in a long time, Mark felt quite optimistic.

But this was only a directions hearing. The guardian's choice of expert was endorsed, and was to report on the impact of the three choices outlined earlier. An order was made to observe contact between Charlie and Mark. Emma insisted it remained chaperoned by her neighbours. Emma's statement was to be admitted for the next hearing in May. There was another order permitting Mark to have indirect contact by post with Charlie, and Emma assured the court that she would hand over any letter Mark sent, to Charlie.

When the judge first came into the court he had had only an hour to look at the bundle of documents, but he had not seen any of the position statements. Charlie's solicitor apologised to the judge and then produced copies for him, Mark's one and a half pages and Emma's forty-nine pages. The judge retired for only ten minutes to look at them. When he returned he made a passing remark that judges always appreciated brevity. Emma's position statement was actually a collection of statements, letters and reports going all the way back to the beginning covering the cruelty to animals charade. There were also letters from neighbours and friends supporting Emma and accusing Mark of all sorts of extraordinary things aimed at undermining Emma and causing her stress. There was a statement written by her making all sorts of allegations against Mark, supported by people like Charlie's friends parents, and attesting to Emma's brilliant parenting skills. The first few times Mark read this rubbish he was amazed at the sheer energy and doggedness that Emma had in collecting all this paperwork. It also demonstrated just what spin she had put on the facts to her support network. If they had known the truth of what Emma actually did they would have been shocked. For Mark, divorce and the battle to see Charlie was private and a painful part of his life that he only discussed it with close family and Karen.

Mark had brought up the question of continuing or restarting counselling for Charlie at school or privately. The guardian had reported that the school counselling had finished at Easter and that Charlie's behaviour had deteriorated at school again in June and July to such an extent that the school had contacted Social Services. Emma suddenly announced that she had already instructed her GP to set up counselling and that it was to start imminently. After the hearing Mark contacted the surgery and they confirmed that they had made a referral but Emma never attended with Charlie. Emma's answer to Charlie's problems was to change his school yet again in January 2008. In early November Social Services got involved again. In her report the social worker stated that anonymous concerns for Charlie's welfare at home had been passed on from the NSPCC. At the same time the school had also reported concerns for Charlie at home, from comments Charlie had made to teachers at school. The concerns appeared to be about Emma's treatment of Charlie, with his mother screaming and yelling at him and locking him in his room. The anonymous caller alleged that the mother's behaviour was becoming worse and unpredictable. Mark was completely in the dark about all of this till he saw the report in documents brought before the court from the guardian. Emma predictably accused Mark of being the anonymous caller to the NSPCC. But Mark knew that she and Greg had fallen out not long before. Mark guessed that he was either involved or Emma had made the calls herself in order to label Mark as being determined to cause her as much trouble as possible! Mark shuddered as he realised that she could really be that underhand and devious with not a care, it seemed for their son's welfare! But it turned out it was not a serious issue for social services as they wrote that no further action was necessary, the case was closed.

The following January Emma moved legal firms yet again and instructed new solicitors in Slough. Mark was beginning to get cold feet about being LIP in Reading in May. Mark had his doubts about the aggressive nature of the advice and approach from Adrian, not to mention the likely cost! He wanted to represent Mark properly in court like a lawyer. By mid-February Mark had decided to use his barrister again. Adrian was very supportive and even stayed in contact to see what happened. When Mark eventually made it clear he could no longer pay for advice Adrian generously gave his time and advice over the phone for free.

Now though Mark's concerns were no longer financial but rather the impact and effect the situation was having on Charlie. Adrian opened Mark's eyes to the procedures, protocols and archaic rigidity of the legal system. In many ways he was a breath of fresh air blowing through a fossilised regimented and stuffy system. He relished attacking the judges in their lazy, cosy, unaccountable fiefdoms. Before Mark worked with Adrian he had already perceived that the judges and their attitudes were probably the biggest problem in the justice system, in the Family Division. Now he felt his spirits fall. If the system was indelibly flawed—what hope did he have?

Chapter 22

The Uneven Playing Field

When Mark re-engaged fully with Ian Hamilton as his child matters solicitor Mark made it clear that he wanted an economy deal. He was not interested in Ian attending court but in order for Mark's barrister to act for him, he had to be instructed by Ian. Mark also asked him to keep the other costs issues separate. He knew that he could only afford one or two more hearings.

When Mark had lived with Karen, she had done most of the background work on researching schools and after school clubs etc. This was in preparation for the change in Charlie's residency in 2007 that was to be supported by the guardian. So when the judge asked Mark to produce a detailed plan for May 2008 Mark updated all the previous information, contacting schools for the latest Ofsted reports, checking there was still a place available etc. Mark asked his GP to give a report on his health for the court. Emma had claimed Mark was unfit to look after Charlie because of the health problems he had suffered.

A month after restarting with Ian Hamilton, Mark was informed that the solicitor no longer worked there. Mark could not get a straight answer or explanation out of the senior partner as to what had happened to Ian. When Mark asked if he had been sacked he was told Ian had simply disappeared and could not be contacted at all. They did not know where he had gone. Mark was dumbfounded. He had heard the occasional story of a solicitor doing a runner in the media, but he had never expected it to happen to one he was dealing with! Ian had always seemed so laid back! Things went from bad to worse. Peering over the now familiar pinz—nez, the senior partner said he would handle Mark's case. Mark was reeling; he really did not want to this legal fossil representing him but how could he get out of it? Then, four days later Mark was introduced to a very pleasant lady solicitor called Alison Rooney. Mark breathed a sigh of relief, and wrote to the senior partner explaining the arrangement that he and Ian had come to over the costs issue. In reply, Mark was sent a bill for £11,000 for work Ian had billed to him. This apparently included work on child matters whilst Mark was LIP. Mark had a very strained discussion with the senior partner who basically said he knew nothing about any arrangement and insisted that Mark owed the firm £11,000. Mark explained what the arrangement was, and that he had gone LIP and in fact had engaged a Mackenzie Friend, whom Mark had paid. Mark refused to pay any bills prior to February and made it clear that he expected the solicitors to honour the arrangement to pursue the costs issue at their expense, recouping the expenses when the case was won.

It seemed to Mark that he was between a rock and a hard place. In a month Mark was due in court and he wanted his barrister to act for him. If Mark moved solicitors he knew he might have trouble getting the papers out of them in time, especially in view of their claim that Mark owed them money.

Mark put the pressure back on them to demonstrate they were decent, honourable people. Mark reminded them that they had caused friction before by not billing Mark within the agreed parameters and reminded them that he had sorted that problem in good faith. Mark could have challenged the £13,000 extra bill, but had chosen to meet his commitments. Mark maintained that just because Ian had not kept them informed of the arrangement did not mean they were not contracted by it. Mark challenged the senior partner to honour the agreement. Eventually he agreed. Mark felt sorry for Alison as she was in an embarrassing position. Every time she rang Mark she was at pains to point out she was not charging Mark for the call. Mark also made it clear that he was not going to pay for the time it took for Alison to get up to speed with the case. Mark said he would deal direct with his barrister.

In order to reduce costs Mark had asked Ian to inform the other parties about Mark ending his status as LIP as close to the May hearing as possible. This would mean that Charlie's solicitor would retain responsibility for the court bundle (documents). All the statements and documents for the hearing had to be filed through them. There is a fair amount of work involved with preparing the bundle for the judge, sometimes other parties objected to certain documents being included, so agreements had to be reached. The bundle then had to be indexed so when in court the judge could give a page reference to the documents to which he was referring. This is all very time consuming. Needless to say Emma's solicitors had a torrent of correspondence about the bundle. Charlie's solicitor was publicly funded. So Alison did not have management of the case. That saved costs.

When Mark met his barrister at Reading court they had to wait around for a long time whilst other cases were heard first. Mark explained what had happened with the solicitors. His barrister roared with laughter, he thought it was highly amusing. He explained that the firm had a reputation for negotiating hard with all barristers over their costs. So much so that they routinely billed higher than normal knowing that the firm would cut the bill anyway. He explained that if Mark kept control of the witness bundle at the court and kept copies of everything from now on, he should have enough to go to another solicitor if he had to. Apparently Mark could go to any solicitor and still instruct his barrister to act for him. He said, like most barristers, he was not insured to act directly for Mark but had to be instructed by a solicitor. Mark felt better, at least he had a fall back position. When Mark got home he spent hours copying the bundle.

When Mark had been involved with Adrian he was aghast that Mark did not use a computer or email.

"What are you talking about man? This is the 21st century, you have to get with it! The only way I communicate is by email, it keeps an electronic record, it's all I do, apart from emergency texting! Have you even got a lap top?"

"Yes, I bought one in the January sales in 2007 but I haven't used it yet. All my 2003 computer course notes are buried in a barn!"

"Well unbury them, go on a course, anything but you've got to get up to speed!"

Mark realised Adrian was right, he had just been going by trial and error. He was grateful that Adrian had forced him to use the computer and by the time Mark was back with his barrister he could email his chambers with information direct without going through the solicitors.

At the end of March Mark had his interview with Mrs. Lovelock, the expert child psychologist. Mark spent over three hours in her office. The next day Mark was due to have contact with Charlie, supported by the chaperones and observed by Mrs Lovelock. The interview was fairly straightforward. She spent most of the interview on the history of Mark and Emma's marriage from his perspective. At one point Mark found himself getting quite tearful about all the external pressures there had been on the marriage over the years. Mark was surprised that she asked very few questions about Charlie and him, or about previous contacts. She said she would invite Mark back for a follow up interview after the contact. She said he could ask questions then. The contact with Charlie the next day was difficult. Mrs Lovelock's idea of observing was to micro—manage the entire contact period. They met at the park at a children's playground and Mark caught his breath as he saw how much Charlie had grown. But Charlie was not pleased to see Mark and hung back. Eventually father and son played hide and seek. Then as Charlie came down a long slide Mark popped up and said "boo". Charlie burst into tears and ran off to Steve. It then started to rain so they all went into a Hotel. Mrs Lovelock insisted that Mark sit furthest from Charlie. The conversation was difficult, mainly about school; Charlie's replies were monosyllabic. Mark had not seen Charlie for over a year, yet Mrs Lovelock expected Mark to maintain a constant dialogue with Charlie who was clearly wary, and did not want to do that. Mark had brought some presents and that helped break the ice a bit. They looked through some photos Mark had brought. Eventually Charlie said he was hungry so Mark went to buy him some chips. Charlie came to join Mark in the queue, an unexpected surprise. Mrs Lovelock got up to observe. Charlie did not like that so he went back to his seat scowling. After a difficult period Mark went off to feed a parking meter. On his return they all trooped off to the swings till it rained again. They retired to a coffee shop. Mark persuaded Charlie to play snap. They all played (except Mrs Lovelock), and Charlie ended up sitting on Steve's knee. Mark found this challenging. The whole experience was quite a shock for Mark. Charlie refused to touch Mark, let alone kiss Mark or hug his father, and would not let Mark hug him. Mark felt sick as he realised how alienated his son was from him. The feeling of injustice and sorrow was almost overwhelming. A few days later Mark rang Mrs Lovelock' office to arrange the follow up interview. Mark was told it would not be necessary. Mrs Lovelock was going to write a report based on that contact as the evidence of the father/ son relationship. Mark felt a cold feeling in his stomach; he had a distinct feeling that he was about to be stitched up.

Mrs. Lovelock produced a report of 87 pages. There was an extremely detailed analysis of Charlie. Mark was struck by the complete lack of any discussion with any person connected with Charlie and Mark. In her preamble Mrs. Lovelock catalogued hours of interviews with Emma's associates including several neighbours, her so-called partner Alex and Charlie's new schoolteacher. Given the immediate history of the case Mark thought it very odd that she did not speak to anyone from the previous school. One thing was certain though, she flatly refused further discussion with Mark. She did not contact any of Mark's support networks who knew Charlie: such as Tony and Tilly, his sister Laurie or Karen.

At the hearing Mark raised these objections and Mrs Lovelock agreed she wanted another observation of contact. Mark made it very clear that he was not going to be micro-managed in the same way. The judge ordered her to observe and not to interfere. The contact venue was fixed at a local petting zoo, and the arrangements were agreed in court. Mark was specifically allowed to bring Karen if he wanted. At the hearing and in his report before the court the guardian had indicated that ongoing contact was not likely to be a viable option given the history of obstruction by Emma. He said on balance he thought Charlie, for his long term development, would be better off moving to live with Mark. Because there was only a short time in the day for hearing evidence Mrs Lovelock did not express her views. Her report left various options with outline scenarios for each.

The judge ordered a final, final hearing to be heard over three days towards the end of June in Reading again. He ordered Mrs. Lovelock to produce an addendum report by early June.

Mrs Lovelock changed the venue after the hearing. She overruled all Mark's other suggestions and she insisted that contact be observed at the park again. The day before contact her secretary rang to tell Mark that Karen could not come to the contact. Infuriated, Mark arrived the next day with Karen. Mrs Lovelock got angry when she saw Karen. And asked her to leave. Mark agreed wearily.

Charlie was fretful and kept saying that he could not be late back to his mother.

"Why is he saying that? I have never ever brought him back late?" Mark asked Mrs. Lovelock

The woman shrugged.

"No idea" she said.

"Well don't you think you ought to find out? As I said, Charlie has never been late back from a contact."

Mrs Lovelock looked at him frowning deeply, and said.

"Look Mr. Richards, I did ask you not to bring Karen, but you ignored me!"

"But she's going now, what has that to do with Charlie worrying about being late back?" Mark said trying to control his anger.

Eventually Karen took charge of the situation, as Mrs Lovelock seemed unable to hear or understand anything Mark said. Karen left and waited in the town for the duration of the contact. Mrs Lovelock went on to control and manage the contact session much as she had on the previous occasion. Charlie was more relaxed, on familiar ground and spent less time clinging to Steve. Mrs Lovelock went on to describe in her addendum report in fairly minute detail her perceived failure of Mark to empathise and connect with his son. Mark made a detailed complaint and rebuttal to most of her points to the guardian and later to the judge. On the contact there were moments when Mark would have liked to discuss things with Mrs Lovelock. Her whole attitude came over as "I am the professional, I question you, you do not question me!". It is what Mark called a professional's arrogance. They had a personality clash and Mark considered Mrs. Lovelock to be hostile. But the repercussions in court were far more serious.

At the fourth final hearing over 25th, 26th and 27th of June the positions were laid out by the three barristers. Then Mark gave evidence, followed by Emma. They were questioned by each of the barristers, and sometimes the judge would ask questions to clarify a point. For most of the second day Mrs Lovelock gave evidence. The judge questioned her at length. She was asked by Emma's barrister to give an assessment of Emma as a mother. She went on to give a glowing account of Emma and went further to say that in her professional opinion she believed Emma had had a complete conversion on how important good contact for Charlie with his father was. She believed Emma would encourage and support such contact. Mark's barrister leapt up to object as Mrs Lovelock had not been engaged to professionally assess Emma, and the opinion contradicted that of other professionals. The judge overruled him. She was then asked to comment on the possibility of transfer of residence to the father. Mrs Lovelock said Mark did not have the necessary parenting skills, nor did Mark have sufficient empathy or put Charlie's needs before his own to permit her to make a recommendation for Charlie to live with Mark. Mark's barrister objected repeatedly that an assessment based on two contacts and one interview were not sufficient grounds for this. Mrs. Lovelock went on to say that Charlie had indicated that he wished to see his father. Mrs. Lovelock was confident that contact could be restarted with Charlie's wishes defining that contact.

She said that Emma had already offered more contacts than the suggestion of 4 short contacts with chaperones each year. Part way through Mrs Lovelock's oral testimony, the guardian and Charlie's barrister stood up to say that the guardian withdrew his support for a change of residence because he could not go against Mrs Lovelocks' professional opinion. He did add that he was sceptical of Emma's conversion, given the history of the case.

The case collapsed.

In his judgement judge Travers explained that he understood Mark scepticism over Emma's apparent conversion but agreed with Mrs Lovelock that Emma had had a complete change of heart over this. On that basis he went on to outline the future of contact, expecting the chaperones to be weaned away from contact in three months and with staying contact to be resumed within a year. He set out an order for a few short contacts and ordered Mrs Lovelock, Emma and Mark to meet in September to plan the structure of contact going forward. He also ordered that any deviation from the orders made, including the loss of just one contact would trigger a return to court before him within 7 days of such a notification. He was confident that, as Mark had demonstrated " the patience of Job" in dealing with this case, Mark would go along with the process to rebuild his relationship with Charlie. Mark's barrister had been pleased when Mark had told him they were before judge Travers, as he described him as one of the golden boys of the system. He had a reputation for getting things done. Mark was reasonably optimistic that he may be able to control Emma. He had a good control of the proceedings and did not let discussions drift off course.

Two things immediately struck Mark and had alarm bells ringing. Mrs Lovelock wanted Charlie to have paramount control of how contact proceeded. To Mark's mind Charlie was completely under his mother's influence and Mark foresaw Charlie being put under incredible stress to comply with Emma's wishes over his own. The other was the obvious bias from Mrs Lovelock. One extraordinary comment from Mrs Lovelock during her oral evidence was that she said that what had happened before was no longer relevant to the case. Every other professional involved with Emma and Charlie indicated that Emma did not put Charlie's needs and wants before her own. Judge Travers himself in his opening remarks had said that the very unusual but obvious observation of the whole case was that from the very beginning Emma had fought over every single area of the divorce. He said it was quite rare for this to happen as most people contended specific areas of dispute like, for example, finance. In Mark's evidence he had pointed out that this was Emma's third apparent epiphany, so why should it be any more credible than the previous two? Mark also pointed out that the guardian had stated in his report before the hearing that he felt contact was not the way forward given the history of the matter. When Mark left the court on the final day he happened to walk out with the guardian. He wished Mark luck with the new orders but he said he knew they would not work and that Mrs Lovelock was completely wrong,

Emma had fooled her completely.

When Mark stopped to discuss with his barrister what they could do now, he repeated what the guardian had just told him. In his opinion the case had been a close run thing until the guardian's position collapsed. He was extremely disappointed with the guardian, but given his actions in the past he was not surprised that he had taken the opportunity to 'bottle out'. He felt that had the guardian challenged Mrs Lovelock's testimony and voiced his opinions the judge would have listened. That was the guardian's job. In his barrister's opinion this happened all too often with state employed people pitted against privately engaged professionals whose next job depended on their reputation. Mark said that he had often complained to Karen that the guardian was more concerned with managing his job rather than doing it as far as Charlie was concerned. At the end of the hearing the guardian asked the judge if he could resign from the case. There was some discussion about possibly requesting a NYAS person to do the job. In the end the judge ruled that the guardian had to stay on but in the role of "keeper of the files". As such he was not expected to do anything. The judge felt that now that Emma had completely changed her attitude, the guardian had no active role anymore.

After a few days thinking about his options, Mark sought his barrister's advice on appealing the outcome. He said application to the court of Appeal would be expensive. If Mark lost he would have to pay, if not all, a high proportion of the costs for everyone else. That scenario would put Mark into debt. He also said that the appeal judges would most likely support Travers and allow him the latitude to try contact one more time. Mark dearly wanted to appeal but the advice he was being given was that the financial risk was too great. Mark was already having to subsidise his earnings from his savings to live, so if he got into debt there was no way he would be able to repay it. Mark had had financial help from his ex-brother-in-law for several hearings up until the third set of final hearings that finished in February 2007. He felt uncomfortable accepting any further money with no good result to show for it.

Following the hearings in Reading the driving agency Mark worked for lost two contracts that Mark usually did for them. As a result, work almost dried up. At that time Mark was also about to take his final driving instructors exam so he left the agency to practise for his exam. In mid-July Mark cancelled his regular maintenance payments to Emma for Charlie. As his agency payments had been erratic and Emma demanded that Mark pay by standing order, Mark had worked out a figure for regular payments each week. The idea had been to adjust the total amount every year to that agreed with the CSA. As it happened Mark had paid more than the legal requirement calculated by the CSA. When Mark wrote to Emma explaining that he was not earning and so had cancelled the standing order, this became an excuse for her to complain about his lack of financial support for Charlie at every opportunity, including at her meetings with Mrs. Lovelock.

As ordered Mrs Lovelock explained the outcome to Charlie. There were many understandings outlined in the preamble to the orders. For example one understanding was that " the mother recognises and accepts that Charlie needs to have, for his own emotional development, a proper relationship with his father and that the goal should be that Charlie would have free and unsupported contact with Mark". It outlined the role of the chaperones and stated that Mark was to have unfettered access to the school. One of his immediate areas of contention was that Emma only agreed to contact at places that to his mind were very boring venues for a seven year old boy. Mark felt this was a deliberate move to make contact more difficult and less fun for Charlie. In the past Charlie and Mark had done active things together. Mark was specifically refused permission to allow Charlie to visit Tony and Tilly or his sister Laura's house and indeed to have anybody other than Karen accompany him on contact meetings.

Mark was given a list of six dates over the next 10 months, each for three-hour contacts. In September this was to be looked at again and amended or built on when moving forward with contact to include the reintroduction of the staying contact. There was an order for Charlie to contact Mark indirectly every three weeks initially by cards or letter. It was going to be left up to Charlie to decide if he wanted to phone Mark.

In his summation the judge talked at some length about what he called Emma's previous 'demonisation' of Mark to Charlie. He accepted that Emma had now changed. But he emphasised that in order to help Charlie rebuild a relationship with his father Emma had to actively reverse the demonisation. He said this would be a major indicator of the change in attitude by Emma.

The ball was firmly in Emma's court. Judge Travers went on to say that he had got an understanding from Emma that there would be no restrictions over his involvement with the school or any other area of his parental responsibility such as Charlie's health. The judge had ordered that Emma and her legal team draw up the order with the agreements and understandings in Emma's own words so that she could not, at a later date, claim she did not understand them.

When the judge ordered that the guardian be relegated to the role as keeper of the files, Mark saw the guardian as a mechanism to register his complaints and objections concerning the case which could be referred to when, as Mark believed they would, things went pear-shaped. When Emma had been assessed previously, she had waited a year to raise any objections to the report. As it happened the objections and criticisms about the report centred on descriptions of the untidiness of the home and in particular the piles of unwashed clothes, pots and pans and crockery in the kitchen. The substance of the psychological analysis was not challenged. Judge Grey heard the complaints and was critical of the personal and unnecessary nature of descriptions of the living conditions at Charlie's home. But he was also critical of Emma for taking over a year to object. With that in mind Mark wrote several times to the guardian over the next year to voice his anger and frustration at the continued shenanigans consistently being used by Emma to frustrate Marks attempt at rebuilding a relationship with Charlie.

Mark was uncomfortable about having Emma's friends and neighbours, Steve and Melanie Jackson, as Charlie's chaperones on contact. Emma and Mark had known them for nearly ten years. They had entertained each other in their respective homes, and on one occasion Mark had even invited them to Christmas lunch. One thing Mark had the most difficulty with was that they had made it plain over the years that they were not interested in having children. Children were too much of an intrusion in their lifestyle. Instead they devoted themselves to their four standard poodles. They had made it obvious when Mark was living as separated but still in the house, that they took Emma's side. Emma was always talking to them. They both wrote statements in support of Emma for the court. Steve made a personal attack, Melanie was more neutral but despite their obvious bias, apparently Charlie could not have anyone else.

The first contact was at Town Museum in Newbury, within sight of the park they usually went to! Mark asked Karen to accompany him, partly as a witness to the proceedings and partly to take photographs of Charlie with Mark. Karen was brilliant in making sure that they came to contact armed with lots of fun things like colouring books and crayons, cards and the Frisbee to play with. Charlie was very awkward to start with, refusing even to say hello or engage. In the museum he thawed out a little but kept his distance.

As they sat in a little café having tea and ice-cream, Charlie started colouring a book.

"So Charlie, are you enjoying school?" Karen asked brightly

"Yes, I got two stars last week!" Charlie said proudly

"Well done you!" Karen said , "What did you get your stars for?"

"Reading and another one for tidying the classroom!" Charlie said, casting wary glances in Mark's direction.

As they crossed the road to where the canal separated the quay from the park, swans and ducks were crowding together as people threw them bits of bread.

"Can I throw some Mister?" Charlie asked and Mark felt a lump in his throat, it had been a long time since he had heard the old familiar name from Charlie.

"Of course, I'll go in and get some form the café."

Charlie began to interact more with Mark as the noisy birds ran towards them to get the bread. The boy was laughing out loud now and even ducked behind Mark and held onto his leg as one greedy swan tried to take the bread right out of his hand! It was a reasonably successful contact. Charlie wanted to come back and see the swans and go to the park the next time they met in September.

In early July Mark had written to introduce himself to Charlie's new preparatory school as his father. Mark had been sent a prospectus and an invitation to tour with the headmaster.

Emma and Mark attended the meeting with Mrs Lovelock as ordered by the court. Mark had expected Emma to become more and more difficult over time, but not so soon after the court hearing. Emma tried repeatedly to lambaste Mark for not paying maintenance. Mrs Lovelock found it difficult to keep Emma on track about contact. Apparently none of the venues Mark put forward were acceptable. For some reason Tony and Tilly's house was vetoed by Mrs Lovelock, even though in the past Charlie had spent many contacts there. Charlie had actually loved the second contact at Newbury between the swans and the park. There was lots of activity to do together there. Emma vetoed this even though Charlie had asked to return there. Mark pointed out that some venues were just too expensive by the time Mark had paid for four adults and a child. Emma, in order to appear friendly, suggested that Charlie and Mark could picnic on the farm. Mrs Lovelock was very impressed and said so in her report to the court. In court Emma denied categorically that she had ever made such an offer. It had obviously been just a ploy to soften up Mrs Lovelock.

The next problem came totally unexpectedly. The school had referred Mark's letter of introduction to Emma for her response. She had written back to the school that Mark was not to be allowed to visit the school except in the case of a specific school event. Her ability to split hairs in the use of certain words that she herself had written in the court order was extraordinary. The judge had been perfectly clear in his summation. But Mrs. Lovelock had not attended the last day at court and she took Emma's side in the argument and then claimed in her report that Mark had agreed with her decision that he could only go to the school on an open day or at Charlie's invitation. Mark could not have been more opposed to her attitude. He vehemently challenged Mrs Lovelock' position that Charlie should have any authority over his involvement with the school. Mark said repeatedly that putting the onus on Charlie to decide about everything was simply piling more stress on the boy. Mark actually said that just because she was an expert did not make her right! Mark knew his son, and understood what was really happening. He was frustrated and felt exhausted. He really did not know how much longer he could go on, facing obstacles at every turn. This woman who doubtless thought she was very good at her job, was playing God with the most precious relationship, that of a father and his son.

Why could no-one see what was going on?

Chapter 23

The End of The Line

Mrs Lovelock described de-demonising Mark as reframing situations for Charlie to see Mark in a positive light. But trying to get Emma to address this was a struggle. Emma was adamant that it was nothing to do with her. It was all up to Charlie. By the end of the meeting Mark knew for sure that Emma's apparent conversion had been a hoax. Yet Mrs Lovelock, despite all the evidence to the contrary, wrote in her report that Emma both understood and would engage in reframing. Mark simply could not believe how Mrs Lovelock could justify coming to that conclusion. They went on to plan the future of contact. It was immediately obvious that Mrs Lovelock was not interested in even attempting the time scales the judge had outlined. The chaperones were to accompany Charlie for at least 9 months and would only be weaned off with Charlie's agreement. Staying contact was not even going to be considered until well into 2010 so was not discussed.

Mark gritted his teeth in frustration. He knew that if he wanted to see Charlie he had no choice but to agree. It was deemed too early for Charlie to ring Mark. After the meeting and after Mark saw Mrs. Lovelock's report he wrote to the guardian to register his complaint and objections to Mrs Lovelock' involvement and bias.

The school offered Mark an open day tour and an appointment to see two of Charlie's teachers. Mark had no wish to antagonise the school, so he attended the open day.

The facilities at the school were impressive, but so were the school fees! The teachers described Charlie as a troubled child who had difficulty concentrating. When Charlie was in a good mood though, apparently he was a lovely child.

The third contact was supposed to be at half term, but it was cancelled. Charlie had asked to go to a friend's party on the same day. Mark acquiesced and asked for another day instead. Emma offered the next day, the Sunday. Mark explained that he was moving house and that the Sunday was the formal hand-over to the landlord. Emma refused to offer any other day. Mark was extremely disappointed but despite the impotent rage he felt, let the matter rest.

Mark had moved back in with Tony and Tilly. At the end of November he wrote to the judge to explain his fears for future contact and to make him aware that there were ongoing problems. He got no reply.

At the final hearing in June 2008 the judge had said he saw no reason for the stay on the costs matter imposed by Judge Grey to remain. He lifted the stay, making it free to pursue the matter. Emma's solicitors said they did not act for her in the costs matters. Emma asked for time to seek legal advice. By October Mark realised that he had little choice but to go back to being LIP, except for the costs matter.

The next contact was just before Christmas at a Victorian Costume museum. Mark did not think this was going to be an easy venue for a young boy. Steve had a close connection to the museum and he spent a lot of time explaining things to Charlie. After an hour Charlie said he was bored and asked to go for an ice cream. The restaurant closed at 4pm so they went to Burger King. After much persuasion Charlie was coaxed into opening his Christmas presents. After the presents Mark asked Charlie to think about the chaperones and how much longer he would need someone with him.

"I will always need Steve, he makes me feel safe!" Charlie said and Mark could almost hear Emma in his voice.

"I see Charlie, can you tell me why you would not feel safe without him? Maybe I can change things?"

Charlie looked down at his feet and shrugged.

"Come on Charlie, I would never do anything to hurt you, you know that, tell me why you don't feel safe?" Mark prompted gently.

After a long silence Charlie said,

" I hate your family and I don't want to see them again!"

Mark was shocked at the outburst. Again it was almost as though Charlie was speaking with his mother's voice.

He wondered how much further Emma was going to be prepared to go to pursue her alienation strategy.

Mark explained to Steve as they left that Charlie needed help to adjust to the situation without chaperones. Mark said that Emma needed to address this. Steve said nothing.

The next contact should have been in the February half term. On the 4th February Mark left Tony and Tilly's to live with Karen as a lodger. The recession was affecting her income so the arrangement was good for both of them.

Mark failed his driving instructor final exam. Now that it was evident that Charlie was not going to be living with him Mark decided not to pursue that career. His brother John had appeared at Christmas from Thailand and invited Mark to return with him for a visit. He generously offered to pay the fare on his air miles.

Mark spent a month travelling around Thailand. He was loosely based from John's apartment in Bangkok. The effect of being away from Emma's toxic influence was amazing: most of the stress related symptoms caused in essence by Emma's endless bullying, melted away.

At the beginning of February 2009 the south of England had unusually heavy snowfalls. The evening before contact Mark rang Emma to find out what the roads were like in her area. The radio reports spoke of 9 inches of snow at Bristol airport! They agreed that the contact should be cancelled. Steve was also concerned about driving in the snow. Mark asked Emma for another day over the half term to make up for the one lost. She claimed she and Charlie were going away for the rest of the period. Mark suggested that he pop down to see Charlie just for an hour or so the weekend following half term. Emma was adamant that Mrs Lovelock had said that contact could only take place in holiday time. So yet again, Mark had Mrs Lovelock to blame, this time, for not being able to see Charlie. On a later contact Steve and Charlie both said they had not gone away for half term. Whilst on the phone Emma had the gall to tell Mark she had to change the 4th April contact to 28th March. Mark told her he had to check his diary and think about it. Mark discovered that Charlie was to break up from school the day before, so he would be exhausted. It was yet another clever attempt at sabotage.

In order to cover her tracks for the judge Emma sent Mark two letters dated 5th and 8th February, during the half term. The second offered to ask Steve if he would fit in another day, over the half term. The two letters arrived in the same envelope with a post mark dated 13th. So it had been posted the first day after the end of half term. Luckily Mark kept the envelope as evidence of Emma's deviousness. It was typical of her to be so obstructive about something, and then actively spin the story to try to prove how conciliatory she was for the benefit of the court.

At the end of March the hearing to sort out the cost issues from the appeal hearing in 2005, nearly four years before, came to court. Emma had got an adjournment in February. Reading County Court managed to confuse the hearing as a child matters hearing so had Judge Grey presiding. Mark had left the case in Alison's hands. She had instructed a barrister. Mark did not attend. It turned out that Emma had refused to pay the bill as presented to her in November

2008; hence the arranged hearing. The barrister had drawn up a skeleton argument, as previously ordered by judge Grey, and when it was presented to Emma, she suddenly agreed to pay. But she refused to pay the outstanding costs incurred in forcing her to pay. This was the third hearing on the matter, in addition to the hours of work done by his solicitor over the years to get her to pay.

The judge ordered Emma to pay the outstanding bill plus only £750 for the court costs. Judge Grey said the costs applied for were wholly disproportionate to the sum being claimed and were excessive. He summarily slashed the costs by 80%! The irony was that his past actions were largely to blame for the high costs, together with Emma's relentless determination to fight everything. Judge Grey appeared to be angry that this matter had come back to court to inflame the ongoing child matters proceedings.

Mark could barely contain his anger at the judge. It was he and he alone who had kept this festering battle going for four years!

If, in the customary manner, Mark had financed the recovery of the costs, then Mark would not have seen any of the £5,400 owed to him. The solicitor and barrister's costs would have been deducted first. As Mark had told Ian originally Mark had no confidence that he would ever get any of the money out of Emma.

The courts, it seemed, were a minefield of prejudice and incompetence. As it was the solicitors ended up considerably out of pocket.

When Mark complained to judge Travers about the loss of contacts and other breaches of the orders, Mark asked him to trigger the clause in his order to bring the matter back before him within 7 days.

The judge instructed Mark to make a C2 application in the normal way. (This takes months). So Mark applied through Reading County Court. They muddled the application. The case was referred to judge Travers but somehow judge Grey got involved again. Because of the muddle at the costs hearing judge Grey instructed Mark to apply direct to judge Travers via his Clerk at the Royal Courts of Justice in the Strand in London. So instead of going back before him within seven days, it was to take three months!

The only beneficial side effect was that now that Emma knew Mark had referred the contact problems back to court, she was now back on good behaviour.

Because the court had ordered Emma to ensure Charlie sent cards and letters every three weeks, Mark got a steady flow of letters. The initial letters explained what he was doing and were written by Charlie in longhand and signed by him. After Christmas 2008, however, everything was done on computer and generally consisted of only one or two sentences saying thank you for something. They were also no longer signed by Charlie. One exception was in response to Mark's visit to see the school on the open day and seeing his teachers. That produced a picture of a man's face with the caption "stupid man", drawn by hand. Alongside, written by hand, were demands for Mark to stay away from his school and the farm. In the contacts father and son rarely talked about the future, but on a couple of occasions Mark did ask Charlie if he had talked with Emma or the chaperone about contact. By the spring of 2009 Mark asked at the end of contact whether the chaperone would be coming on the next contact. Charlie's response was extraordinarily aggressive.

"I told you I *HATE* you, I don't want to see you in the first place and I will *NEVER* come and see you without a chaperone!"

Mark bit his lip to stop the tears coming. He knew that he would have to be patient.

Largely contact was good. There was a pattern. At the beginning Charlie would be aloof and ignore Mark and Karen if she came with him. After an hour the boy would relax a bit and be friendly and they would be able to do things together. But Charlie would be clock watching and for the last half an hour or so the barriers would go up again and he would often go to Steve. When it was time to leave he would get agitated and be visibly stressed. It was perfectly obvious to Karen and Mark that little or no reframing or de-demonising had been done. In fact quite the opposite, by the time the hearing in Reading was arranged Charlie was noticeably troubled. Up to this time all his school reports indicated that he was troubled and not settling down. All the teachers commented that he lacked concentration, that his work was erratic. Charlie could be moody and withdrawn.

On the surface contact with Charlie seemed fair, but Mark had a nagging feeling that Charlie was a volcano waiting to erupt. It was almost impossible to talk about anything with him and he always kept his distance.

After several delays a hearing was arranged in Reading before judge Travers again. The judge kept it very informal: just Emma, Mark and the guardian in court. Mark had produced a proper bundle with chronology.

Emma and Mark produced position statements and relevant evidence such as letters to support their arguments. The guardian said he had no role to play in the proceedings so was merely an observer.

The judge said he had read the bundle and asked Mark to explain why he had called for a hearing. Mark outlined the main points to substantiate his claim that Emma's conversion was a hoax. Every time Mark spoke Emma interrupted or spoke over him. Mark had to ask the judge to intervene. The judge asked Emma to respond. Naturally she claimed everything was going brilliantly. But she took the opportunity to go over old history and to whine that Mark was not paying any maintenance. The judge asked the guardian for his comments. He had none.

In his position statement Mark had made some strong criticisms of both the guardian and judge Grey. The guardian had remained purposely and pointedly aloof in the waiting room before going before the judge. One of Mark's main appeals to the judge was the lack of progress in weaning off the chaperone. It was a year since the hearing where he had expressed a wish that the chaperones were withdrawn within three months and staying contact re-established within a year. Mrs Lovelock' plan had called for the withdrawal of the chaperones over the spring or summer. Mark's complaint was that Charlie was against it because Mark believed he was not being encouraged to think about it positively; neither, Mark said, was there any evidence of reframing or de-demonising. Mark had lost two of the six contacts so far!

The judge closed the bundle and said he was not inclined to deal with the frictions or the matter of Emma's commitment or lack of it. He was happy that Mark was having contact, albeit in his words, with minor problems. Bizarrely he then ordered that the chaperones be weaned off by early next year and to have a review hearing in March 2010. In effect he gave Emma a further six months to keep the chaperones.

After the hearing Mark informed Alison of the outcome. She and Adrian, his Mackenzie friend had asked to be kept informed of progress. Alison's reaction was that Mark should either appeal, with all the stress that that would entail, or Mark should consider backing off for a few years till Charlie was older. For a couple of years Mark had been voicing concern that this continual battle was undermining Charlie and his schooling. If Alex had left his wife and married Emma, as he claimed he wanted, Mark would have backed away knowing that there was a reasonable father figure for Charlie. But it was now apparent that everything about Alex and Emma was not as it seemed. Alex had faded away. Adrian was more interested in the psychology. His first thought was that had Mark been represented the judge would not have been able to take his lazy attitude over the case. Secondly he felt that most judges had big egos and Mark had made the judge face the fact that he had been completely wrong in his previous judgement. Emma had obviously hoodwinked him. That was an embarrassing viewpoint. The judge had ignored the evidence, and because Mark was awed by the court's power he had gone along with it. Adrian had been and was right, Mark was not assertive enough.

Mark had a contact with Charlie from 11am to 4 pm at the Living Rainforest about ten days after the hearing. Karen accompanied Mark and they took a picnic for everyone. Charlie arrived late with Steve. For a long time he was aloof and distant. At lunch he started to interact, largely by trying to kick Mark under the table. After lunch there was talk in the courtyard about the charity and some of the animals they had seen. Charlie said he wanted to go to the play area. Mark took his hand and they slunk off. Charlie climbed up a climbing wall to about twelve feet then he lost her nerve and swished down on the safety rope. The others came to watch. Next Charlie and Mark did some pond dipping together, which he seemed to enjoy. They went to the shop at the exit as the contact was nearly at an end. Charlie spent ages trying to pick a present to take home. He was so anxious by this stage that he was unable to choose. Karen helped him. On the walk back to the car park Karen held the chaperone back as Mark tried to talk to Charlie about how he felt about contact. It was as if Mark had turned on a switch. Charlie became quite vacant, staring at the ground repeating like a mantra that he hated Mark and did not want to see Mark again. Mark got no real sense out of him, but he was visibly distressed.

"Come on Charlie, we had a nice time didn't we? Contact is supposed to be a fun time for us both." Mark said. Then taking a deep breath he said. "If you really hate seeing me I will take a step back. It's up to you!"

Charlie looked down at his feet.

"Look Charlie" Mark said gently, "I, won't see you again until you want to see me, how would that be?" Before Charlie could answer Steve joined them and Charlie went to him.

Mark explained what he had discussed with Charlie and expressed his thanks to Steve for his help in trying to make contact successful.

"Look Steve, I just can't continue with this. It's cruel! The alienation seems now to be so bad that seeing me is just exacerbating the problem for Charlie. So basically what I am saying is that I am not going to see Charlie for the foreseeable future."

"Look, I'm sorry, sorry for all of it. But I think you could be right. We arrived late today because Charlie was hysterical and refusing to go on contact!"

Mark bowed his head.

"Sorry to have to tell you this Mark, but Charlie hates being forced to write cards and letters every three weeks."

Mark sighed. " I knew there was a problem with the letters. For some time now they have been reduced to one or two sentences and unsigned."

"Really? I didn't realise that." Steve said, " I thought they were longer letters." The two men stood in silence for a moment then Steve said,

"Look, I might as well be honest with you, ever since Charlie used to stay with you for the longer contacts in 2006 he was more and more worried about not being returned to his mother."

"But that's crazy I was never so much as a minute late back, you know that!" Mark said.

"I know but Charlie was convinced that you wanted to take him away from his mother for ever!"

"Well why didn't Emma reassure him? I have done everything I could in good conscience but I'm not going to put Charlie through anymore of this cruelty!"

Steve nodded and put his hand out. Mark took it and the pair shook hands.

The simple truth was that Mrs Lovelock' plan to put Charlie at the heart of decisions about contact just put too much pressure on the boy. Charlie was desperate to please everyone, but his bond with his mother was far stronger than his bond with Mark, and given Emma's extreme hostility Charlie was in an impossible position. The other serious flaw was that Mrs Lovelock was completely fooled by Emma's so-called conversion. Because of that blinkered attitude, nothing was ever going to work.

Extraordinarily, although Emma claimed to love her son so much, she was prepared to put him through endless stress and turmoil to secure sole control over him. And now a father, that had done nothing wrong, and had nothing but love to give, had to sacrifice his relationship so that Charlie could have some stability and peace in his young life.

Mark wrote to tell the judge what he had decided about Charlie's contact and the reasons why. Mark asked him if he had any ideas on the matter. The judge replied that it was Mark's decision, adding that he did not condone it and that if Mark wanted to do anything about it Mark should apply to the court in the normal way. Mark was pretty angry at this heartless response. At the final hearing the judge had said that if the contact did not work, he had plenty of other things at his disposal in his armoury. His constant assurances that he would do everything in his power to support Charlie to have a good relationship with both parents were as hollow as his promise to deal with a parent that constantly obstructed contact. The hypocrisy was sickening.

Mark mulled over what to do for the rest of the summer. He wrote to Charlie regularly but had no way of knowing if he received the letters. In September Mark emailed the judge's clerk to say that he would attend the hearing scheduled for March to discuss a way forward.

Mark wrote to Steve to thank him for his help over contact and to the District Domestic Violence Liaison officer to update the history of the case and to close his dialogue with that office.

Mark also wrote to Mrs Lovelock explaining why he had ended contact and expressing his criticisms of her handling of the case in general. Mark wrote to Emma outlining why he had decided not to continue to see Charlie and wrote to the school to advise them of the news and that there might be a reaction from Charlie. Mark wrote to Charlie explaining again what he had said to him the last time they had been together.

Mark received a thank you note from Charlie for the Christmas present he sent the boy. A week before the March hearing Mark rang the Reading court to check it was still listed and was assured it was. Mark went to Reading for the scheduled hearing only to be told that they had no record of it. He was referred to the listings officer. She told Mark the court hearing had been cancelled months ago. On further investigation she explained that the judge had closed the case and files in October 2009 and had discharged the guardian. Mark was almost lost for words that no one had thought to inform him! He had always been told that as the applicant in the case he was the only person that could close the case or at the very least it would require his agreement to do so.

Mark wrote to the judge for an explanation. He replied that as Mark had ended contact with Charlie there was nothing else the court could do for him. As a result the judge had closed the case. Mark's instinct was that as the case was one that the judge really did not want to have to deal with properly, he had leapt at the first opportunity to wash his hands of it. Mark suspected there were no other options in his armoury, other than having to deal harshly with Emma. And both this judge and his colleagues had studiously avoided that option.

A few weeks later Mark embarked on a 500-mile walk across northern Spain, along the ancient pilgrimage route to Santiago De Compostella, called the Camino Frances. In the five weeks, as he walked, in the right kind of atmosphere and mentally rejuvenated, Mark had plenty of time to ponder his future with Charlie.

Galling as it was Mark recognised that Charlie was showing signs, at last, of settling at school. Obviously what he needed most was stability and consistency to give him the chance to reach his potential. In the short term it would be better for Charlie to settle with his mother; and for Emma to de-stress about keeping Mark out of Charlie's life. But, Mark knew, in the longer term, it could be very damaging for Charlie to remain completely dominated by such an abusive mother. Until Charlie was older and able to express himself more and assert his own wishes there was nothing constructive that Mark could do. Whether the alienation continued as Mark expected it would, or whether one day Charlie would wish to judge Mark for himself remained to be seen.

The likelihood was that Charlie would be conditioned to follow the same twisted emotional life path as his mother. There has already been two generations of abuse, possibly more. Children that are groomed so negatively would not easily be able to escape some amount of emotional scarring.

On his walk Mark pondered how best to change the culture of denial, incompetence and prejudice that so pervaded the Family Law Division. How could the outcome for children like Charlie be improved; abused by one parent with an extreme attitude and alienated from the other? How could a system be fashioned that was wiser, cheaper, quicker and above all fairer? From his experience, Mark realised that

The Family Court failed on all counts, and was plainly not fit for purpose.

While he was writing an account of his experiences in the summer of 2010 Mark learned from Charlie's school report that he was being moved to another school. How shocking that now that his school reports suggested he was settling down and producing some good work at school, Emma had decided to move him again! Charlie needed stability. Emma had moved the child from nursery school to nursery school, now school to school. Charlie had never been anywhere for more than two years. He had no chance to build up a good group of friends as he stayed such a short time in any one place. Was this yet another sick strategy to keep Charlie completely dependent and tied to his mother? Mark wrote to Emma asking for information on Charlie's new school.

After some delay she replied that if Mark paid her £55,400, she would send the information. Rather than react to the blackmail Mark sent a further three letters over the next five months: all of which were ignored.

Finally, in October, Mark applied to the High Court for a hearing to ask the judge to enforce the order of 2008, which had enshrined his parental right to be involved with Charlie's schooling and health matters without interference from Emma. Judge Travers declined to hear the matter and passed it over to a more junior judge, judge Brownlow, the case to be heard in Reading again. Mark was eventually notified that the hearing would be in January. At the time there was considerable disruption with heavy snowfall in the south of England, together with the usual Christmas postal rush. As a consequence Mark decided not to risk sending a small bundle to the court in the post, but decided to take it with him on the day of the hearing.

When Mark arrived at the county court, he was informed that the courtroom had been damaged by water from burst pipes. They adjourned to the Magistrate's court. Mark asked the Usher if he would take the small bundle for the judge. He declined. When they went before the judge, he declined the documents again and proceeded to question Emma, after ascertaining from Mark that this was a single-issue hearing. He questioned Emma as to what she saw as the problem with Charlie's father knowing the identity of the boy's school. Her repeated answer to questions around this subject was that she had no problem but Charlie was adamant that his father should not be told. She claimed that Charlie had demanded to leave one school as he could not trust his father not to turn up at the school. Emma went on to claim that during his time at the previous school Charlie's behaviour had deteriorated very badly, following allegations of cheating and stealing. Judge Brownlow fixed Emma with a purposeful stare.

"So do you always do what your son demands?"

Emma smiled at him disarmingly,

" Goodness no! But your honour, in this instance Charlie was so adamant that I had to support him." She let her smile fade to be replaced with a look of concern.

"You could ask him yourself!" she said.

"The boy is here?" Judge Brownlow said frowning. He was very displeased and explained that Charlie should not be informed of any of the legal process. Emma had been criticised by nearly every professional involved for including Charlie in the court process. As Emma claimed she could not explain Charlie's reasons for wishing to exclude his father from his school, the judge decided that Charlie explain them to Mark in person. He had a recess to allow time for Charlie to talk to Mark. It then took 40 minutes to persuade Charlie to even see Mark. Mark met Charlie in the company of Steve again. Charlie would barely look at Mark, most of the time he looked down at the table. Eventually he muttered.

"I don't like you and I don't want to see you!"

"But why Charlie, why do you feel like that?" Mark asked

"Because I don't trust you!" Charlie refused to explain why until, as Mark pressed him gently, he blurted out

"You hit mummy!"

"Ok Charlie, listen to me, that simply is not true, do you hear me? It's not true!"

But the wary look in his son's eyes as he glanced at him briefly stopped Mark in his tracks, he couldn't put the child through any more.

Mark said gently "Ok Charlie, but I will continue to be informed of your progress at school. At your age you do not have the wisdom to choose a school for yourself, but you can and you must complain if you are unhappy there.!"

Charlie looked up at him doubtfully,

"Look son, it is a parent's duty to monitor a school and to make sure a child is receiving the best education available. I am afraid that whether you like it or not I am going to do that, check on you and on your school."

For about ten minutes there was a difficult one-sided conversation, going round in circles. Charlie became more and more hostile, so Mark withdrew. The judge reappeared, and was disappointed to learn that Charlie had been unable to express his reasons.

Mark asked the judge to consider making a statement ruling that Emma had broken the order. He refused to address the matter and instead went on to make an order that Emma should write once a month to Mark informing him of Charlie's progress at school and in his life in general, including photographs. He ordered that Emma would supply copies of any school reports edited so that the school identity remained hidden. The application was adjourned till the end of August. Mark was refused permission to appeal.

Mark left the court reeling with the realisation that the judges' repeated assurances that they would support him and would ensure that Mark would maintain a link with his son was a complete sham. What should have been an open and shut case of breaking a court order was sidestepped and the judge had gone on to countermand a more senior judge's order and what should have been enshrined as Mark's civil right as a parent. This was another example of blatant prejudice. Because Mark was refused permission to appeal there was now nothing Mark could do to complain.

He had reached the end of the line.

Chapter 24

What was the point?

In the days that followed, Mark was so angry that he had to allow himself a week to cool down before thinking of what he could to address the injustice. Mark wrote to several newspapers and investigative programmes like Panorama. He also determined to publicise what had happened to him by having the account that he had written for Charlie, rewritten by a ghostwriter

As he struggled through the days on autopilot, the same question went round and round in his head; what is the purpose of the civil court? Most people would probably say—to deliver justice. This would certainly be the case if you were applying to the civil court for redress for some harmful action against you. The Family Court, however was totally different. At his second hearing, before the only lady judge Mark had encountered in his fifty odd appearances in court, Mark was told bluntly that the court had nothing to do with justice: it was all to do with the interests of the child!

Mark had been brought up with the imperial spin that, like most things British, the courts and the justice system were the best in the world. Being educated in the private school system he was often preached to that the British value of fairness was one of our most famous national characteristics. If it was not fair, it was not cricket! Once he was caught up in the legal system, for a long time, Mark had the unreal expectation that the great British justice system would prevail and everything would come right. When he became a member of Families Need Fathers Mark began to get a sense of the anger and frustration of so many fathers' with the apparent lack of basic justice in the system. In the fathers4justice meetings Mark met some men whose anger and bitterness was consuming them; even one or two trying hard to hide the menace of violence. Every so often the media reports cases where fathers who are denied proper contact or, in their eyes, not enough contact, take the extreme action of suicide and the murder of their children. Mark did not condone such actions but now, sadly, he had a real, if appalling sense of how these tragic situations could arise. The biggest injustice in the system was that men and women were not considered emotionally equal. Mark had encountered this prejudice repeatedly. When it comes to raw emotions, Mark thought, we are still animals. In nature there are two dominant emotions; to procreate and to protect our young. The way society has progressed or evolved men had been programmed not to show any emotional weaknesses to those outside the family; in case those weaknesses could be exploited. It was perfectly acceptable for women to show their emotions in our society in most situations. Mark appreciated that in his lifetime many of these old doctrines were being overturned and many men were experiencing some confusion over this. It was also a given that most fathers are not as expressive in describing their emotional links with their children as mothers are.

When the idea of changing residence became a serious option Emma was repeatedly questioned by barristers, judges and experts as to how she would feel if Charlie was taken away from her. Her consistent reply was that it was so inconceivable that she could not come to terms with it. Nobody ever asked Mark what it was like not to see his son. In one hearing before judge Grey at the end of a discussion about a possible change of residence the judge demonstrated his prejudice by closing the hearing saying that as Mark had not produced a detailed plan for how he was going to look after Charlie, he was adjourning the case. Firstly, Mark reflected, he could and should have indicated before the hearing that Mark should produce such a plan. Secondly he could have spent ten minutes questioning Mark if he was really interested. When, at later hearings, Mark produced such a plan it was never even referred to.

Mrs Lovelock was given three options to consider for the court about Charlie having a relationship with Mark. One of the options was to change residence; she was to question the effect on Emma and on Charlie. She conspicuously failed to address any of this in her report. It became obvious from her oral examination in court that she did not intend for this to be an option. She also failed to interview any of Mark's supporting friends or partner to explore Mark's emotional links with Charlie. The overriding impression in court was that as a father Mark had less emotion invested in Charlie than his mother had. Mark was not saying that he felt the same as Emma, because Mark recognised that men and women felt differently about things. What Mark resented deeply was that Mark was automatically a 'second class parent.' On the few occasions that Emma or Mark spoke in court, when the subject of a change in residence came up, Emma would, without fail, do a great emotional act with tears and sobs. These always made judge Grey uncomfortable and usually produced a pithy comment from Mark's legal team. On one occasion the guardian leant across and said "Oscar performance this time!"

Mark had spent hours waiting in court ante-rooms before going before a judge at the County Courts. On occasions Mark's barrister would explain the workings of the system. Mark was rather disconcerted to hear him describe the guidance of a case as like a giant game of chess. It was important to know in advance what was likely to happen and be said. He would never ask a question to which he did not already know the answer. It always seemed to Mark to be very wasteful of time in court when detailed statements for viewing could just as well be written beforehand. The result was that most of the time in court was spent reiterating the substance of those statements, with the other side trying to trip you up or catch you out. Of course for most of the hearings Emma and Mark never said a word. Mark would guess that to be a barrister you would have to be in the top 10% of the population academically and intellectually. Plainly barristers were not stupid. Judges are selected from barristers. That's not to say several judges were not foolish! Mark's own barrister hoped one day to join the Bench. Mark drew the assumption that barristers wanting to be promoted to the ranks of judges were not going to overly criticise the body in public. One criticism aired occasionally was that having spent years at barristers meetings and dealing with the worst side of divorce and warring parents, when elevated to the Bench much of that insight apparently disappeared! When they discussed why that was, Mark learnt that part of the problem lay in how judges were promoted. It was explained to Mark that the success of a judge was measured by his having the least number of successful appeals against him. Mark would have thought a measure of success would be how fast you successfully dealt with a case. The longer a case ran, the more expensive and intractable it becomes: by any measure, less successful. The penny dropped! Mark understood why judge Grey endlessly adjourned the case with review after review instead of dealing robustly with it. It also explained the great reluctance of most judges to transfer residence, because it was such an emotive order that it was almost always bound to be appealed. The system actually rewarded judges that obfuscated and procrastinated. Mark realised that if Emma's bad behaviour had been dealt with properly early on, the situation would not have gotten so out of hand with Charlie ending up being so emotionally abused by his mother.

If Emma had been dealt with robustly or even harshly by being sent to prison or being made to pay for the endless review hearings, then she may have appealed. If the appeal judge upheld her complaint then it would have affected the original judge's promotional prospects. This then was a system that operated with the unintended consequences of prolonging cases and doing more damage to the children involved. Mark complained time and again about judge Grey's attitude to costs. His favourite escape clause for Mark's case was "It is not in the best interests of the child".

In Mark's case Charlie had inherited far more than Emma and Mark from their share of the divorce settlement. If

Emma had been ordered to pay the costs of the hearings brought back to court because she had broken the latest contact order, then there could have been two consequences. First the financial pressure could have curbed Emma's behaviour, or secondly she may have carried on till her finances required her to sell the farm. In which case she could have moved into Charlie's inherited house two miles away. The judge said it was not in Charlie's best interests to be moved from the family home. At what point does incompetence become prejudice? Mark was advised that if she were eventually proven to be the cause of breaking the contacts then Mark would be able to recoup most, if not all of the costs to that date.

She was found guilty of contempt of court, she appealed, and lost. After that judge Grey went out of his way to shield her from paying any of those costs except for two small hearings. He then enabled her to avoid paying these for years. His prejudice over the costs debacle was extraordinary. He was the major cause of Mark's second great complaint of the system. Why should Mark have to lose £200,000 trying merely to see his son when Mark had done nothing wrong while Emma was found guilty and criticised by nearly every professional involved with the case. British justice?

Mark took issue with those judges that constantly hid behind the excuse not to act by stating that it was not in the interests of the child. In Article 8 of the European Convention of Human Rights, it states, amongst other things, that everyone has the right to respect for their family life. The courts have taken the view that while a balance must be struck between the competing interests of parents and children, the welfare principle continues to predominate as laid down in the Children's Act 1989. Predominate does not mean to be exclusive. Several judges appeared to refuse to deal with situations even when they had criticised Emma for doing something wrong. They effectively did nothing to punish her, claiming it was not in Charlie's interests. The attitude over the family home was a case in point.

Mark listened to an interview on the radio with Mrs Hodge, a minister in the labour government. For much of the interview she was vehemently denying there was any bias in the Family courts against fathers, or more particularly non-resident parents (nearly always fathers). Mark listened with incredulity, wondering which planet she lived on. The spin was relentless.

Mark found the most marked difference in the use of judge's powers to intervene. In the injunction hearings the judge used some draconian measures against Mark. Mark had admitted three or four occasions to retaliating to Emma's storm of harassment. This is typically where the law was an ass. Mark's admission of a few instances of harassment compared to the daily barrage he was subjected to by Emma, meant Mark was the guilty one. Mark continued to deny the allegation that he had interfered with the business. But the judge found these things proved. His response was to order Mark out of the family home and put up an exclusion zone. The judge was made aware that it would be very difficult for Mark to maintain contact with his son. Mark was also ordered to sell his half of their company to Emma for £1. In effect Mark was ordered to leave his home, sell his company, resign from his job and give up his lifestyle choice to be a farmer. In short Mark was ordered to give up everything he held dear in life. Very few men in a divorce lose their jobs too. Most men keep that anchor, at least, in their lives. The fact that Emma had gone to live with her mother two miles away was immaterial. The judge could have ordered her to live with her mother who was dying, and where she was to spend much of her time anyway. Yet when it came to child matters and enforcing contact orders, the judges claimed they had little power.

Over the years Mark's legal team put forward many ideas to help get over the contact problems. Mark did not remember any being accepted or implemented. Emma seemed to have the power of veto over everything. The only modifying influence on Emma's behaviour was the threat to move Charlie to live with Mark, and to counter any threat of this she usually adopted good behaviour and reconciliatory advances just before upcoming hearings. When judge Grey finally removed that threat, Emma continued to frustrate contact by endlessly delaying procedures and intimidating the guardian.

The higher up the court ladder they progressed the more the judges exclaimed they had more options to deal with the problems. Judge Travers in particular said several times there was more he could do to help sort the problems. And yet, Mark reflected, they had never put forward any new ideas. They seemed wedded to the idea of contact, even though the history of the case demonstrated the problems that there had been with that, or the lack of it. Towards the end of the process Mark put forward some ideas from outside the box. The judge had said it was important to rebuild his relationship with Charlie but that staying away from home would be too stressful for Charlie. Mark had suggested that he order Emma out of the house for the summer holidays and following term. Mark could then move in and live with Charlie and the boy would get the chance to rebuild his relationship with his father, from within familiar surroundings and friends. This would, Mark though, shock Emma into realising the court was serious and if after this period things did not improve then Charlie could be moved to live permanently with Mark. This and more unconventional ideas were never even acknowledged by the judge. Mark had eventually written and told him he was out of ideas and surely from his experience of cases like this, the judge could offer something useful. But although often claiming to have other options, the judge never put any forward. Mark encountered this two-faced attitude from the judges consistently; they would say one thing and then do another, undermining any respect for their status.

Mark sought advise from all sorts of quarters. Mark saw an advisor from the Citizen's Advise Bureau. He happened to be a barrister. The conversation ended up in the area of the European Convention of and Court of Human Rights. Mark pursued advice from charities like Liberty and the Aire Centre in London. Liberty said it was not their kind of case. Mark got good initial contact with the Aire Centre, but his case handler left to go and work for another employer and Mark lost continuity and eventually, contact with the charity.

Whilst Mark was LIP, he contacted and saw about twenty different firms of solicitors with a view to pursuing the angle of Clause 8 of the European Convention on Human Rights. Most said Mark would be wasting his money and it would take years to get to court. One of the interviews was with a very generous lady solicitor in Western Super Mare.

She gave Mark about three times the free introductory discussion time. She described a case where she had pursued the breach of contact orders with six penal notices till eventually the resident parent was jailed. She thought Mark should pursue the case getting repeated penal notices till Emma was jailed. Mark pointed out that Emma already had two penal notices against her and that his own costs had been more than £200,000. When Mark asked how much her client had spent, she said "hundreds of thousands of pounds". Mark left her office thinking there was something badly wrong with a system that allows a judge to order something six times, and have it broken six times, before he does something about it. If you are the non-resident parent and you break a court order without good reason or mitigating circumstances, you are summarily punished by the judge. It seemed from Mark's experience and anecdotal evidence that the resident parent (usually the mother) got away with breaches of all sorts time and time again.

In Mark's experience the same attitude pervaded the police. Whenever Emma broke the contact order Mark was ordered to leave and take the matter back to court. They knew that was a process that took months. Most times when Mark rang for assistance it was denied. The Domestic Violence Liason Officer said that they had responded 22 times for Emma. Mark was repeatedly told and threatened by the police that if Mark did something wrong Mark would be arrested. On the matter of allegations of domestic violence, the senior police sergeant told Mark he would not win in those situations. Mark must actively avoid them or suffer the consequences. The police Domestic Violence Liason Officer later explained that they had Home Office guidelines to arrest after the third complaint, whether they felt it warranted it or not. In the Family court during the divorce and contact hearings Emma alleged all sorts of domestic violence. It was obvious that the court, using the precautionary principle, viewed Mark as guilty or at best suspect until he proved himself innocent.

Even when it became a matter for consideration, comment and then analysis by professionals no such precautionary principle for Emma's emotional abuse was deemed necessary. Even judge Travers's explicit denunciation of Emma for demonising Mark in Charlie's eyes did not elicit any precautionary steps. Even though Emma had had two previous 'conversions' of her negative attitude to Charlie having a relationship with Mark, the judge grasped at the third conversion wholeheartedly without applying any precautionary principle. Mark had found it irritating and expensive that early in the divorce proceedings Emma could make an allegation of domestic violence or abuse, and even though, over months, the allegation was found to be groundless, she could make another allegation and they would be launched again on another lengthy process. What surprised Mark was that there was no financial cost levied against her for bringing these untrue allegations or for wasting court time. Mark had to pay all his own costs to fight the string of allegations. In his opinion and after his bitter experience, Mark believed that the courts should allow only one hearing for all allegations, for any further allegations, if they were found to be baseless, the person making the accusations should be made to pay all the court hearing costs as a deterrent. Mark saw this as the only way to deter those that just wanted to delay proceedings or to smear their opponent.

The third most serious criticism of the system Mark had was the time it took to do anything. To Mark there were critical periods in a child's development that the courts should do their best to accommodate. These periods revolve around education. The first and crucially important is when a child started formal school aged 5. In Mark's case the court had been aware that there were problems from the age of 15 months. By the time Charlie was two years old the court was well informed of the contact problems. If the case could be handled robustly, it was surely best to do that before the child-started school. If, as in Mark's case, the parents lived far apart, before school was surely the best time to try the more extreme remedies like longer staying periods or even residence change. Other times to avoid would be the run up to important educational goals like GCSEs and A levels. One of the major reasons for not seeing Charlie was to give him some stability and peace at school. Mark thought it was tragic that Emma had moved him again, causing more upheaval for Charlie. The judges should expedite the course of a case to these ends. Where there are children of mixed ages this would obviously not be so practical.

Children are resilient. Mark's own parents separated when Mark was 12 years old. Mark had learnt to adapt to the two different households and two lifestyles, one in a town, the other on a farm. One area Mark was initially very ignorant and naïve about was the impact on very young children's learning of patterns of behaviour and attitudes to life: the earlier the lesson learnt the more ingrained it may be. Mark knew nothing of the training that judges received. From what Mark gleaned from the attitude of the judges Mark went before, Mark doubted whether they received much training about the psychological impact on a person's life that is laid down in the earliest years. Some say that your life patterns are laid down or learnt by the age of one and a half years. The Jesuits claimed that if they had a child for the first seven years of its life they could control that person for life. From what Mark had learnt from counsellors, psychologists and therapists in general and from what Mark had read, her behaviour and what Emma was saying to Charlie before the age of two would have enormous repercussions on Charlie throughout his life. Mark felt that senior judges should undergo a degree of training in psychology, so that it is not necessary to have so many experts in court. It would be cheaper to train experienced judges rather than publicly funded experts.

When Emma's mother disowned her, Emma seemed genuinely shocked and distressed by the experience. When Mark had begun to get an inkling of what her mother had done and said to Emma after walking out on Emma's father, Emma had had been adamant that she would never do that to Mark nor treat a child so abominably. Yet when she became pregnant she appeared to morph into a clone of her mother. With the benefit of hindsight it was now apparent to Mark that after Charlie was born Emma became overtaken or possessed by the grooming or indoctrination of her mother that she had absorbed as a very young child. It seemed as though she was unable to override this learned behaviour. Mark wondered, if their marriage had been just a sham? Was it simply that when Emma finally got the prize she wanted, a child, a switch went on in her head and the groomed attitudes and behaviours surfaced? Emma was not stupid and could follow all the arguments and criticisms of her behaviour by the court and its hired professionals: and yet she remained in complete denial of her behaviour.

How could that be? Mark had often heard it said that if you repeat a lie often enough you begin to believe it. Yet it remains puzzling, and to some extent scary, that Emma attended therapy, albeit under coercion from the court, and yet emerged apparently saying the right things to get her off the hook and under the radar, while remaining fundamentally in denial and unrepentant. Emma had been described as anxious and claimed to be afraid of Mark and afraid of what Mark would do to Charlie. One thing Mark was certain of was that Emma had never been frightened of him. She had attacked him physically at least seven times in their marriage. Although Mark defended himself by retreating and leaving the scene, that invariably made her even more angry; Mark had never hit nor hurt Emma in anger. Once they had separated she had said that she thought Mark was weak and pathetic. Mark realised after a while that Emma had fully expected him to give up and leave them alone. If Mark had known then what he knew now, Mark would have walked away, saving himself from financial ruin and emotional devastation, while his son was legally kidnapped and groomed to hate him.

Emma had never had any cause at all to expect Mark to harm Charlie. Charlie was never late back from contact. Mark never received any complaint, nor did the court, for any injury sustained on contact. Allegations were made but they were never specific, always vague and unverifiable by a professional. Even the allegations that Charlie was sick after contact and had nightmares were never corroborated by anyone else. When professionals were engaged to look out for these things or visit the house after contact, they could find no evidence of Emma's concerns and allegations.

What is the role of Cafcass? From Mark's experience it would appear to be as legendary exponents of the 'jobs worth' mentality. In the beginning Mark had a lady officer who did an accomplished job in producing her reports on time. It was unfortunate that she apparently took early retirement due to ill health. Her replacement, Mark was told was one of the most senior officers with more than 20 years experience. Rather naively Mark assumed that would be good news. He was a likeable, approachable man. For the early years, whilst contact seemed the right way forward, he seemed to be biased towards Emma, Mark accepted that and even agreed in principle that for very young children and obviously those children still on the breast, the child was best with the mother: unless there is a serious threat to the child. As the case progressed and contact became more difficult to support, Mark's concern was not so much the bias towards Emma so much as his apparent unwillingness to engage and do his job. As guardian he had considerable powers that he did not appear to use. Mark was very surprised that judge Grey never questioned him over his inability simply to see Charlie, let alone criticise him for not dealing with the schools and other professionals more closely. There appeared to be very little constructive dialogue with Social Services. At some point it was pointed out to Mark by his barrister that there was a turf war going on over budgets between the two organisations. Social Services, when Mark first contacted them months after starting the separation, refused to get involved as the matter was already before the courts. They seemed not to understand that first, in court, one was rarely allowed to speak, and second it took months to get to court. When the school called in Social Services over their concerns for Charlie's behaviour, there appeared to have been little inclusion of Cafcass. Other people complained to Social Services about Emma's behaviour to Charlie. Mark only found this out from documents brought before the court. Mark felt a bitter stinging resentment of the professional bodies who either through ignorance or incompetence refused to include the other parent when concerns were raised. Many professional bodies refused to acknowledge parental rights. In fact on two occasions Social Services advised other professionals not to release information about Charlie to Mark; in contravention of the law. So Mark had to get his solicitor to educate them at his own expense.

Mark smiled to himself ruefully as he thought that his own father would have described the guardian as a professional civil servant. By that he meant a person who spent much of his time looking after his job rather than doing it. Mark failed to see how the guardian could possibly claim to have acted for Charlie in the last three years. Mark's solicitor and Mark himself were baffled by some of his excuses. But the biggest criticism of the guardian was that he failed to stand up for what he privately thought and verbalised, in court. Mark always had the greatest respect for anyone who stood by their principles and opinions even if Mark personally took an opposing view. When the guardian finally expressed his opinion about Emma and Charlie's future in court and in his reports, he quickly retracted them when another professional expressed the opposite view. Rather than do his job and fight for what he thought was best for Charlie, he withdrew his opinion. Indeed he then tried to resign his role. If Mark had thought he had genuinely changed his mind he would have accepted that in good grace. However he made it plain shortly afterwards that he still thought the other professional was completely wrong.

Mark thought back over his experience with solicitors. It had been mixed. There are two reasons for using a solicitor. First, they are the first place to get legal advice for your problem. They also prepare and do some of the legwork for your barrister. The second reason for a solicitor is that you have to have a solicitor to instruct a barrister. It's a cosy arrangement. One of the risks of this symbiotic relationship is that you may chance upon a good solicitor, but they may then instruct a poor barrister. You do not know if a barrister is any good in court, until you are before the judge!

Mark's first solicitors were a small town firm. With hindsight it became obvious that they simply did not have experienced enough family law solicitors to deal with Emma's antics. It was also Mark's misfortune to have a brash young barrister thrust upon him. There are two important qualities to look for in a barrister. First is the quality of their advice; second their action in front of the judge. Unfortunately Mark's first barrister had been a disaster on both counts. But as someone with no experience in these matters Mark took the advice of his solicitor. After all, he reasoned, that was what you paid them for. When Mark decided to change solicitors he was exasperated to be charged £750 for photocopying all the documents to be sent to a new solicitor. When Mark felt he might have to move to new solicitors a second time Mark was mindful that they may charge Mark several thousand pounds for copying his documents. As a precaution, Mark realised too late, it is wise to keep copies of everything and get copies of the witness bundle at each hearing. It was unfortunate that the replacement solicitor, Ian Hamilton had given rise to such misunderstandings over billing and the pursuit of costs. Mark did make the general observation that solicitors, like veterinary surgeons, expect to be paid for whatever they do, irrespective of the result of their advice.

On the other hand Mark thought barristers worked very hard for a modest fee. Sometimes the barrister only appeared for half an hour, at other times he will be before the judge all day. They often incur a lot of travelling and nights away from home. Mark's travelled from London to Reading for each hearing. Those costs were always in his fee, whereas the solicitor charged everything else as extra, even parking the car! The barrister has to have a nimble brain, often refreshing the case hours before appearing in court. His chambers will have a small team preparing some of the case but it is largely down to him to deal with it. Mark imagined that it was quite different for the multi-million pound divorce cases and for celebrity client's cases. Mark's solicitors charged approximately £130 per hour. The barrister's costs would vary from £600 per day for a directions hearing to £1,200 per day for more substantive hearings with more preparation.

In 50 odd hearings Mark had been before 16 different judges. Mark was brought up to view judges with respect and as pillars of society. By the end of his involvement with the courts Mark felt that that respect had evaporated. That is not to say they are not honest, decent people, Mark was sure they were. When you consider that they are drawn from the more successful barristers, why do they become like timid old ladies once they get behind the bench? In a fit of pique after one hearing Mark had rounded on his barrister and had said;

"Why is it that when judges leave home in the morning do they leave their balls behind?"

His barrister expressed some sympathy with Mark's view and opined that he had noticed that many vociferous, passionate barristers became timid on the bench. He thought there was a culture of "don't rock the boat" amongst judges.

But Mark's biggest criticism of judges at important hearings was their unabashed use of hollow words. Many times Mark heard strong words from the judges on how they would deal with miscreants, and that the courts were not to be ignored. But time and again the judges did not remonstrate with Emma for her behaviour. She soon learnt that she could get away with anything. The only judge to read the riot act was the lady judge, who unfortunately never sat for an important hearing.

The only judge who commanded a vestige of respect from Mark was a judge at the injunction hearings. Although Mark did not agree with much of his judgement and thought much of it flawed, he took some bold decisions. Most judges declared that they would do what they could to improve the situation for Charlie. Mark was particularly disappointed by judge Travers's decision to close the case without even consulting Mark. It demonstrated to Mark that after assurances that there were plenty more things he could do if contact did not work, all he really wanted was to get rid of the case at the earliest opportunity.

Mark got heartily sick of hearing judges say to Emma that they took a dim view of obstruction to contact and that if it continued they would deal with her. It was a commonly aired view at the father's support group meetings that many judges prolong the cases by doing nothing and in the end, the father would give up. If any domestic violence was admitted then the advice was not to bother going for contact through the courts, as you would not stand a chance. Mark wished that either the way judges were promoted was changed or they were paid in line with results. They should get a bonus if cases are resolved with a good ending produced quickly and reducing pay for cases that drag on and on or end unsatisfactorily or remain unresolved. It reminded Mark of a conversation Mark had had with his father after a couple of years of litigation. His opinion was that the courts rarely solved anything and they soon parted you from your money. He said that even Mrs Thatcher, who took on the unions, would not take on the judges. They had too many friends in parliament to allow any serious reform. At the time Mark thought this view was rather jaded. Mark was not so sure anymore. For some reason Mark kept thinking of turkeys voting for Christmas!

Something that always struck Mark as odd and extremely unhelpful in the court process was that once a judge had made an order, for example for costs, the judge did not follow it through and check that the order was obeyed within a certain time limit. It would be simple for the clerk to enquire from the other side's solicitor as to compliance. But no, bizarrely it remains up to the opposition to pursue, often at further cost and time. This automatically made the atmosphere between the two warring parents worse. It should not even have to be dealt with in another hearing, but by correspondence. Judges seemed to assume no responsibility for their orders! It would be hard, Mark thought, to invent a more dysfunctional system!

What Mark would favour would be a system of mediators with the power of a judge to intervene and to order reports from any experts necessary for a case. The mediators would see the parents for child matters only. There would be no legal representation allowed except for parents with handicapped intellect or communication skills. The rough outline would be to have a morning or afternoon per family once a month.

Initially meetings would be with each parent, then both together. The mediator would stay with the case. A good mediator would get to the bottom of the problems face-to-face fairly quickly. Cafcass or similar organisations could be engaged to report on schools and housing arrangements etc. These reports could be graded for useful detail and paid for with a reflection of the grade. In the vast majority of cases the problems would be identified within 6 months or 6 sessions. Each session would be recorded and the mediator would keep a file of notes and reports. One of the big problems with the law dealing with family matters is that, as seems currently to be assumed, *one size does not fit all!* With an open society and different types of parental partnerships case law does not meet today's more complex needs. Case law would not apply. At present the law is only changed if a successful appeal is made at the highest level. The judges at the highest level are elderly and generally out of step with modern Britain. In essence the law does not adapt quickly. The government need only to give a broad outline of the basic principles for child matters. The rest is for the mediator and parents to agree. What one couple agrees to does not have to apply to others. The system would do away with legal aid. Orders from the mediator would be written on the spot for each couple, to be shown to police or other agencies as necessary.

The whole system could be simpler, cheaper, quicker and fairer and above all not so confrontational. Both parents would be continually consulted. The present system has many parallels with the NHS dealing with psychologically based illnesses. The judge is like the doctor who never has time to talk to the patient to properly understand the problem. Instead the patient goes off to see experts to treat various symptoms. The system rarely deals with the cause of the problem. Once a symptom is dealt with the treatment is concluded till the next symptom appears.

One of the things Mark seriously disliked about the family court system was that he had to put life changing decisions in the hands of a legal representatives who did not know Mark, and whom Mark did not know. But it was all in the lap of the gods. If you happened to get a barrister or a judge on a bad day your life could be ruined. Most legal representatives are not expert across the whole range of topics in child matters. A barrister may be good at negotiating with the other side or presenting the case to the judge, but he may be hopeless in asserting a position for reclaiming costs. The law is very complicated with lots of procedures and protocols. There are nasty legal traps for the uninitiated. If you were LIP you needed to be good at talking in public, to be assertive with a quick brain. An ability to read legal documents and case law at speed is also useful. For someone like Mark that hated to be reliant on other people the legal system is best avoided. Although Mark considered himself to be middle class, Mark acknowledged that his upbringing had been in the advantaged spectrum of society. Mark noticed that the judges he went before were from similar or more advantaged backgrounds. In Mark's own childhood the Christian religion was an important element in private school education. He had been brought up to view motherhood as portrayed by the Virgin Mary as sacrosanct. Mark postulated that amongst judges, and they are overwhelmingly male, there is a cultural bias born of their backgrounds to view motherhood as pure: certainly not evil.

Mark also found the aura of secrecy that pervaded the Family Court to be fundamentally misplaced. Mark had always believed that an adult should be responsible for his or her actions. If a man beat his wife then he should face public scorn. If that impacted on his children's' attitude to him, then so be it. Part of society's problems, Mark thought, lay in the refusal to blame and hold people responsible for their actions. That element of reputation for most people acts as a curb on their behaviour. Most people do not want to be labelled something unpopular, so act to reduce that likelihood. If you are brought up with a conscience, the sense of guilt can be very powerful. When things are proven in the Family court they should be available for common knowledge. In some circumstances, like mine, where the child is alienated, it should be possible to name and shame the adult. The child should have some sense of truth from an official site. Public scorn is society's cheapest, swiftest, most profound deterrent for bad behaviour. Charlie is being brought up thinking his father is bad and his mother wonderful; a position being reinforced by the court. Charlie will hopefully learn the truth later in life. Mark had to hold on to that hope. As a child he had the resilience to accept things and deal with them quickly. The truth now would be beneficial to Charlie. Mark would like to name everyone he encountered on this journey through his struggle but is forbidden by the rules of secrecy till Charlie is 18 years old. Mark realised that he believed that public officials should be open to public criticism, and some named and shamed, just like rogue traders. Mark knew that he did not now have the money to continue legal proceedings or make complaints through the proper channels. His previous experience of complaining about a judge had proved a complete waste of time.

Mark believed some people had been negligent, and others had severely failed Charlie.

With the current levels of bias, incompetence and cost Mark realised that he would advise any father in a similar situation to avoid using the courts. The best advice Mark was given was to keep a detailed diary. As he sat now looking though the thousands of words, he wished he had recorded how he actually felt at the time rather than just the facts of the matter. This is an area with no easy, quick solution but, Mark thought, the court had made the situation much worse, put him through an emotional wringer and ruined him financially. What it had done to Charlie, Mark could only guess.

As the sun set and Mark watched its fading rays, he closed the diary, and blinked tears from his eyes. This was it, it was over, and while he missed the sound of his son's laughter and his presence with an almost physical pain, he knew he had done everything he could reasonably do for his son, short of going to prison. Mark watched as the last of the light disappeared over the horizon. His conscience was clear and that was as important to Mark as his son, his Charlie. He had tried, he had failed but he had never wavered in his enduring love for his child.